# KINFOLKS

ALSO BY LISA ALTHER:

**Kinflicks**

**Original Sins**

**Other Women**

**Bedrock**

**Five Minutes in Heaven**

# KINFOLKS
## falling off the family tree

### The Search for My Melungeon Ancestors

# LISA ALTHER

**Arcade Publishing**
**New York**

FIRST EDITION

Doris Ulmann photograph *Two Melungeon Boys* from *The Appalachian Photographs of Doris Ulmann* (Penland, N.C.: Jargon Society, 1971). Used with permission of the Doris Ulmann Foundation, Berea College, Kentucky.

Frontispiece: author's family tree, courtesy of author

*Library of Congress Cataloging-in-Publication Data*

Alther, Lisa.
  Kinfolks : falling off the family tree / Lisa Alther. —1st ed.
     p. cm.
  ISBN 978-1-55970-832-6 (alk. paper)
  1. Alther, Lisa—Family. 2. Authors, American—20th century—Biography.
I. Title.

PS3551.L78Z46 2007
813'.5—dc22                                              2006101353

Published in the United States by Arcade Publishing, Inc., New York
Distributed by Hachette Book Group USA

Visit our Web site at www.arcadepub.com

10 9 8 7 6 5 4 3 2 1

Designed by API

EB

PRINTED IN THE UNITED STATES OF AMERICA

For my parents,
John Shelton and Alice Greene Reed,
and my grandparents,
William Henry and Hattie Elizabeth Reed,
with gratitude for all the love
and all the genes

Mine heritage *is* unto me *as* a speckled bird,
the birds round about *are* against her;
come ye, assemble all the beasts of the field,
come to devour.

—Jeremiah 12:9

# Contents

# Introduction

MANY PEOPLE ARE BORN believing they know who they are. They're Irish or Jewish or African-American or whatever. But some of us with culturally or ethnically mixed backgrounds don't share that enviable luxury.

My mother was a New Yorker and my father a Virginian, and the Civil War was reenacted daily in our house and in my head. My Tennessee playmates used to insist that Yankees were rude, and my New York cousins insisted that southerners were stupid. I knew I was neither, but I had no idea what I might be instead. Hybrids have no communal templates to guide them in defining themselves.

In my life since, I've often lain awake at night trying to figure out how to fool the members of some clique into believing that I'm one of them. For a long time I lived with one foot in the PTA and the other in Provincetown. I also moved to several different cities, hoping to find a homeland. But each time I discovered that joining one group required denying my allegiances to other groups. In Boston, New York, and Vermont, I pretended not to hear the slurs against the South. And in London and Paris, I remained silent during anti-American rants.

But I have gradually become grateful for this chronic identity crisis because it has fostered my career. Everything I've ever written has been an attempt to work out who I am, not only culturally but also sexually, politically, and spiritually.

I rationalized my penchant for protective coloration by reviewing what I knew about my hapless ancestors, who were usually in the wrong place at the wrong time. They were Huguenots in France after Catholics declared open season on heretics; English in Ireland when the republicans began torching Anglo-Irish houses; Dutch in the Netherlands during the Spanish invasion;

Scots in the Highlands during the Clearances; Native Americans in the path of Manifest Destiny; Union supporters in Confederate Virginia. I concluded that I'd inherited genes that condemned me to a lifetime of being a stranger in some very strange lands.

Then I met a cousin named Brent Kennedy, who maintained that some of our shared ancestors in the southern Appalachians were Melungeons. The earliest Melungeons were supposedly found living in what would become East Tennessee when the first European settlers arrived. They were olive-skinned and claimed to be Portuguese.

Conflicting origin stories for the Melungeons abound. They're said to be descended from Indians who mated with early Spanish explorers, or from the survivors of Sir Walter Raleigh's Lost Colony on Roanoke Island, or from Portuguese sailors shipwrecked on the Carolina coast, or from African slaves who escaped into the mountains. Brent himself believed them to have Turkish ancestry. Before the Civil War, some were labeled "free people of color" and were prohibited from voting, attending white schools, marrying white people, or testifying against whites in court. After that war, some were subjected to Jim Crow laws. A friend who worked as a waitress told me she was ordered to wash down the booths with disinfectant after Melungeon customers departed. She also said that her mother warned her as a child never to look at Melungeons because they had the evil eye.

Growing up, I'd heard that Melungeons lived in caves and trees on cliffs outside our town and had six fingers on each hand. Brent's showing me the scars from the removal of his extra thumbs launched me on a journey to discover who the historical Melungeons really were and whether my father's family had, in fact, been closet Melungeons.

For nearly a decade I read history, visited sites, and interviewed people related to this quest. In school I'd learned that what is now the southeastern United States was an empty wilderness before the establishment of Jamestown in 1607. But my research taught me that it was instead filled with millions of Native Americans. It was also crawling with Spaniards, Portuguese, Frenchmen, Africans, Jews, Moors, Turks, Croatians, and British, among others — all roaming the Southeast for a variety of reasons.

In their wanderings these (mostly) men sired children with willing or unwilling Native Americans. Although an estimated 80 to 90 percent of Native Americans eventually succumbed to European diseases, some of their ethnically mixed children survived because of immunities inherited from their European and African fathers. They, in turn, had descendants, some of whom found ways to coexist with the encroaching European settlers.

I assembled plenty of clues about Melungeon origins, but DNA testing finally gave me some answers — and also explained why a sense of belonging has always eluded me. After a series of tests, I learned that I'd been walking around for six decades in a body constructed by DNA originating in Central Asia, the eastern Mediterranean, the Indian subcontinent, the Middle East, and sub-Saharan Africa. This in addition to the contributions from England, Scotland, Ireland, France, Holland, Germany, and Native America, which I already knew about through conventional genealogical methods.

For weeks after receiving these results, I wandered around in a daze, humming "We Are the World." A lifelong suspicion that I fit nowhere turned out not to be just idle paranoia. But once the reality of my panglobal identity sank in, I realized that I'd finally found my long-sought group. It consists of mongrels like myself who know that we belong nowhere — and everywhere. This book chronicles my six-decade evolution from bemused Appalachian misfit to equally bemused citizen of the world.

# KINFOLKS

# The Virginia Club

M Y YOUNGER BROTHER BILL is clutching his teddy bear, the noose still knotted around its neck. My older brother John and I sit on a carpeted step in the front hallway as the gray-haired babysitter with crooked brown teeth informs us that the Melungeons will get us for having hung the bear from the upstairs landing, just out of Bill's reach in the downstairs hall.

"What's the Melungeons?" I ask.

"The Melungeons has got six fingers on each hand," she says. "They grab mean little chilrun and carry them off to their caves in the cliffs outside of town."

John and I glance at each other uneasily.

When my parents get home from their tea dance at the country club, John and I wait for Bill to tell on us, but he doesn't. He's a good kid. The Melungeons won't be interested in him when they arrive.

In her silvery cocktail dress and the spike heels that make her look like a toe dancer, my mother is very glamorous. The top of her head comes to my father's chest. He's the tallest man we know. He claims he has race-horse ankles. He's madly in love with my mother and is always coming up with corny new ways to tell her so.

Tonight, right in front of the babysitter, he says, "Kids, isn't your mother just as pretty as a carnival queen at a county fair? If

I put her in a pageant, she'd win the four-hundred-pound hog. But how would I get it home?"

Her face freezes halfway between a smile and a frown as she tries to decide if this is a compliment. She was a model at the University of Rochester. In my favorite photo, she's wearing a satin evening gown, standing inside a giant wine bottle, her black hair bobbed. But at home she resembles Harriet Nelson more than Loretta Young because she hates to buy clothes. My parents share a horror of spending money. Having grown up during the Great Depression and World War II, they say you never know when the next ax will fall.

Since my mother is from upstate New York, she doesn't gush like normal mothers. She used to teach high school English, so she's always coaching us to pronounce "cow" in one syllable. Our friends look at us as though we're lunatics whenever we say "cow" as she recommends. But our cousins in New York still mock our southern accents when we visit them in the summer. They say southerners are stupid. Our Tennessee playmates say Yankees are rude. But I've met plenty of rude southerners and stupid Yankees.

My mother's hobby is curling up in an armchair with the library books from which she's always quoting. When she makes us take naps so she can read in peace, she announces, "I'll but lie down and bleed awhile and then rise up to fight again."

Once at supper, as she was carving a chicken, she looked up and said, "Children, always remember to stab low and pull up."

"Why?" I asked.

"That way you sever the aorta." She illustrated this in the air with her knife.

In the car on the way home from dropping off the babysitter, my father, a doctor, confirms that some babies in East Tennessee are born with extra fingers, which are usually removed at birth. He indicates on my hand the joints from which they can sprout.

Before turning out my light that night, I look under the bed and in the closet for lurking Melungeons. I'm often bad, and apparently the Melungeons, like Santa, have their ways of finding out. At least I know how to stab low and pull up.

Lying in the dark, I convince myself that I'm safe as long as my body is completely covered by the top sheet. It's summer, and we don't have any fans. We don't buy things that aren't on sale, and who ever heard of a fan sale in the South? The air that drifts through my window, carrying the screeching of the night insects, is hot and humid. But the thought of being seized in my sleep by six-fingered cave dwellers is so appalling that I endure the sweaty sheet. I become alarmed as I try to figure out how to stay encased in my magic sheet if our house catches fire and I have to jump out the window.

John, Bill, and I are crammed into one seat on the Ferris wheel. Spread out below us are the throngs of milling townspeople and the lights from the carnival tents and rides. As we hurtle toward the ground, I can see my mother standing outside the ticket booth. She's frowning. I wave as we swoop past her and head skyward, but she doesn't notice.

When we stagger off the ride, my mother tells us that we have to go home because her baby will soon be born and she needs to go to the hospital. Back at the house, my grandmother arrives, and my mother departs with my agitated father.

The next morning my grandmother informs us that we have a new baby brother named Michael. Shrugging, we race outside to ride our bikes in the driveway.

Toward dusk my father drives us to the hospital. Children aren't allowed inside except as patients. So we sit cross-legged on the lawn while the frogs in the valley take turns burping. My mother comes to her third-floor window and tilts a blanketed bundle in her arms so that we can see Michael. He looks like an unpromising playmate, but we do our best to act excited.

My mother vanishes. Then she reappears without the bundle. She opens the window and tosses foil-wrapped candies down to us. They turn out to be chocolate-covered cherries — my favorite — so the evening hasn't been a total waste.

One day in Miss Goodman's second-grade classroom my nose starts bleeding. I lean my head back, but it doesn't help. Miss Goodman sends me to the nurse. She can't stop the bleeding either, so my mother comes to get me.

That night I wake up to find my pillow soaked with blood like in some horror movie. Can this be the revenge of the Melungeons that I've long been expecting?

As my mother changes the sheets, my father packs my nostrils with cotton. I smile because, while explaining what he's doing, he's finally called me Betsy. I've changed my name to Betsy because Lisa, pronounced "Liza," is too weird. My only ambition is to be exactly like every other student at Lincoln Elementary, none of whom is named Lisa, pronounced "Liza."

Tucking me in, my mother says, "There! Isn't it nice to have fresh, clean sheets?"

"Dot in the biddle of the dight," I mutter.

The next morning my mother drives me to the hospital, explaining that my father is already there, reading about my nosebleeds in the medical library. She rolls me in a wheelchair to a room and helps me undress. Black and blue bruises cover my entire body, like one of those tattooed natives in *National Geographic*. I put on a gown that ties in the back and climb into the high, narrow bed.

My father, wearing green scrubs, booties, and a cap, comes in. He tries to act silly, but he looks tired and worried. His doctor friends and my grandfather come and go in their scrubs, poking at my bruises and murmuring to each other. Nurses arrive to remove the bloody cotton wads from my nostrils and to pack them with fresh cotton. I can feel the blood seeping down the back of my throat. Sometimes it makes me gag.

This continues for what feels like several years. But it's probably just a few weeks. I don't really know. Day after day the light outside fades to black. Then the night gives way to dawn. I lie there, dissolving squares of strawberry Jell-O in my mouth and repeating the name of my illness in my head — idiopathic thrombocytopenic purpura. It has a rhythm like a poem. It's nice to have a name for what's happening to me. I never imagined my body could let me down like this. I never imagined until now that my body and I weren't one and the same.

Sometimes I raise an arm to inspect my bruises. The new ones are black or midnight blue. Then they turn to shades of purple. When they're almost healed, they fade to yellows and greens. It would be beautiful if it weren't my arm.

One morning, I realize that the nurses and orderlies have been calling me Lisa. I'm still a Betsy, trapped in the bloodless body of a Lisa, but I'm too weak to protest. With a sigh I bid Betsy farewell and let her go.

My father and his friends decide that I need a transfusion. But I have rare blood, and no donor can be found except my grandmother. As my father explains this, I feel a stab of panic. I picture myself as her blood flows into me: my hair turns silvery blue; I develop wrinkles on my face and a slight stoop. I express these concerns to my father, and he laughs for the first time since this all began.

In the end, the blood of another doctor matches mine. After the transfusions my own blood starts to clot again. No one knows why. I am pleased to be a medical mystery.

Soon I'm back in Miss Goodman's classroom, listening to our Bible teacher recite the Twenty-third Psalm. When she gets to the part about the valley of the shadow of death, I understand that's where I've been.

But the only lasting consequence is the realization that I need to choose another career. My father describes each day's operations to us at the dinner table. He also tells about a man in jail who swallowed a spoon so he could escape as they drove him to the hospital. Once he'd escaped, he realized he had a spoon in his stomach and needed to go to the emergency room, where the sheriff was waiting for him. My father has so much fun at the hospital that we all want to be doctors, too. But who ever heard of a doctor who's afraid of blood?

My parents have bought a three-hundred-acre tobacco farm eighteen miles from town. We spend our weekends peeling ancient yellowed newspaper pages off the chinked log walls of a cabin at one end of our new valley. My father has hired a man with a bulldozer to make a dam so we can have a swimming pond. The water from the spring in the hillside keeps draining into underground caves, leaving only a mudflat. My mother calls it Shelton's Folly.

John and I form the Electric Fence Club. To join, the younger kids are required to touch the electric fence, which they do, to their regret and our delight.

My grandmother has to drag my grandfather out from town to see our farm. My grandfather was orphaned in southwest Virginia when his father died of pneumonia and his mother of gallbladder disease before he was six. Like an episode from *Oliver Twist*, the uncle in charge of the estate sold their farm and squandered the money.

My grandfather, one of eight children, was raised by an older sister named Evalyn who was married to a farmer who put him to work in the fields. My grandfather ran away when he was a teenager, hiking a hundred miles through the mountains to join two older brothers in Kentucky. He worked as a logger to put himself through medical school. He has earned his lack of enthusiasm for rural living.

We own a brown Saddlebred named Nora, who used to be a show horse before she got too old. She plods grimly around the pastures with us kids on her back swatting her with switches. Once my grandparents arrive, my father insists that my grandfather take Nora "for a spin." When my grandfather first practiced medicine in the Virginia mountains, he kept a stable of six horses for house calls into the hills, so we figure he must know how to ride.

My grandfather finally agrees — to humor my father. He swings up onto the equally unenthusiastic mare. Next thing we know, Nora is leaping along the dam like a ballerina. Our mouths drop open.

My grandfather runs Nora through her five gaits as though shifting the gears on a race car. At his command she backs up. In response to pressure from his thighs she prances sideways and then switches her lead leg in mid-stride. Attempting to copy these moves later that week on a pony we keep in the backyard in town, I will gallop under a wire clothesline and nearly decapitate myself. Trying again a couple of years later, I will ride Nora into a barbed wire fence and require thirty-six stitches in my left leg.

Nora and my grandfather return to the cabin. He slides off her.

"Nice horse," he says, tossing the reins to my speechless father.

We continue to stare at our grandfather and Nora.

"Can we go home now?" he murmurs to my grandmother.

Pam, Martha, and I, along with half the other kids in town, are riding the new escalator in J. Fred Johnson's Department Store. No one could believe the advance reports of a self-propelled staircase, but it's all true!

As we dash through the lingerie section to the stairs that glide back down to the ground floor, we pass dozens of high school girls stalking along with textbooks balanced on their heads, weaving through armless plaster torsos clad in brassieres and girdles. The girls are students from the charm class that's held in a room off the hair salon, where they're learning the skills necessary to become the next Miss Kingsport. If your posture is perfect, the sky's the limit.

J. Fred Johnson was a revered town father. His widow lives next door to us on Watauga Street. After the War Between the States, when many in our region were starving, he teamed up with some Yankee bankers to found our town. Its nickname is the Model City. In 1918, J. Fred, as everyone calls him, invited my grandfather, William Henry Reed, from Virginia to open a hospital.

We tear ourselves away from J. Fred's new escalator because it's time for the cowboy special at the State Theater. The Lone Ranger, Roy Rogers, Gene Autry, Hopalong Cassidy — you never know which you'll get until he appears on the screen. One of my grandfather's claims to fame, in addition to being able to operate with either hand, is that he performed an appendectomy on Tom Mix once when Tom was in town for a wild west show.

We amble up Broad Street, the axis of the Model City. When my grandparents moved here, the street was packed clay. There were few stores and many vacant lots. The workmen building the town lived in a city of canvas tents near where the Piggly Wiggly now stands.

Martha is on my right. She has wavy blond hair and blue eyes. Although a year older than I, she's a lot shorter. But she's still the boss of the neighborhood, except when her brother Nic is around. Nic wraps his stack of comic books with a swing chain and locks it with a padlock so no one can read them without his permission.

To my left is Pam. She's as tall as I, with curly black hair and glasses with thick lenses. Her mother works at a grocery store, and they live with her grandmother on the street behind ours. Whenever Martha and I ask Pam where her father is, she replies, "None of your beeswax and shoe tacks."

Behind us is a traffic circle surrounded by four steepled churches of red brick — one Baptist, two Methodist, and one Presbyterian. My family's church, St. Paul's Episcopal, is a low stone manse with a door the color of dried blood. It looks as though it belongs on a windswept moor. Instead, it squats atop a hill, looking down on the other churches.

My father used to be a Baptist, but he says he doesn't want his children threatened all the time with burning in hell. His mother, my grandmother, Hattie Elizabeth Vanover Reed, assures me that he's never been happy since he turned his back on the

Baptists. But he seems happy to me, except when she stops ˅ ˎ remind him that only Baptists will pass through the Pearly Gates.

Ahead of us is a boarded-up train station of maroon brick. Since freight trains are now the only rail traffic, there's no need for a station except as a clubhouse for our drunks. Branded liquor is illegal, and moonshine is expensive, so they're said to imbibe liquid shoe polish and after-shave lotion at their socials in the vacant building.

The plaintive howls of the locomotives whistle in my bedroom late at night as I lie there fretting about marauding Melungeons. The trains clatter past Riverview, where the Negroes live in low red-brick apartment buildings. Then the trains stop at the Tennessee Eastman plant by the river to unload mountains of shiny black coal and to collect camera film, ammunition, and bolts of rayon.

But the train we kids care most about is the Santa train, which creeps down from Virginia at Christmas. The railroad workers toss candy, pencils, and toys to the children along the tracks. This mission ends in the Model City with a parade up Broad Street. Santa transfers to a hook-and-ladder truck, from which the firemen throw candy to us town kids.

My grandfather's first hospital was located above a drugstore down the street from the defunct train station. He had four beds in two rooms. In his teens, my father worked as a soda jerk in the drugstore. On the sidewalk outside it, some farmers now cluster for their usual Saturday in town. They wear limp-brimmed hats, pressed overalls, and high-topped work shoes. Some also wear suit jackets and starched white shirts. They talk quietly, or not at all, occasionally squirting tobacco juice into the gutter. We've already seen their children sadly eying the counters at Woolworth's, which are full of wind-up toys from Japan that their mothers in housedresses sewn from floral-print flour sacks can't afford to buy.

The spot in which the farmers are standing is where an elephant, later labeled Murderous Mary, killed a boy in a circus parade up Broad Street shortly before my grandparents' arrival. She stopped to pick up a piece of watermelon someone had tossed her. The boy leading her gouged her with his goad. She seized him with her trunk, threw him against a wall, and squashed him with one foot.

The town concluded that Mary had to be executed. The sheriff shot her several times, but the bullets didn't penetrate her hide. She was loaded on a flatbed car at the train station and transported to a town down the line called Erwin, where there was a construction crane. A chain from the crane was wound around Mary's neck. The crane hoisted her into the air as she trumpeted indignantly. The chain snapped, and Mary crashed onto the track and broke her hip. However, a second chain didn't snap, suspending her until her struggling ceased.

Mary's carcass was lowered into a pit dug alongside the track with a steam shovel. We have a newspaper photo at home of Mary hanging from the crane. Everyone makes fun of Erwin as the town that lynched an elephant.

Every time this story comes up, my father claims to have done an autopsy on a Ringling Brothers elephant that died in Boston when he was a medical student at Harvard. He insists he and some fellow medical students cut a trapdoor in the elephant's chest and crawled around inside her collecting specimens. Listeners always exchange glances, trying to figure out if this could be true. My father is famous for his embellishments.

I hand the gum-chewing woman in the admissions booth at the State Theater my dime, and she returns a penny. I glance uneasily at the iron staircase outside the building, which leads to the balcony where the Negroes sit. It's neat to sit up high like that — but it's less neat not to get to buy popcorn or candy first.

Once we find some seats, howling Indians on horses, faces painted in alarming patterns, fill the screen. They circle a flaming farmhouse, shooting arrows and hurling tomahawks. The problem isn't the Indians, who possess a certain mute dignity.

Nor is it the settlers, who are bringing dance halls and repeating rifles to the frontier.

The real problem is a surly Indian named Two Hearts. The Lone Ranger tells Tonto that Two Hearts is "a low-down, lying, thieving, and deceiving half-breed." Tonto, in contrast, is as loyal as a teacher's pet. Two Hearts has incited the otherwise amiable Indians to murder and arson because he hates his white trapper father, who has rejected him and his Indian mother. The unhappy Two Hearts is slain by the disgruntled Indians — as studded with arrows as an Easter ham with cloves. Harmony reigns in Buffalo Flats, and the Lone Ranger rides off into the sunset on Silver with Tonto by his side.

As we stroll back down Broad Street, we discuss why the Lone Ranger is called "Lone" if Tonto and Silver are always with him. This will remain one of life's many mysteries.

I inform Martha and Pam that we're walking atop a field of gore. At school I've studied the Battle of Long Island Flats, fought in 1776 beneath what are now the streets of the Model City. The settlers defeated the Cherokee, led by Chief Dragging Canoe, and forced them to hand over Long Island, where the red-brick factories and round holding tanks of Tennessee Eastman now sit. Long Island had been a sacred site where the Cherokee negotiated peace treaties. I offer to tell them how Dragging Canoe got his name, but they don't care.

Back at our house my mother is clipping the boxwoods up the front sidewalk with scissors. There are one hundred sixteen bushes, and she trims four a day all year round. That way we never need to pay a yardman's exorbitant rates.

Our house is a white brick two-story Georgian with green shutters. Shortly after moving to town, my grandmother had this house designed and constructed on the street where the Yankee plant managers were living in their white-columned plantation houses. Watauga Street runs along a ridge that overlooks Tennessee Eastman, with Bays Mountain as a backdrop. At night, thousands of factory lights down in the valley flicker romantically in the mist that creeps up the Holston River and the smoke that swirls from the plant stacks.

While the house was being built, my grandmother didn't like how the brick wall out back was being laid, so she fired the mason and took over herself.

Watching her slap mortar on a brick with a trowel, the embarrassed mason said, "Excuse me, ma'am, but you can't build a wall like that."

She looked up and replied, "Sir, not only can I — I am."

When it was finished, the architect praised my grandmother's workmanship.

She replied, "Mr. Dryden, I know this wall will stand because I've studied Thomas Jefferson's brick walls at the University of Virginia."

And it's still standing, despite the best efforts of climbing ivy to drag it down.

My father grew up in this house. When he returned from Europe after World War II, his parents gave it to us. One of my earliest memories is of visiting my grandparents in the cabin they rented after moving out. I can picture a brown snake slithering across black-and-white-checked linoleum. My eyes are at knee level to the alarmed adults. Way overhead near the lightbulb in the ceiling I can see the handsome stranger in the olive jacket who claims to be my father. I've been calling him Daddy just in case it's true. My mother says my grandfather ushered the trapped copperhead out the back door, where he chopped its head off.

My mother stops snipping the boxwoods to ask about the movie. After our summary, we head to the backyard, rounding up my brother Bill and Martha's brother Nic, Stacy and Stanley from the house behind ours, and Molly and Carol, who're visiting their aunt next door, Mrs. J. Fred Johnson. Although we persuade them to reenact the movie, no one will play Two Hearts. He seems pathetic, being neither cowboy nor Indian. So we switch to Trail of Tears instead. To my amazement they agree that I can perform the Dying Eagle dance. Although everyone covets this role, I usually hog it because I own the wings.

A father on Catawba Street has organized the boys down there into a tribe. They've built a huge tepee in his backyard, and they make war bonnets and armbands from the beads and feathers he orders from a catalog. Girls aren't allowed to join. But since my brother John belongs, I've stolen some of his supplies to decorate my cardboard wings, which I now tape to my arms. My loincloth is a dish towel secured by a leather belt.

My dance around the imaginary campfire is inspired as my wings lift and droop and flutter. When the soldiers (wearing the same blue caps we use for War Between the States) arrive to drag me off to Oklahoma, I swoon to the ground. It's my finest performance yet — at least until the soldiers start piling moldy leaves on me to bury me.

Sometimes we play circus acrobats, performing gravity-defying routines on our teetering swing set and trying to lure our lazy mutts over jumps with dog biscuits. Other days we play pioneers in Stacy's playhouse, forcing Bill and Stanley to be either Indians or buffalo. Either way, we slaughter them with our wooden rifles. We also play World War II, dressing in camouflage clothes and my father's too-large captain hats and crawling around the backyard with our rifles cradled in the crooks of our arms.

But our favorite game is War Between the States. Despite the fact that my mother used to sing "Sherman's Dashing Yankee Boys" to my brothers and me as a lullaby, nobody wants to be a Yankee. So we insist that Bill and Stanley do it as the price of playing with us older kids. We turn our tool shed into a field hospital and administer transfusions via lengths of string attached to bottles of water dyed red with food coloring. We listen to each other's chests with one of my father's old stethoscopes. We also fill the empty pill capsules he gives us with flour, mustard, dirt, whatever is handy. Our Yankee prisoners, heads wrapped in gauze, are required to swallow them with water from my father's World War II canteen.

*

Our family is driving along the Holston River. John is lying on the backseat shelf. I'm stretched out on the backseat, and Bill lies on the floor, legs propped up on the hump in the middle. Michael is up front between my parents.

I sit up so I can see the huge house where my grandfather set up his second hospital. It's been turned into the Boatyard Apartments. Down the road is the Netherland Inn, which housed travelers in the nineteenth century when the port for which Kingsport was named was flourishing. The early settlers headed west in flatboats from its docks. The road we're on was a path other settlers followed to the Cumberland Gap.

We pass beneath forested cliffs. This is where I've pictured the caves of the Melungeons. But I don't see any people at all among the trees — six-fingered or otherwise.

We turn off the highway and wind up the hill to my grandparents' new house. Originally a nightclub owned by a moonshiner who was sent to prison, it has a wide porch that overlooks the river and the country club golf course on the far bank, with Bays Mountain beyond.

My grandfather is standing in the side yard, still dressed in his Sunday slacks and monogrammed silk shirt. A golf ball is teed up before him. Getting out of the car, we watch him drive the ball across the river to the fairway of the ninth hole. He used to be a semiprofessional left-handed baseball pitcher, and his smooth, powerful swing is the envy of the club. Because there's no bridge for five miles, he keeps a boat chained to a tree along the riverbank so he can row over for a quick game whenever he can escape my grandmother's plans for him. He's been written up by *Ripley's Believe It or Not* as someone who can drive a golf ball onto a green from his yard but has to drive his car twelve miles to reach the course.

As my parents and grandfather stroll toward the house with a toddling Michael, John, Bill, and I detect the roar of an approaching train. We race for the wall above the valley through which the tracks run. We get there just as the train does. It clatters past, coal cars mounded high with black chunks, some of which dribble over the sides to bounce along the tracks. Other cars carry huge tree trunks bound for the paper mill in town or bales of cotton for the textile mill. The boxcars have names stenciled on their sides. Many say "Carolina, Clinchfield, and Ohio," the company that owns this line. But some stray cars read "Frisco Line," "Atlantic Coastline," "Louisville and Nashville," "Central of Georgia," "Denver and Rio Grande."

The brakemen on the porch of the caboose wave to us as they vanish around the bend, off to experience adventures in a vast world about which I know nothing. I vow that I'll go there some day. I find this notion both thrilling and terrifying.

In the echoing silence that follows, the names painted on the cars continue to parade through my brain to the beat of the wheels pounding on the steel tracks. They recur time after time, like a nagging tune you can't get out of your head. Or like the rhythm of "idiopathic thrombocytopenic purpura" when I lay in that hospital bed.

In the kitchen, my grandmother, wearing an apron over her Sunday suit, is molding a ball of dough into a Parker House roll. Two dozen others, brushed with melted butter, are already rising beneath a damp dish towel. She hands me some Saltines, and I go back outdoors to the fishpond and crumble the crackers into the water. The giant goldfish are lurking beneath the lily pads, pretending they're invisible. Cautiously they glide toward the floating crumbs, waving their filmy fins and tails. Then, throwing caution to the winds, they battle to see who can gulp down the most Saltines.

I join my parents and my grandfather on the porch to look down at the river, which is frothy from a chemical spill at Eastman. Dead fish are bobbing in the current.

My mother says that if we'd been standing here in 1779, we'd have seen a flotilla of thirty flatboats passing by, beginning their thousand-mile journey to Nashville. The boat in the rear carried settlers with smallpox. Downriver, some Cherokee attacked and killed them, much to the warriors' later regret, because they too came down with smallpox, passing it along to their entire village.

She points to Bays Mountain. Its forested ridges are fluted with coves like a pinched green pie crust. She explains that the mountain was named for a bay stallion who used to roam free there in the nineteenth century and lure domesticated mares into the wild. She's like a walking *Encyclopaedia Britannica* (which she's read from A through Z). I've never asked her a question she can't answer.

My grandfather smiles at her. They like each other. They're similar — both smart and quiet. My grandmother's and mother's feelings about each other are another matter.

We sit down at the gleaming mahogany table. As silver bowls and platters of shelly beans, mashed potatoes, sweet potatoes, molded Jell-O salad, and rolls circulate, my grandfather carves the roast beef. He can make the pieces as thick or thin, as rare or well done, as anyone wants, slicing with either hand. I'm intrigued by this talent, except when I reflect that he practices by carving similarly through human fat and muscle during the week. This involves blood, which I can't yet bear to think about.

On the wall beside us stretches a mural that features a white plantation house and a hoop-skirted belle who is entering a horse-drawn carriage. In the foreground, slaves on a wharf are loading cotton onto a sailing ship. But my grandmother, born in 1887 amid the coal fields of southwest Virginia, wouldn't have known a cotton boll from a hockey puck.

Her father farmed near a village called Darwin. When she and my grandfather first met, he was her teacher. They turned out to be second cousins. After they married, both taught in rural schools, until she persuaded him to pursue his dream of becoming a doctor (a dream perhaps fostered by his watching helplessly while both his parents died).

My grandfather attended the University of Louisville, hopping freight trains to visit his wife, who was still teaching in Virginia. The next year he won a scholarship to the Medical College of Virginia in Richmond, where he tended Confederate veterans at the Soldiers' Home. My grandmother joined him in Richmond, where she sold cosmetics in a department store and worked as a matron at a women's prison, once fighting off some attacking inmates with a hat pin. During the summers, my grandfather sold aluminum pots door-to-door and cut timber. He was also paid to pitch in a semiprofessional baseball league.

As I try to picture my elegant grandmother fencing Cyrano-like with a hat pin in a prison, I listen to my father and grandfather reminisce about the preacher at their Baptist church when my father was a boy. One Sunday he demanded during a sermon that everyone who agreed that golf on Sunday was a sin stand up. The entire congregation, including my grandfather's Sunday golfing buddies, stood except for my father and grandfather. When my grandmother saw them still sitting, she sat back down. But when she saw her bridge club standing, she stood back up. Then she sat. Then she stood. Then she sat.

That afternoon the preacher came to pray over his two unrepentant sinners. Spotting him walking up the sidewalk, my father and grandfather raced out the back door and headed for the woods, the preacher in pursuit. They managed to outrun him. Later that week he was committed to Lyon's View, the state mental hospital.

My grandmother's face is pinched. She doesn't like this story. But the rest of us are laughing, so she says nothing.

As time passes, so does my fear of Melungeons. Communists take their place. Some older kids from North Carolina, who're visiting an aunt down the street, invite me to be their brainwashing victim. They tie me to a grape arbor and demand my grandmother's name and address. They claim she's a spy, and they plan to torture her, too. When I refuse, they threaten to drive bamboo splinters beneath my fingernails. But I will never betray my grandmother, whatever they may do to me. They push broom straws under my nails until they bleed, but my jaws remain clenched. Luckily their aunt calls them home for lunch. Untying me, they congratulate me on my courage.

I've learned on the playground at Lincoln Elementary that the best defense is a good offense. Recently a trashy-fifth grader from Highland Park was standing beside me at a stoplight as I walked home from school. She was wearing a red silk windbreaker embroidered with a dragon, which some older brother or uncle must have bought in Korea, and she was smoking a cigarette. I was nervous because some Highland kids were said to carry switchblades.

"Are you John Reed's sister?" she sneered.

"Yeah," I sneered back. "You wanna make something of it?"

Fortunately she didn't.

My grandmother is a founder of our town's Virginia Club. To be eligible you must be born in Virginia, sport a silvery blue perm, and wear white gloves downtown. Mrs. J. Fred Johnson belongs. My mother, the New Yorker, does not. The Virginia Club meets every month to discuss famous Virginians, such as Captain John Smith, George Washington, General Robert E. Lee, and Mrs. Mildred Spencer, the 1952 Pillsbury Bake-Off National Champion, the first to use mayonnaise in chocolate cake to keep it moist.

The Virginia Club also discusses the superiority of Virginia over Tennessee and the number of acres in each member's ancestral land grants from King James I. A feature in our town newspaper has reported that the Virginia Clubbers come from "old Virginia bloodlines and money." My grandmother refers to them as "those fine Colonial ladies." It's not unheard of for a member, upon going into labor, to insist that her husband drive her the eight miles across the state line so her baby can be born a Virginian.

Yet we never go to Virginia, despite the fact that my grandparents between them have fourteen brothers and sisters there, plus many aunts and uncles, nieces and nephews, and cousins. My grandmother's mother died of pneumonia when my grandmother was thirteen, and my grandmother didn't get along with her stepmother. Could this be why we've never met her family, or even seen photos of them? When my father was a boy, the drive took ten hours on unpaved roads. The road is paved now, but we've gone only once. I recall picking through a slag heap at a coal mine to find amazing fossils of prehistoric plants and insects, but I don't remember any relatives.

My father has mentioned a Cherokee ancestress. When I ask my grandmother about this, she speaks of the recent rainstorm and current warm spell.

As I continue to bug her, she finally snaps, "My family may be a tiny bit Indian. But it's not a Cherokee. It's Pocahontas. Pocahontas was a Virginian."

Not only have I not been born in Virginia, I am now a left tackle on the Longview Losers. Our coach, the father of Sam (who will go on to become a quarterback at West Point), tells my team, all of them boys but Ellen and me, that if they'd play with my grit, we might win a game or two. I don't tell him that it's not grit, I just like the body contact.

One stormy afternoon we play a team from the mill village called the Stampede. Joe, their captain, is a son of the butcher at the Piggly Wiggly. I slog through the mud with my usual fervor, but the final score is 96–14 in their favor. In parting, Joe says sympathetically to Johnny, one of our halfbacks (who will soon become my first boyfriend, bringing me a real stuffed baby alligator from Florida), that it must be hard to have girls on your team. As the rain pelts down, our team, caked in orange clay, turns as one to gaze at Ellen and me, and we realize that our gridiron days are numbered.

The boys have an ally in my grandmother, whose silver Cadillac is lurking in our driveway when I get home. I tromp into the living room in my muddy uniform to find her perched on the sofa in a suit of raw silk. Her permed hair encases her head like a helmet of silver feathers. Her face contorts as she struggles to convey her displeasure without frowning, since she's trying to starve her frown lines. I'm hurt. I've endured broom straws under my fingernails for her. But clearly she's a Two Hearts, not a Tonto.

I'm standing on the rose-and-aqua Persian carpet in my grandparents' living room, surrounded by adults I don't know. I've figured out that the tall, lanky men who look uncomfortable in their suits and ties are my grandfather's cousins from Virginia — Reeds and Artrips. Others are doctors or patients, plant executives, Virginia Clubbers, all come to pay their respects to my grandmother.

My father looks as though he might start crying. He adored his father, who took him on house calls once he was old enough to help. My father administered ether during operations on kitchen tables in remote hollows.

He credits this with helping him through World War II. While assigned to a troop ship in the north Atlantic, he had to perform an appendectomy during a German submarine attack. After strapping himself to the operating table to prevent his being hurled across the room by the depth charges, he discovered that the ship hadn't been supplied with medical instruments. Using a trick he'd picked up from his father during those house calls, he transformed dinner forks into retractors.

In France, my father had to climb down a ladder into a deep pit full of German prisoners to treat the ill and injured. But he says it was no different from confronting a houseful of mountaineers, who might bury you in an unmarked forest grave if you botched an operation on one of their kin. Once he was operating on a German prisoner when German paratroopers landed outside the tent. They burst in, waving their rifles. But thanks to the sangfroid he'd learned from his father, he just kept operating.

Realizing that the patient was one of their own, the paratroopers thanked my father in perfect English and left.

There's a fresh snowfall, so my mother sends my bored brothers and me outside to play. As we careen down the icy hill on our sleds and saucers, I try to figure out what it means that my grandfather is dead. He'd had a heart attack and then cancer, so he'd been even quieter than usual lately. But I'd thought that since I'd gotten better after my nosebleeds, he would, too. I feel indignant at the notion of never seeing him again.

My mother says that when my father departed for boot camp right after my birth, my grandfather insisted on holding me whenever he was home. And he was sad when my mother, John, and I hit the road in an old Ford, following my father to army bases in Wyoming and Texas. When my father was shipped to Europe, we drove back to Tennessee and then to New York to stay with my mother's family. Upon my father's return for a stint at Walter Reed Army Hospital, we drove to Washington, D.C., to join him.

We moved seven times in my first two years. (As an adult I will suffer from chronic wanderlust.) My car seat was an orange crate on the floor of the backseat. My mother says that when she removed me from it at day's end, I'd just sit motionless in my playpen like a baby Buddha. Chipmunks would climb through the bars and eat my teething biscuits as I watched in silence. Although this sounds to me like someone who needed medication, it may be when I learned to prize solitude — and kind people like my grandfather, with sad smiles and sky-blue eyes.

Our parents didn't let us attend the funeral at the Baptist church because my grandfather's casket was going to be open. They said they wanted us to remember him as alive and active, not as a waxy corpse wearing bad makeup. Without seeing his inert body, it's hard for me to believe he's dead. But maybe that's what our parents hope we'll feel — that although my grandfather's body may be dead, he himself is still with us.

# My Inner Hillbilly

WHAT I MISS MOST ABOUT THE LONGVIEW LOSERS is the cama-
raderie. Being pounded into the mud by hoods from across
town on a weekly basis is a bonding experience like no other.
Because of my early years alone in the orange crate, I have a
great longing to belong, coupled with an inability to do so. Consequently, I will join almost any group, but only briefly.

To prove that I'm now one of the girls, I accept a bid from a
sorority at my high school named the Queen Teens. Our nickname is the Q.T.s, pronounced "cuties." Our archrivals, the
Devilish Debs, sometimes call us the Cooties. They're envious
because, although we're regarded as trashier than they, we throw
better parties.

Each Q.T. initiate is instructed to submit a bra and panties.
These are returned dyed purple, the club color, with holes cut
out for the nipples and the crotch. At the initiation slumber
party, we new members model our lacerated lingerie for the old
members. Many old members are Baptists who are going steady
with the burly footballers with whom I used to butt helmets. But
the erotic charge in the small ranch house during this twisted
fashion show is palpable as the smoke from their mentholated
Salems wreathes the old members' bouffants.

Meanwhile, I've experienced a religious conversion. I've announced to my parents that I don't believe in God. The truth is

that I no longer believe in the Episcopal God. I've come to believe instead in my grandmother's Baptist God because He provides hayrides for His youth groups. The Baptist Youth have been reared to regard anything fun as a sin, so they think sin is fun.

After a few quick verses of "This Little Light of Mine" for the benefit of the chaperones in the truck cab, each Baptist boy piles up a barricade of hay bales while his Baptist girlfriend hollows out a nest in the loose hay that pads the truck floor. As the truck creeps slowly along the country roads, driven by someone's salacious dad, the Baptist Youth have been known to make a believer out of more than one lapsed Episcopalian.

I've also joined the marching band. In our town, the Friday-night high school football game is almost as important as church on Sunday. It's certainly more entertaining. I play the clarinet. I'd have preferred the trumpet, but our family owns an ancestral clarinet, so everyone who wants to play something must play that. John played it before me, and Bill will play it after me.

I'd also have preferred to play sports rather than the clarinet. But when a group of us girls presented the school board with our plan for a basketball team, the head of the board informed us that competitive sports were injurious to the emotional health of young women. (She will be hospitalized for bipolar disorder several years later, despite never having played basketball.)

My new plan for escaping the family clarinet involves becoming a flag swinger. At halftime the drum major leads the band onto the football field, followed by the school mascots, an Indian brave and squaw, both dressed in feathered headdresses and fringed buckskins. Our squaw is Jewish. Her father owns the nicest clothing store in town. The band director insists she's the only student who looks Indian enough for the role. (As an adult, this woman will move to Atlanta and become president of the Hadassah.) After the Indians come the majorettes in their white boots, short shorts, and uniform jackets, led by the head majorette, who twirls the fire baton once the bonfire is lit and the stadium lights are extinguished.

Behind the majorettes come the half dozen flag swingers, also clad in white boots, short shorts, and uniform jackets. Their maroon-and-gray flags (the school colors) are the size of bridge tablecloths. They're attached to four-foot staffs with bulb handles. By grasping the bulb you can wave and swirl the flag in hypnotic patterns, making snapping sounds. This is done while marching with your knees brought so high that your thighs are parallel to the ground. It's like rubbing your stomach and patting your head at the same time.

One of the flag swingers, although a Devilish Deb, is willing to break ranks and help me realize my dream. She teaches me the routines in my backyard. I march up and down the driveway practicing them for months. The toddlers from next door watch me with round eyes. The dogs try to shred my flapping flag. My family members snigger from the windows of the house.

The day for the tryouts arrives. My flag swinger pal tells me I've got it made: grades count in the final computations, and I'm second in my class. Although I perform my routine flawlessly before the band director and the gym teachers, when the list of winners is posted, my name isn't on it.

As I turn to walk away, I realize why. My grades are high, and as I march my knees nearly touch my chin. But the flag swingers and majorettes are drop-dead gorgeous. I'm okay-looking in a wholesome, camp-counselor kind of way. But I'm not perky or frisky. I'm awkward and shy. Worst of all, I lack vim.

For the first time, I turn to the balm of writing, soon discovering that those prevented from living the life to which they aspire can write about it instead. I produce my first short story. I've been reading Faulkner novels from the town library, and I'm entranced by stream of consciousness. In the fourth-grade play, I was Miss Noun, who was married by the preacher to Mr. Verb. It is exhilarating to learn that a famous author writes in phrases that sometimes divorce the two.

My story is told from the perspective of Nathan Hale on the morning of his hanging by the British for spying during the

American Revolution. He watches through his prison bars as the boots of the approaching soldiers crush the autumn leaves, and he reflects on the brevity and futility of life. Through Nathan Hale I express my own despair at having failed in the flag-swinging competition, at facing another tedious football season playing the family clarinet in the fourth row of the marching band.

"Leaves falling. Rust and scarlet and gold. Boots tromping, smashing, crushing. In front of the courthouse, dangling above the scaffold in the red from the rising sun, a noose. . . ."

The story is published in the school newspaper because I'm also the feature editor to whom I've submitted it. But when it appears, I don't recognize it. It reads, "Brightly colored leaves were falling to the ground outside the bars across Nathan's window. The soldiers marched through them on their way to the jail to escort him to the gallows. . . ."

I race into the classroom of the faculty adviser, Mrs. Hawke, who's my English teacher and the wife of a local sheriff. She's tall and bony with a face that always looks pained. I say, "Mrs. Hawke, something awful has happened to my story!"

Looking up from her desk, she says, "I bet you think that story was pretty good?"

"I didn't think it was so bad that it needed to be completely rewritten."

"Well, let me tell you something, little lady: that story wasn't even written in complete sentences."

After a long pause, I say, "Mrs. Hawke, if you're going to rewrite my story, you should put your name on it, not mine."

"And if you're going to speak to me in that tone of voice," she replies, "you need to march right down to the office and see what our guidance counselor has to say about students who are rude to their teachers."

She writes out a referral slip and hands it to me. I stomp to the office. The guidance counselor suggests that I go home for the rest of the day and contemplate the consequences of being disrespectful to my superiors.

\*

When my mother hears of this, she drives us both to the school. She drags me into the principal's office and insists I tell him what's happened. Shaking his head, he rescinds my expulsion and sends me back to class.

But Mrs. Hawke and I are now archenemies. One of her test questions asks for the definition of *perdition*. I write "damnation," and she counts it wrong because it's not "hell."

I race to the library and look up *perdition* in a dictionary. The definition given is "damnation." I carry the dictionary to Mrs. Hawke's classroom, lay it on her desk, and point this out.

She says, "Well, I bet every dictionary doesn't define perdition this way."

I reply that one is enough to make my case.

Gazing at me through narrowed eyes, she agrees to give me half credit. But it's clear she has me marked out as a troublemaker.

In the summer of 1959, I work as a receptionist in my father's office. I'm impressed by how much time he spends with his patients and how kind he is to them. But I'm most impressed by the fact that he charges them only $3 per visit. Some can't afford even that, so they pay him with cakes or country hams or sacks of beans.

One evening as he's driving me home, we pass a poor part of town. I make a snotty-teenager remark about the people who live there.

Very quietly he says, "Those people are my patients and my friends, and I never want to hear you talk that way again."

Later that summer we take a family vacation to a South Carolina beach. When we pull into our driveway upon our return, Stanley from next door greets us wearing a suit, even though it's not Sunday.

As I climb out, I ask Stanley, "Why are you all dressed up?"

"We've just been to Martha's funeral," he says, and explains that Martha, my best friend from childhood, has died in a wreck at church camp in a car driven by a youth minister who was showing off by racing around the mountain curves. His car veered off the road and rolled down a cliff. Martha, who was sitting by an open back window, was thrown partway out. The car landed on top of her.

I walk upstairs to my room and lie down on my bed. I'm completely numb, as though my arm has just been lopped off. (When I think of this, even forty-five years later, I'm still numb.)

Once we get our drivers' licenses, my friends and I spend most of our lives in our parents' cars, like gypsies in their pony carts. Marty and Jane are my most frequent companions because they live nearby. Marty's father is a doctor and her mother is on the school board. She's very well coordinated and, like me, would love to ruin her emotional health by playing organized sports. Instead, she's dating the star of our basketball team. Jane, a popular cheerleader whose father is a businessman, is dating our quarterback.

My boyfriend, Harold, is a good baseball player, but he doesn't have time for sports. He works almost full-time at Sobel's, the clothing store owned by the father of Linda, our Dobyns-Bennet High School squaw. Harold is the best-dressed boy at our school. He reminds me of my grandfather — tall and slender with beautiful clothes and a diamond pinky ring.

Hour after hour, day after day, week after week, Jane, Marty, and I drive up Broad Street to the train station, U-turn, and descend Broad to the church circle. Teens arrive from all over southwest Virginia and East Tennessee to join us. At night, Broad Street is like a Los Angeles freeway during rush hour. Cars stop as passengers from one hop into another, or as people flirt or argue with those headed in the opposite direction.

Constantly picking up or dropping off any of a dozen other friends, we eat fries and burgers at drive-in restaurants. We go to drive-in movies. Our favorite prank is to move the car when one of us goes to the refreshment stand, so the abandoned one has to hunt through the rows of parked cars with their panting occupants to find us. Smoking Pall Malls, we cruise the new road to Bristol, the first divided highway in our area, with the same excitement as when we rode the new escalator at J. Fred's.

Dates with boyfriends take place entirely within cars — at the drive-in restaurants and movies and in secluded spots with fogged-up windows and radios softly purring.

A girl soon leaves town chubby, only to return skinny a few weeks later. As their bellies swell, a couple more girls drop out of school to elope with traumatized, baby-faced boyfriends.

One night I find myself attired in a white strapless Scarlett O'Hara gown with a hoop skirt, waltzing at the country club with a tuxedoed and cummerbunded Harold. I'm taking as much pleasure in my Merry Widow corset and satin spike heels as I used to in my shoulder pads and cleats. I, too, am now proud of the Tidewater land grants my fine colonial ancestors received from King James I. My grandmother sits at a table with my parents, smiling like the Cheshire cat in her sequined gown.

Meanwhile, my sister Jane has been born with an olive complexion. Swaddled in a flannel blanket, she resembles a papoose. My mother, descended from New England Puritans, once proclaimed the idea of extramarital sex as unappetizing as using someone else's toothbrush, so there's no possibility of genetic intervention by some Native American milkman. Years later, when a plausible explanation emerges, some acknowledge having noticed Jane's exotic coloring. But at the time, as in all polite southern towns, no one says a word.

My brother John was my rebel without a cause while we were growing up. He threw snowballs with rocks in them at passing cars. He tapped into the phone line and made free calls all over the world until the president of the phone company informed my father that John would go to prison unless he stopped. He built a shortwave radio to play chess matches with people behind the Iron Curtain.

I used to hide in John's closet to watch him hypnotize his friends, stretching them board-stiff between two chairs, their heads on one and their feet on the other. He'd tell them that when they awoke, they'd walk into the shower fully dressed and turn on the faucets. Afterward they'd stand there in the shower in their soaked clothing, totally bewildered.

When John dropped out of high school to join the navy, my father hunted him down and shipped him north to Deerfield and then to MIT, where he grew the first beard Kingsporters had ever seen on a young man from a respectable family. He edited the campus humor magazine and orchestrated such pranks as planting a large cardboard missile from a military recruitment display nose-first in the floodlit MIT dome and then painting a crack down the dome as though the missile had crash-landed there.

Since John is my hero, I take his advice when he tells me to come north to college. In any case, I'm intrigued by my mother's homeland. I'm also intrigued by my father's madcap adventures at Harvard Medical School. So I hop a train up there, and John drives me to interviews at several colleges.

I like the woods and the lake on the Wellesley College campus because they remind me of home — apart from all the anxious young applicants in their Bergdorf Goodman suits, who are strolling the paths with their equally anxious parents prior to their interviews. I've bought a suit made from a material that resembles mustard-colored burlap. The red paisley blouse matches the lining of the jacket. It had seemed chic at J. Fred's on Broad Street. But up against all that gear from Neiman Marcus, I realize that I resemble June Cleaver en route to the dentist.

I sidle toward a turreted stone structure that looks as though it might house the Addams family. As I present myself to the receptionist, I doubt if I have a chance here. I have a bad suit and no parents.

I'm ushered into a room with stained-glass windowpanes

and enough elaborately carved oak furniture and paneling to have fueled the fireplace in our cabin for an entire winter. My interviewer, an older woman in a Pendleton plaid suit, doesn't seem to notice my burlap fashion error. But she does ask where my parents are and how I've gotten here from Tennessee. I mumble something about my mother's having a baby and not being able to get away. The interviewer studies me as though I've escaped from Tobacco Road.

An ornate silver tea service sits on a table beside her needlepoint-upholstered chair. She asks if I'd like some tea.

I accept.

Organizing two Limoges cups and saucers, she inquires whether I'd like lemon or milk.

I've never drunk hot tea before, but I like milk and lemon, so I say, "Both, please."

She raises one carefully tweezed and penciled eyebrow. A corner of her lip-brushed mouth twitches. Gritting her molars so that her jaw muscles pulse, she pours milk into my cup, followed by tea. Then she briskly places a slice of lemon on my saucer and passes it to me.

After I squeeze the lemon into my tea, the milk begins to curdle, and I realize I've committed a faux pas. I also realize that my quest is hopeless. Whatever made me think that a mongrel like me could sprint with these Ivy League greyhounds? Did I learn nothing from the flag-swinger debacle? I'm wearing a suit sewn from a feed sack. My parents aren't interested enough in my future to accompany me. My brother at MIT is a juvenile delinquent. I don't know not to put both milk and lemon in hot tea. And my SATs are well below Wellesley's average.

A month later, I'm accepted at Wellesley. Everyone is incredulous, especially me.

My grandmother arrives at our house in her silver Cadillac demanding, "What's wrong with Duke or Vanderbilt?"

I reply that nothing's wrong with them, but I want to see the world.

"Boston is hardly the world," she snaps.

After enduring many years of condescension from the Seven Sisters wives of the Kingsport plant managers, she's pleased I've been deemed bright enough to function at Wellesley (an assumption that soon proves questionable). But she also seems sad. It was a giant step from Darwin, Virginia, to Kingsport, Tennessee, and once she'd taken it, she rarely looked back. The step from Kingsport to Boston is even more drastic, and she doubts John and I will look back either.

Her own son went up north to the University of Rochester, one of five promising Kingsport students given scholarships there by George Eastman (who killed himself shortly afterward, hopefully for unrelated reasons). After Harvard Medical School, a residency at the Roosevelt Hospital in New York, and a tour of duty in the field hospitals of France, my father finally came back home for good. But he brought along a Yankee wife, a Congregationalist whose idea of a good time is to read the *Encyclopaedia Britannica*. The Virginia Clubbers asked my grandmother why my father couldn't have married a nice Virginia girl, and she repeated this to my mother.

As I skim the results of the senior class poll to be published in the next edition of the *Indian Tribune*, I descend into a state of terminal chagrin: I've been elected Most Studious. It was bad enough not to make flag swinger. Now this!

In the first place, I'm not studious. I cruise Broad with the best of them. In the second place, I didn't need to be studious to become salutatorian. Any idiot could have done well on the true-false quizzes that determine our grades.

In fact, but for the machinations of Mrs. Hawke, I'd have been valedictorian. At the end of the term, she gave us several spelling tests in which she mispronounced the words, leaving us to guess at what we were supposed to be spelling. The boy who became valedictorian is one of her favorites.

Although I couldn't have hoped for Most Popular since I

lack vim, I did think I had a shot at Best Smile. I practiced in the mirror all year long, and my smile was definitely among the best at D-B.

I feel unable to face graduation. But I have to because, as salutatorian, I must deliver my speech. It showcases a quote from Shelley: "Naught may endure but mutability." I point out to my yawning classmates assembled in the gym that although we can never be sure how things will change, we can be sure that change will occur.

Afterward, a flag swinger, looking like a crow in her flapping black robe, asks me if this Shelley is Shelley Fabares who sings "Johnny Angel." I reply yes in a sad attempt to undercut my image as Most Studious.

Once we arrive at Wellesley in John's yellow convertible, piled high with my possessions as though we're the Beverly Hillbillies headed for Hollywood, I understand why they've accepted me: they pride themselves on geographical diversity, and there are only three Tennesseans in the whole place. I'm a token Tennessean. This is fine with me. Every college needs a few students who know all the lyrics to "Louie, Louie."

Wellesley also prides itself on uplifting the disadvantaged. I pause to wonder if they've somehow learned about the Melungeons and mistaken me for one.

Fortunately, one of the three Tennesseans is a junior from Nashville named Ophelia, who's been assigned to me as Big Sister. She takes me under her ample wing and explains the mysterious codes that govern the incomprehensible behavior of our Yankee classmates. She, too, has a doctor father, a Yankee mother, a sister, and three brothers. Apart from her bright red hair and heavier build, we could be twins.

What I find most shocking at Wellesley isn't just that the other students raise their hands in class and volunteer to talk. It's also the fact that nobody smiles or comments on the weather when we pass on the campus sidewalks. In Kingsport, I conducted endless discussions — with clerks I'd never seen before — of their latest operations and the delinquencies of their children. Some days I'd wanted to punch a clerk in the mouth to get him just to sell me a damn Coke without intruding on my private turmoil with his sordid family sagas.

But soon my early training in the orange crate kicks in at Wellesley, and I begin to cherish my invisibility. When I wear my nightgown to class beneath my trench coat, no one notices. In Kingsport, such sartorial behavior would have been critiqued for weeks.

My only complaint is that after having accepted me for being a Tennessean, Wellesley immediately tries to transform me into a Wellesley Girl. I'm forced to take a speech test. Because of my mother's extensive coaching on how to pronounce "cow," I'm able to conceal my true accent and win exemption from the remedial speech class.

The posture test requires us to strip down to our underwear and be photographed from several angles, as in police mug shots. Because of the Q.T. initiation fashion show, I know how to strut my stuff in a bra and panties, so I pass with high marks.

However, I'm unable to sidestep the Fundamentals of Movement class, held weekly in the gym. For half a year we're given instruction in how to sink into a sofa while balancing a cocktail glass and how to get into a sports car in a skirt without flashing too much thigh.

My hopes are high that I'll one day need these skills, but each blind date is more excruciating than the last. Few experiences are more demoralizing than spending a rainy weekend at Yale with a surly preppy who hates you. I soon realize that my problem is the same as when I auditioned for flag swinger: I'm not a fun person.

My parents don't drink alcohol. It gives my father migraines, as it did his father. Also, a coalition of preachers and bootleggers — strange bedfellows indeed — has conspired to keep Kingsport dry. Moonshine is available, but some partakers suffer blindness and lead poisoning. To buy branded liquor, you must drive to Virginia. But if you get caught by Tennessee patrolmen on your trip home, you forfeit your car. Hence, the popularity of iced tea in East Tennessee. My blind dates in New England find me a drag because my idea of a bacchanal is half a beer.

However, I'm soon fixed up with Richard from Cornell. He belongs to a fraternity in which the brothers drink so much that nobody notices or cares that I'm sipping the same cocktail all night long.

Education at Dobyns-Bennett consisted of the memorization of dates and facts. At Wellesley, I soon learn that facts aren't facts. Math has always been my favorite subject because the answers to problems are either right or wrong, as opposed to the multiple shades of gray in the humanities. But once I learn in calculus about the existence of imaginary numbers, I decide not to major in math after all.

In Bible 101, I discover that even the word of God has been put into His mouth by ancient Christian spin doctors. With magic markers we highlight the verses inserted into the gospels by various factions trying to bolster their own grip on power.

One day in English class I experience my first true thought. As we discuss "Flowering Judas" by Katherine Anne Porter, I notice the recurrence of the word *silver*. In a flash of illumination I realize that Porter has done this on purpose to suggest a parallel between one of her characters and Judas Iscariot.

My mind promptly retreats into darkness. But I know I've discovered a new function for it. Southerners are always trying to prove how nice they are (even when they aren't), and Yankees are always trying to prove how smart they are (even when they aren't). It's the difference between leading with your limbic brain or your neocortex.

But now that my neocortex has been jump-started, there's no stopping it. Soon I'm critiquing situations I've always blindly accepted, like a brat pulling the wings off butterflies. Along with this newfound ability to tear anything apart comes chronic melancholy. I feel like Eve after her expulsion from the Garden of Eden as she starts to realize that she and Adam are two separate people and that the talking snake is not really her friend.

Since these are the Martin Luther King Jr. years, I quickly grow less proud of my grandmother's alleged ancestral land grants in the Tidewater. After the murder of some civil rights workers in Mississippi, a hallmate bursts into my room to announce, "You southerners make me sick!" Another muses over a pot roast dinner one night, "It's so interesting to hear you say something intelligent in that accent of yours." This, despite the fact that I've passed their damned speech test.

I'm bewildered. Back home I was teased because my mother was a Yankee and my pronunciation of "cow" was so bizarre. I'd always longed to be a real southerner. Now I'm being accorded that honor, but it's been transformed into a badge of shame. We learned in school that southerners fought the Civil War to protect our homeland from invasion by immigrant Yankee riffraff. But my hallmates tell me its purpose was to end slavery. I have to admit that, if true, this seems a worthy goal.

After a couple of days in the library employing my newly activated neocortex, I discover that I'm not even a pseudo-southerner. East Tennessee is so mountainous that most of its antebellum farms were subsistence operations, so there weren't many slaves. These struggling farmers, many descended from indentured servants, resented those large landowners and merchants who were profiting from slavery. Also, many mountain families took pride in ancestors who'd fought to free the colonies from Britain and were appalled by the notion of dissolving that hard-won union.

In 1819, a Quaker named Elihu Embree founded the nation's first abolitionist journal, the *Manumission Intelligencer*, in Jonesborough, the town in which my family's farm is located. When Tennessee seceded from the Union, East Tennessee tried to secede from Tennessee, as West Virginia had from Virginia. During the Civil War, 30,000 East Tennesseans joined the Union army, comprising one-third of all white southerners who fought against the South. Guerrillas in East Tennessee burned railroad bridges there to cut Confederate supply lines. Mountain men called "pilots" led Confederate draft dodgers and deserters and escaped Yankee prisoners to the Union lines in Kentucky.

My neocortex collapses into a whimpering stupor. Since I'm taking a creative writing class, I decide to write a short story set in East Tennessee to sort this out. As Flannery O'Connor once wrote, "The Southerner knows he can do more justice to reality by telling a story than he can by discussing problems or proposing abstractions. . . . It's actually his way of reasoning and dealing with experience."

In the resulting tale, one character says to another, "Law, honey, where'd you get that hat at?"

When my professor returns the story, she's scribbled in the margin, "Real people don't talk this way." I've never before known that the people I grew up among weren't real. This might explain why I'm so confused.

Embracing my newly excavated Appalachian heritage, I buy a banjo and learn to play it badly. Ophelia plays a guitar, and our favorite tune is "They Are Moving Grandpa's Grave to Build a Sewer." The hallmate who's sickened by southerners offers to cover our waitress shifts in the dining hall if we promise never to play it again. To punish her insolence, we sing eight verses of "Are You Washed in the Blood of the Lamb?" All around the courtyard windows slam shut. But even Ophelia good-naturedly ridicules East Tennesseans as white trash who make a laughing-stock of the entire state.

Undeterred, I continue to court my inner hillbilly, lounging around the dorm in bib overalls, an undershirt, and bare feet. When my housemother, Mrs. Bradner, complains, I accuse her of cultural imperialism. I explain to my profoundly uninterested hallmates that the Deep South is to Appalachia as mint juleps are to Pepsi. That if the plantation South is the land of moon-light and magnolias, the mountain South is the land of moon-shine and magnum rifles.

I take my final exams in the infirmary, where I'm incarcerated for a month with carbon monoxide poisoning acquired on a trip home from Cornell in a car with a faulty exhaust system. I also have mononucleosis from the stress of trying to function in such a bizarre place.

But I do survive the cut my freshman year, despite feeling like the first amphibian ever to lie gasping on dry land. And I've learned the most important lesson of an Ivy League education: Ivy Leaguers are no different from anyone else — except for the fact that they don't know this.

Sealing my exit from the South (just as my grandmother has feared), I marry Richard from Cornell after graduation. The re-ception takes place in our backyard in Kingsport beneath a huge revival tent erected for free by an evangelist who's one of my fa-ther's many grateful patients.

A New Jersey native, Richard is working at an ad agency in New York City. By bribing several Dickensian characters lurking in a basement office, we manage to rent an apartment with high ceilings and parquet floors in a prewar building overlooking the Hudson. The only drawback is that getting from the subway on Broadway to our building is like negotiating the no-man's-land between the British and German trenches during World War I.

As a wedding gift my father gives me a box of bullets and the .38 special his father carried in his medical bag on house calls in case of attack by a drug addict. My father kept the pistol in his sock drawer at our house in town for the same reason. But the West Nineties clearly trump the streets of Kingsport when it comes to danger. So I take the pistol to a gun shop on Broadway to get it cleaned. When I pick it up, the dealer tells me I'm lucky

I didn't fire it because a metal guard is missing and I'd have blown my hand off.

As I walk back to our apartment, I imagine a scenario in which I shout at an attacker, "Stop or I'll blow my hand off!"

I've spent my first two decades struggling with whether I'm a southerner. Since my mother is a New Yorker, I feel genetically entitled to spend my next two decades struggling with whether I'm a Yankee. So I put my banjo in mothballs, buy some suits at Saks, and start work as an editorial assistant at Atheneum Publishers. Richard and I attend operas, concerts, and ballets. We eat at ethnic restaurants all over the city and attend plays both on and off Broadway. On weekends we join the nearly inert lines of traffic in and out of the city in order to ski in Vermont and swim off Long Island. We eat lobsters on Cape Cod and cotton candy on the boardwalks of New Jersey. I conclude that I like being a denizen of my mother's motherland.

My mother's grandmother, Ruth Griswold Greene Pealer, was a piano teacher and choir director who rose to the rank of national genealogist for the Daughters of the American Revolution. En route, she traced eleven lines of her family back to England — and one to the *Mayflower* (along with six million other Americans). Late in life she modeled for a bust included in an international exhibition called *The Family of Man* under the label "Caucasian Female." A cast of it sits on our piano back home.

Ruth lived in South Danville in upstate New York. Her husband, Phillip Greene, died of Bright's disease when her son, my maternal grandfather Floyd Greene, was five. She married again, this time to a farmer and state assemblyman named Peter Pealer. Peter had lost several fingers in a fireworks accident (in a novel variation on my childhood horror of extra fingers).

Caught up in the fight for women's suffrage, Ruth delivered a speech entitled "Woman and Her Advancement" to community groups. In it she maintained that since God made the creatures of our world in order of increasing significance, Woman as the last created was intended as "the crowning work of the Creator." This was confirmed, she insisted, by the fact that Woman was the "last at the cross and the first at the sepulcher" and that it was to Woman that Christ first appeared after His resurrection. However, because of Eve's having been unjustly blamed for the expulsion from the Garden of Eden, "eternity has no time and words no power to express the despairing anguish and woeful heart experiences which have been the lot of Woman through all the ages."

Upon discovering that she was a third cousin once removed to Elizabeth Cady Stanton, Ruth longed to go where the big-league suffragists roamed. In a letter to her teenage son Floyd she explained, "If I don't get out of this town, I'll go crazy." So she left Floyd to finish high school while living with an uncle, and she dragged Peter Pealer to Washington, D.C.

Hating housework, Ruth insisted they live in a hotel. While Peter worked at the Bureau of Engraving and Printing, Ruth joined the Women's Christian Temperance Union and Wimodaughsis (short for Women/mothers/daughters/sisters), a suffrage association. She also served as president of the Women's National Press Association.

Ruth attended rallies addressed by Susan B. Anthony and commented in letters to my grandfather on the beautiful hats and dresses of the audience. She marched up and down Pennsylvania Avenue in a hat piled high with fake fruit and flowers, demanding the vote. About her fellow suffragists she wrote to her son, "People outside have no idea of the 'push,' interest, and determination of the women to win their cause. There is no such word as 'fail' with them, and that is a force that men will find it impossible to break."

Sadly, Ruth sliced her finger on the edge of a page in the *Saturday Evening Post* and died of septicemia before seeing women enfranchised. The deciding ballot in favor of national suffrage for women was cast, coincidentally, by a young legislator from East Tennessee. The night before the vote in Nashville, this young man received a letter from his mother in the mountains saying that she counted on him to do right by her and his sisters. The next day he switched his vote from con to pro. Afterward he had to jump out a window to escape an enraged mob of opponents.

In emulation of this refreshing new role model, I volunteer as a birth control and abortion counselor at Planned Parenthood, having been permanently traumatized in high school by seeing the lives of some of my classmates destroyed by a lack of such services.

Wearing a gold enamel bracelet of Greatgrandma Pealer's that my mother has given me, I march on Washington at the drop of a hat. Each time I round the corner and start down Pennsylvania Avenue through the gauntlet of jeering men who hate everything I represent, I draw courage from the image of Inez Milholland in her white robes, riding a white horse, leading Greatgrandma Pealer and her cohorts through similar mobs in 1913. I try to do my tiny bit to keep their ball rolling, but I avoid the *Saturday Evening Post*.

# Insects in Amber

SOON WEARIED BY THE TRAFFIC JAMS of Gotham and inspired by the vision of surviving a nuclear attack with a home garden, Richard and I go back to the land in rural Vermont. Living in a crumbling brick farmhouse on a defunct dairy farm, we discover why our ancestors left the land in the first place. As the communes all around us turn on and tune out, I smoke beehives. As they smash monogamy, Richard faints while castrating baby roosters into capons.

When I become pregnant, I realize that I've finally found my calling: I'm an Earth Mother. Dressed in an Indian-print peasant dress, I attend natural childbirth classes, where I learn the breathing techniques that will allow my baby and me to escape poisoning from narcotics hawked by a drug industry motivated by greed.

One night I dream I'm holding our new baby. As I inspect its tiny hands, I discover an extra finger on each one. Although I wake up sweating, I laugh this off to Richard, explaining my childhood obsession with the Melungeons. But when I'm tired, I drive Richard mad itemizing the things that might go wrong. And I know them all from the dinner-table seminars with my father.

When we reach the Burlington hospital, the maternity wing is closed for renovations. My contractions are coming fast as we race for the other hospital. Its overcrowded maternity floor is packed with moaning mothers. I join them on my gurney of pain as a protesting Richard is led away to the fathers' waiting room.

It's hunting season, so many of the obstetricians are stalking deer in the snowy forests. The doctor on call has just had a heart attack during a delivery. Things don't look promising, but I keep panting as I've been taught, like a hound with heat stroke. Never in my wildest fantasies have I imagined such pain. The torments devised by the Marquis de Sade would seem like child's play to any woman who's ever been through labor.

Soon I'm begging for every drug ever invented, delighted at the prospect of single-handedly supporting the entire pharmaceutical industry. I pledge to purchase large blocks of their stock if I survive this ordeal, which looks increasingly unlikely.

This prognosis is confirmed when I hear a soft murmuring above me that includes the name of Jesus. A nun is standing over me telling her rosary beads.

Don't talk to me about Christ's suffering on the cross, I silently rage. Did Jesus push a bowling ball through the nozzle of a pastry bag with his stomach muscles? As I scowl at this presumed virgin in black, the next contraction hits me.

When it's over, I'm enchanted with the results — a tiny baby girl as exhausted as I am. Richard assures me she has no extra digits.

To occupy myself while my daughter Sara naps, I decide that either I can watch *As the World Turns* or I can write my own soap opera. I start my first novel. When Sara is awake, I put her in a backpack and we hike through the woods and pastures. Or she toddles around the yard tormenting the dog as I garden. Or she plays with pot lids on the kitchen floor as I can tomatoes or make raspberry jam.

While she sleeps, I write about a character who doesn't know who she is. She tries on roles as though they're Halloween costumes, but none fits — including Earth Motherhood.

My current problem is that I don't do drugs. When people pass joints at parties, I diligently inhale. But instead of collapsing into hysterical laughter over bad jokes, I fall asleep, confirming my lifelong reputation as a drag.

In addition, because of my occasional bouts of melancholy I'm leery of introducing outside chemicals into the already noxious soup my body can brew for itself. And I've read that magic mushrooms are sometimes dried apples injected with hog tranquilizer.

One of my father's favorite stories concerns his treating a dozen people for lockjaw one night at the Roosevelt Hospital in New York. They all attended a party at which they shot up heroin cut on a dusty mantel. The dust gave all these hip fun-seekers tetanus.

One afternoon I find myself leaving Sara with Richard and driving to the University of Vermont library to look up those six-fingered bogeymen of my youth — the Melungeons.

I learn that they were a group of olive-skinned people found living in what is now northeastern Tennessee by the early European settlers. In 1782, John Sevier reputedly found "white Indians" in that area. They themselves said they were "Portyghee." But certain seemingly non-Portuguese surnames are associated with them — Collins, Mullins, Goins, Bolling, and Gibson being the most common. Most researchers source the name Melungeon to the French word *mélange*, meaning "mixed."

I picture my high school classmates who bore those surnames, but I can't recall any distinguishing characteristics. They had many different shades of eye, hair, and skin, and none had six fingers.

My sources divide into two hostile camps. The Romantics ascribe Melungeon origins to Portuguese sailors shipwrecked on the Carolina coast, to survivors of Sir Walter Raleigh's Lost Colony on Roanoke Island, to deserters from sixteenth-century Spanish expeditions, or to other exotic sources too far-fetched even for someone as gullible as myself. Normally I'll believe anything for a while, but wayward Phoenicians in Appalachia nudge me over the edge.

The Academics, however, insist that the Melungeons are merely one of some two hundred groups of "tri-racial isolates" numbering around 100,000 people, found throughout the southeastern United States as far west as Louisiana and as far north as New Jersey. These communities — with names like the Redbones and the Brass Ankles, the Moors and the Turks — are said to be the product of early mixing on the frontier among natives, free blacks, escaped slaves, European fur traders, et al. Some were labeled "free persons of color" in census records.

In 1891, Nashville journalist Will Allen Dromgoole visited some Melungeons and described them as "natural born rogues, close, suspicious, inhospitable, untruthful, cowardly, and, to use their own word, sneaky."

None of my sources mentions cave dwellings or extra fingers.

I persuade a couple of magazines to commission articles from me — one on snake handlers for the *New York Times Sunday Magazine* and another on the Melungeons for a London sociological journal called *New Society*. Both require me to go to Tennessee, where I've spent very little time since leaving for Wellesley. I've popped in for holidays every year or two. But this time I stay long enough to take a look around.

As I stroll the sidewalks of my old neighborhood, I realize that two kids I played Trail of Tears with are now dead — Martha from the car crash and Pam from lupus. They say the good die young, and my own continued existence gives me pause. Martha and Pam were definitely good people. But it's also possible they didn't have enough time in which to be bad.

Martha's brother Nic works for Tennessee Eastman. Stacy is a long-distance trucker based in Texas. Stanley flies a corporate jet out of Mississippi. It's hard for me to picture the funny little kid who helped my brother Bill burn down our tree house piloting a plane with other people's lives in his hands. But he no doubt feels equally skeptical about my being in charge of a small child.

The girls with whom I cruised Broad Street are now living all over the country. Marty works for Proctor and Gamble in Cleveland. One Jane is a city planner in New Orleans. Another Jane is an executive at ABC in New York. Barbara is a banker in Massachusetts. Portia is a real estate lawyer in Chicago. Susan is an investment analyst in New York.

My brother Bill is in medical school in New Orleans, and Michael is at Vanderbilt. After MIT and Columbia, John joined the sociology department at UNC Chapel Hill. He married his high school girlfriend, a gifted pianist with degrees from Duke and Harvard, and they have two young daughters. He's on the vestry of the Episcopal church. He wears handsome tweed jackets with suede elbow patches, and he smokes a pipe. He has clearly negotiated his identity crisis more successfully than I.

It would be stretching credibility to claim that we're all part of the Appalachian brain drain, but it's true that we've all left town. Even my grandmother has flown the coop. She's commandeered my retired Latin teacher to tour the Holy Land, sending my parents a photo of Miss Elmore and herself, both wearing Arab keffiyehs, sitting astride camels with a pyramid behind them and two sinister-looking Bedouin guides below.

I borrow one of my parents' cars and drive downtown for old times' sake. As I cruise a deserted Broad Street to the boarded-up train station, I discover that J. Fred's has been turned into a discount furniture store. The movie theaters are closed, one having become a cheerleading school. Many stores are vacant. Nobody is walking the streets. The Model City has become a ghost town. Everyone must be shopping at the new mall or eating at restaurants on the franchise strip along the highway. I realize that you really can't go home again, but only because home as you knew it no longer exists.

As I approach the church circle, I study the four red-brick

churches with their white spires. Apart from my wedding day, I haven't been inside a church since I left for college. My grandmother was right to worry that once I left here, I'd never look back. But in order not to, I've performed an autolobotomy, renouncing religion, Republicans, and the Vietnam War. I help distraught women find abortions. My favorite members of my consciousness-raising group are lesbians, a category I didn't even know existed when I lived here. I've attended several of their gatherings, one a costume party at which I dressed as the Virgin Mary in a blue nightgown with a halo made from a foil-wrapped coat hanger. Their indifference to convention is refreshing.

But relics from my past keep surfacing like the bloated corpses of drowned swimmers. For instance, I always sit with my back to a wall because my mother used to tell us that Wild Bill Hickock was shot dead on the one day he played poker with his back to an open door. You can flee the forces that have formed you and join the Witness Protection Program in a foreign land. But like Mafia hit men, they just keep on coming, tracking you down despite your cleverest disguises.

As I drive up Watauga Street past the manor houses of the Yankee factory executives, I reflect that at least my parents still live in the house my grandparents built. Yet they've moved on, too. My father's nearing retirement. He's built a tennis court in the backyard and bought a ski chalet in North Carolina. After a lifetime of fourteen-hour workdays he takes time off now to ski, golf, and play tennis. He and my mother make annual ski trips to Colorado with my sister Jane.

Jane has turned into a striking young woman with her olive skin, dark auburn hair, and pale gray eyes that shift to blue or green depending on what she's wearing. She skis on the ski patrol and plays number 1 on the D-B tennis team. She's also first in her class academically, and she has a wacky sense of humor. On weekends she works as a dancing mushroom at the Land of Oz theme park on nearby Beech Mountain. It's as though she's an only child and the rest of us are Joseph's wicked older siblings in *The Coat of Many Colors.* I warn her never to sit with her back to a doorway.

Leaving Sara with my mother, I drive down to a building sided with asphalt shingles that sits in a forest clearing outside Newport, Tennessee. A sign over the door reads "Holiness Church of God in Jesus Name." Men in green or khaki work clothes and women in housedresses are climbing out of battered pickup trucks. A few men carry small cages such as travelers use for their cats. One carries a guitar case.

The preacher, Liston, who drives a truck for a canning factory, has a pocked face, gelled hair, and long sideburns. He greets me warmly and ushers me inside to a seat on a wooden bench. The church members glance at me with shy smiles.

Once the service starts, Liston asks me to say a few words. I stand up and mumble something lame about appreciating their letting me share in their worship service.

A dozen women and girls in long dresses come forward. The guitarist starts playing, and they begin to sing, shaking tambourines and clashing cymbals —

> *It's God here on the platform.*
> *It's God back by the door.*
> *It's God in the amen corner,*
> *And it's God all over the floor. . . .*

Liston's sermon is quiet at first, with lots of Bible quotes, including the one from Mark 16:17–18 on which snake handling is based: "And these signs shall follow them that believe; in my name shall they cast out devils; they shall speak with new tongues; they shall take up Serpents; and if they drink any deadly thing, it shall not hurt them."

Gradually his voice grows louder and louder, faster and

faster, until he's in the full harangue mode that resembles to-bacco auctioneering. I've heard this style of preaching all my life — on the country radio station where John used to be a disc jockey and at the preaching missions every winter in the civic auditorium. But this is the first time I've understood that the actual words are irrelevant. The power comes from the pounding rhythm, every line punctuated by a loud HAH!

And it *is* powerful. It's the origin of the phrase "preaching up a storm." Possibly the driving beat synchronizes the audience's brain waves so that they cease to be individuals and become a mob. But snake handlers call the state of grace they believe they achieve from it an "anointing." One has described feeling as though warm oil were being poured over his head.

Once the atmosphere in the small room is as combustible as gunpowder, a half dozen men take the snakes from their cages — copperheads, rattlers, and cottonmouths. Others swig from a Coke bottle alleged to contain strychnine. (In 1973, Liston's brother and another preacher died from drinking strychnine during a service.)

The men mill around up front, stroking their pet serpents and shouting incoherent praises to the Lord. Some snakes stiffen and sway like dancing cobras. Eyes glazed over, the men wander around displaying their erect snakes to the enthralled or terrified congregation, some of whom pray out loud or speak in tongues or "shout" (a high-pitched scream accompanied by a lashing, jerking movement of the upper body).

Several men lend their snakes to another man, who ends up with an entire writhing handful that resembles the severed head of Medusa. The newly snakeless jump up and down on stiff legs, arms to their sides. Or they raise both hands to the ceiling with delighted smiles, as though soliciting blessings.

By subduing these snakes, which represent the serpent in Eden, these believers are proving that God will protect those who master evil. (Some seventy-seven of the estimated two to five thousand members of this faith have died from snakebites. Though most of the bitten refuse treatment, my father has tended a few in the emergency room and reports that it's an awful death. Like suicide bombers or kamikaze pilots, this cult may prove self-limiting.)

With a start I realize that if Liston calls me forward, I may go. I'm appalled to realize that my sense of politesse is so exaggerated that I'd even juggle a rattlesnake so as not to appear rude to these overwrought Christians, most of whom look like hardworking farmers, truck drivers, factory workers, and housewives. This is probably the most stimulation they've experienced all week. The famous mountain feuds over who left the gate open so the hogs got out may have entertained their forebears similarly.

Even more stimulating, snake handling is illegal in Tennessee. The state, while upholding religious freedoms, affirmed in court its right "to guard against the unnecessary creation of widows and orphans."

Afterward I bid Liston farewell and climb into my car. One of tonight's snake handlers will soon be sentenced to six years in prison for assault after flinging a rattlesnake at someone during a service. In Alabama, another preacher will be sent to prison for life for banging his cage with a stick to upset the snakes and then forcing his wife's hand inside it. Although bitten twice, she survived and reported him to the sheriff.

As I drive back toward Kingsport, I contrast this mayhem to a typical service at St. Paul's Episcopal. There, men in pinstriped suits and women in mink coats intone the General Confession from the prayer book: "We acknowledge and bewail our manifold sins and wickednesses, which we from time to time most grievously have committed by thought, word, and deed against Thy divine majesty, provoking most justly Thy wrath and indignation against us. We do earnestly repent and are heartily sorry for these our misdoings. The remembrance of them is grievous unto us. The burden of them is intolerable."

I admire the sedate cadences of the elegant language. But I recall a Vermont friend's referring to Episcopalians as God's Frozen People. When the choice is between meltdown or glaciation, is it any wonder that I've left town?

I head out to the cabin on our farm so I can wake up early and plan my Melungeon trip. I get out of the car to open the gate. After driving through it, I get out again to close the gate.

As I return to the car, a huge white shape emerges from the dark, like Moby Dick appearing to Captain Ahab. This apparition races me to the car, but I get there first and slam the door in its face, which upon close inspection turns out to belong to a slavering bull named Caesar. I wave to him with a middle finger.

I let myself into the cabin at the bottom of the hill. It was built around 1820 by a saddle maker named Everett Mahoney on land stolen from the Cherokee. Mahoney was the son of an Irishman who came to Philadelphia from Dublin as an indentured servant in 1773. Much of our area was settled by former indentured servants and their children, who streamed south from Pennsylvania and west from the Virginia Tidewater once they served their terms. Mahoney built this cabin from squared chestnut logs and paneled it inside with planks of black walnut.

I dump my gear in the front bedroom and climb into my father's boyhood bedstead, completely exhausted. It's not every day that I consider cuddling Christian copperheads or get chased by a homicidal bull. As I doze off, I make a mental note for my article that the impulse behind both snake handling and bullfighting is probably the same — to combat rural boredom by tormenting lethal creatures.

The next morning I phone Len, the son of Caesar's owner. Younger than I, he wears his hair hanging loose to his shoulders. He sometimes rides an ATV up the valley to check on the cows, leaping around the hills on it like a mountain goat on speed. Despite his mountain-man persona, no one could be nicer or more helpful. Except perhaps his parents, Paul and Wanda, who are probably the kindest and hardest-working people I've ever known.

As a child, I used to watch them harvest tobacco in the field beside our pond. They cut each leaf from its stalk. Holding a stem in both hands, they'd impale it on a metal spike fitted over the end of a wooden pole. Once a pole was packed with leaves, it was pitched like a tepee with the leaves spread out around it to dry in the sun. Then the poles were hung in the rafters of our barn to cure. One time Wanda ran her spike through her hand. But she just wrapped it in a rag and kept on working.

Whenever one of my brothers expressed interest in dropping out of school, my father would send him to work tobacco with Wanda and Paul so he could experience his future without a formal education. After a few days, he'd be thrilled to limp back to class.

"Len," I say when he answers his phone, "Caesar nearly gored me last night when I came in."

"Oh, yeah," he says, "we was having trouble with him, so we put him in your field."

"Thanks a lot."

"If he bothers you, just shoot him with your shotgun."

"I don't own a shotgun," I reply through gritted teeth.

"Well, get you one, then."

"I don't want a shotgun."

"Well, just reach down like you was gonna pick up a rock to throw at him, and he'll back off right quick."

"Len, get that bull out of our yard!"

"Okay, no problem," he says amiably.

I sit down on the porch and gaze out at the pond, where migrating mallards are paddling around on a rest break. A hunched blue heron stands in the shallows, still as a statue, waiting for some hapless minnow to pass by. Bluebirds and cardinals flit in and out of the bushes behind him.

Beyond the pond stretches the valley. It's narrow and flat

with steep hills on either side. Clusters of black-and-white Holsteins are grazing all along it. At the turn of the twentieth century, a doctor named Horne lived in this cabin and reportedly hosted horse races down that valley.

The silence is soon broken by a racket of grunting and snorting. Len has evidently returned Caesar to his harem. He's now standing at the electric fence that separates the dairy cows from the beef cattle. Opposite him looms the Black Angus bull, whose herd of cows and heifers is grazing behind him, oblivious to his heroics on their behalf. The two bulls snort at each other and paw the ground, as though they've been watching too many documentaries on Pamplona.

They take a break so that each can mount one of his long-suffering cows and show the other what he's got. Then the bulls swagger back to the fence and resume their bellowing.

Len and his father know each of these three hundred cows by name. When I was growing up, we split a cow with them every year for meat. I remember the year we ate the cow named Lisa. So do my therapists.

I try my best to ignore all this testosterone and think instead about my Melungeon article. A few miles away, just down the road from Erwin (the town that lynched the elephant), lies an archaeological site called Plum Grove. The first time I tried to visit it, the forest ranger, worried I might loot the unguarded site for artifacts, refused to tell me where it was. I reminded him that it was located in a national forest and I was a taxpayer. He reluctantly drew me a map to the field, which sits in a wide valley alongside the Nolichucky River.

Plum Grove has been carbon-dated to the mid-1400s. Some researchers believe it to be the ruins of a Yuchi town named Guasili, through which Hernando de Soto marched in 1540. The Guasilians gave the Spaniards baskets of puppies to roast for dinner. The soldiers enjoyed Guasili so much that after they left, they called out "House of Guasili" for good luck when rolling dice.

The Yuchi, called the Chisca by the Spaniards, are thought

to descend from the Woodland period mound builders who occupied the Southeast from around 1000 B.C. to A.D. 800. The Yuchi called themselves Tsoyaha, "children of the sun." Other tribes and various Europeans called them the Tongora, Oustack, Tahogalewi, Hogoheegee, Rickahokan, and Hogologe.

Some Spanish soldiers under Sergeant Hernando Moyano fought a battle with the Yuchi in 1566 at their town called Maniateque near present-day Saltville, Virginia. The Spaniards claimed to have burned fifty houses and killed a thousand people. Soon afterward they attacked a second town called Guapere on the upper Watauga River, where they killed fifteen hundred Yuchi by burning down the huts in which they were cowering.

In 1600 the governor of La Florida (as the Spaniards called the entire Southeast), Don Gonzalo Méndez de Canço, interviewed two Indian women named Teresa Martyn and Luisa Menendez. They'd left their village in Yuchi territory to travel to St. Augustine with a Spanish exploring party. These women claimed the Yuchi were "white-skinned, blue-eyed, and red-haired."

In a 1714 battle with the Cherokee, a thousand residents of another Yuchi village barred themselves in their council house once it was clear they'd be defeated. The young, the old, and the women were strangled by the warriors, who then impaled themselves on arrows or hanged themselves from the rafters with their bowstrings. Some survivors were absorbed by the Cherokee. Others joined the Creek in Georgia or the Seminole in Florida. Still others formed a fierce slave-catching tribe in South Carolina called the Westo. (I wonder if some might have moved thirty miles northwest to become the Melungeons.)

A similar fate met many southeastern tribes when the Europeans arrived. The tribes moved to new locations under pressure from the westward-pressing settlers or from other dislocated tribes. They had multiple names in the various native and European languages. These names were rarely what they called themselves. And when these names were written down, each recorder transcribed his own phonetic version. For instance,

Yuchi was also written as Hughchee, Euchee, and Uge. Reduced in numbers by epidemics, starvation, slavery, alcoholism, and war with Europeans and other tribes, the remnants of weaker tribes merged with stronger ones.

As boys, my father and his friends collected boxes of arrow-heads, spearheads, and potsherds from creek banks and burial mounds all around our area. Their collection is now housed in a museum at the University of Tennessee. My father used to lead us kids on similar excursions. When we'd get lost, he'd say, "Don't worry: I'm just taking you back to the Indians." I used to fret about whether he was kidding — until I realized that the Indians were no longer there to go back to.

I drive toward Sneedville, said to be the epicenter of Melungeon settlement. Compared to the Rockies or the Alps, the southern Appalachians are foothills. But compared to the Green Mountains of Vermont, they seem wild and rugged. Southward-creeping glaciers ground nearly half a mile off the Green Mountains, rounded their summits, and broadened their valleys. But some eighty-two peaks in the glacier-free southern Appalachians rise higher than five thousand feet, and the valleys here are deep and narrow. Twilight comes early to these hollows as the sun plunges behind the parapets of rock.

Once you've wound up and down these claustrophobic mountains on hairpin switchbacks for several hours, your heart leaps into your throat when you drive out into a broad valley, and you can very well imagine what settlers must have felt after spending weeks trudging through these punishing mountains. Valley land here has always been highly valued because it's level and easily plowed. Prior to the Tennessee Valley Authority dams, the creeks and rivers flooded most springs, leaving deposits of rich topsoil. Indians built their villages above these waterways because crops grew well in the floodplain and because the rivers provided water, transportation, and fish.

When European settlers arrived, they, too, coveted this rich bottomland. So, in the largest land grab since the Norman Conquest, they simply took it. Or not so simply, because it required many decades of bogus treaties and bloody warfare, culminating in the Trail of Tears. Although American schoolchildren learn that our continent was a vast uninhabited wilderness when Europeans "discovered" it, current estimates place the native population of North America at somewhere between five and twenty million. These people spoke over five hundred languages. The Ohio River Valley alone contained five thousand villages.

"Free person of color" (FPC) was a category applied in the nineteenth century to anyone whose skin wasn't pale enough to allow him or her to pass for a northern European. This included Middle Easterners, Native Americans, Africans, East Asians, East Indians, Mediterraneans, or any mixture of these.

Of course, many settlers were illiterate and had no record of who their ancestors were. Many hid exotic origins, changing or anglicizing their names, moving to new places, fabricating new ancestors. So in practice, it was darker skin that made you vulnerable to being labeled FPC. Since FPCs weren't allowed to testify against white people in court, those who were edged off their land had no recourse (short of murder or suicide) but to move to a place no one else wanted, like a swamp or a mountaintop.

One such spot is Newman's Ridge. It looms over Sneedville, the county seat for Hancock County, the poorest county in Tennessee, with 29.4 percent of its citizens living below the poverty line.

I drive my parents' Buick up and down the rutted dirt roads across the face of Newman's Ridge, searching for Melungeons. Fifty years earlier, several hundred people lived here. Now all I find on the densely wooded cliffs are a few vacation cabins, a deserted church, and the ruins of some farmhouses and outbuildings in fields overrun with briars and saplings.

The only signs of life I discover are a couple of new ranch houses on the main road and a well-tended cemetery on a slope overlooking the Cumberland Mountains, which stretch ridge upon ridge toward Virginia. Wandering among the headstones, some merely flat rocks with names and dates scratched onto their faces, I find several of the traditional Melungeon surnames — Mullins, Collins, Goins, Gibson. Whatever their hardships while alive, these Melungeons are enjoying in death some of the most spectacular views I've ever seen.

I drive into Sneedville, park, and stroll around the streets past the usual feed store, drugstore, grocery store, hardware store, and funeral home found in any rural county seat. In the eighteenth century, this spot was a favorite meeting place for trappers and hunters, who called it Greasy Rock. The few people I pass look just like the farmers who used to gather on Broad Street in Kingsport on Saturday mornings. I don't see a single extra finger.

I phone a woman with a Melungeon last name, a friend of a friend. She lives close by and comes down to meet me on the main street. An attractive woman in a tailored suit, she looks like an escapee from the Virginia Club. We sit down over coffee in a small restaurant and discuss the weather and our mutual friends. Eventually I tell her about my proposed article, asking her if she's Melungeon and whether I could interview her.

She gives me a look that would wilt a stalk of celery. Too late I remember how to operate in the South: you must never ask a direct question. Most southerners have plenty to hide, but they consider it rude to refuse a request. Therefore, as in China, good manners here consist of never putting another in the position of having to say no.

"My family is descended from de Soto's exploring party in the sixteenth century," she replies icily and with finality.

As I drive back to Kingsport with no material for my article, I remember too late having been warned that calling someone a Melungeon in Sneedville is like calling a black person a nigger. I've been impersonating a Yankee for so long that I've forgotten the southern codes, which have remained remarkably intact, like insects in amber, despite the widely bruited homogenization of

America. In New York, a murderer will walk right up and shoot you. In the South, he'll bring you casseroles until he gets to know you, and then he'll shoot you.

Shaking off my chagrin, I review the more exotic Melungeon origin myths — shipwrecked Portuguese sailors, de Soto's deserters, survivors of the Lost Colony. I conclude that life on the isolated farms of Appalachia is stultifying and that romantic tales about one's glamorous forebears make it less dreary.

When I'm trying to write fiction, I prefer to lock myself in a small room without a view. I turn off the phone and unplug the TV. If I can bear the wait, characters eventually emerge to relieve my boredom, like a child's imaginary playmates. No doubt a similar process of sensory deprivation has produced these unlikely Melungeon myths.

After my arrival this trip, I rode around Food City with my father in a motorized cart, to spare his bad back. Grocery shopping can take him several hours because many store employees and customers are his patients, and they all want to regale him with tales of their latest ailments.

He introduced me to an old woman with no teeth, who was stocking a shelf in the pasta aisle. He told her I was a writer in town to research some magazine articles.

She said companionably, "Well, I reckon readin's good, ain't it?"

Because many Appalachians have been, and are, illiterate, a rich oral culture has evolved. The International Storytelling Center is only a few miles from our farm, and their festivals draw thousands. People need their stories, true or not, and the Melungeons are no exception.

As I drive back to my parents' house, I run a gauntlet of churches in competition over which can post the most clever sayings on its illuminated signboard out front.

Today the Bethel Presbyterian sign reads

**A SHARP TONGUE CAN CUT YOUR OWN THROAT.**

Across the highway I pass the Belvue Christian church, whose message is

**IF GOD FILED A 1040, COULD HE CLAIM YOU AS A DEPENDENT?**

As I ponder this question, I study the marquee at St. Luke's Methodist next door:

**TODAY IS A GIFT. THAT'S WHY IT'S CALLED THE PRESENT.**

The Glenview Baptists across the street warn

**THE WAGES OF SIN ARE DEATH. REPENT BEFORE PAYDAY.**

I like that one, but I decide that today's winner is the New Covenant Free Pentecostals down the block with their

**IF YOU GIVE SATAN AN INCH, HE'LL BECOME YOUR RULER.**


I'm sitting in the backyard of some of my parents' friends whom I particularly like. Throughout my childhood they always bought whatever junk I was selling for school fund-raisers — magazine subscriptions, Girl Scout cookies, chocolate bars, greeting cards. I tell them about my doomed Melungeon article and my failures in the field as a journalist.

Mrs. Shobe stands up and disappears. She returns with her elderly yardman in tow, announcing that he was born in Hancock County to a mother whose maiden name was Collins.

I stand up from my lounger to shake his hand. A tall, lanky man in bib overalls, he has straight white hair and high cheekbones. The whites of his eyes are bright around navy blue irises, and his face looks as though he's been sweeping chimneys.

We sit down and chat interminably about the habits of rhododendrons.

Finally Mrs. Shobe asks, "Buddy, are you a Melungeon?"

I blush furiously. She's from Louisiana. She must not realize that this is a question one doesn't pose.

"Half Melungeon," he replies pleasantly.

"Where did your people come from?" she asks.

"I don't know nothing about it." He describes moving as a child from Kentucky to Virginia, where his parents sold him to a farmer for twenty-five cents a day.

"Sold you?" I echo faintly.

"I worked for him from sunup to sundown ever' day of the year but Christmas."

"When did you go to school?"

"Didn't never go to no school. Wouldn't nobody take me, not the whites nor the coloreds, neither one. I was too dark for the whites and too pale for the coloreds."

He describes his children — one in Indiana, a second in Maryland, and a third an airplane mechanic in Louisiana. "Seem like that they don't much care to come home no more," he says sadly.

Back in Vermont I write my article about going in search of the Melungeons and finding that the only ones still on Newman's Ridge are lying in their graves. The younger generations have fled the stigma, blending imperceptibly into the American mainstream. Once Buddy's generation is gone, there will be no more Melungeons. I mock my quest for these legendary mixed-race people when I myself am of Dutch, French, German, Scottish, Irish, English, and perhaps Native American heritage.

I close with a quote taken from a newspaper interview with a Melungeon bank president in Sneedville: "Any mystery our people ever had is gone — or at least any way of solving it. We are all immigrants in this country."

May the Melungeons rest in peace, I think as I push the envelope containing the article through the mail slot at the post office.

As I write about the snake handlers for the *New York Times*, I realize that although I don't miss church, I do miss God. Eating, breeding, and interior design are terrific, but if this is all there is, why bother?

This thought plunges me into the melancholy familiar from my college years. To combat it I check out an armload of books from the University of Vermont library on the various world religions.

As I read about the Puritans and their almost pornographic fixation on original sin, I begin to suspect that I've inherited my melancholy from my mother's Puritan forebears. The Puritans seem as relentless as Southern Baptists in their preoccupation with the fires of hell and as obsessed as the snake handlers with evil. Virginians slaughtered Indians because they wanted their land, but Puritans slaughtered them because they saw them as Satan.

I find Hinduism with its cast of plotting gods and goddesses amusing, especially in contrast to the cool austerities of the Buddhists. Those two are the East Indian equivalent of Baptists and Episcopalians.

But it's the Cherokee who grab me by the throat and won't let go. Maybe it comes from having spent too much time on farms, but I've always suspected that each creature contains a spark from the same flame. Whether you call this flame God or the Great Spirit doesn't matter. And the best part is that you don't have to handle snakes or even set foot in a church to experience it. You live it every day by the way in which you treat the other creatures who are essentially yourself. The cruel merit pity rather than hatred because their behavior is proof that they haven't yet located this crucial core within themselves.

This notion of God as Mr. Rogers seems much more soothing than that of God as a bipolar Santa who dispenses rewards and punishments to His cowering elves based on whether they've been naughty or nice.

Clinging to this sunny theology as though to a rope lowered to a suffocating miner in a collapsing shaft, I return to my neglected novel. I finally get to be a flag swinger by turning my main character, Ginny, into one. Always a recycler, I invent a Melungeon boyfriend for her, one who becomes a snake handler.

Nodding to my preoccupation with extra fingers, I make Ginny's father lose one in an accident. I give her mother idiopathic thrombocytopenic purpura. And I get rid of Ginny's lesbian lover by decapitation as she rides a snowmobile under a barbed wire fence, just as I myself once rode my pony under a wire clothesline.

By the end of *Kinflicks*, I foolishly believe that I've exorcised my past and am now free to start afresh.

## Wannabes

M Y DEBAUCHED SOUTHERN SELF wants to spend the money my novel has earned on a new Jaguar. But my thrifty Puritan self, knowing that I may never earn another penny from my writing, wants to invest it so I can pay myself a salary and continue to write what I please. Having finally realized that I'm a bisectional, I decide to honor both selves by salting some away for the famine and using the rest to take Richard, Sara, and me to London for a couple of years. I've always wanted to live in a foreign country, so I persuade Richard and Sara that they do, too.

We rent an apartment in Hampstead across the road from the Heath, the eight-hundred-acre park that overlooks the city. I expect to fit right in here because of the eleven lines of Great-grandma Pealer's family that hailed from England and because of Grandmom Reed's ancestral land grants from James I.

But in a nightmare flashback to my own childhood, Sara immediately comes home from school in tears because her British classmates have mocked her accent.

"Tell them that if it weren't for people who talk like you do, they'd be speaking German," suggests my brother John, who's visiting.

Eventually we make some friends. Sara's is an urchin named Phoebe, who conducts her around the neighborhood along the tops of the walls that divide the backyards. Phoebe regularly steals all the fruit from our fruit bowl and teaches Sara how to shoplift.

I fall into a nest of feminists — socialist feminists, Marxist feminists, cultural feminists, radical feminists. Although they spend lots of time arguing about their differences, I can't tell them apart. They all seem like bright, attractive, excessively rational young women. But the only thing they share, ideologically speaking, is a hatred of America as the seat of power for the capitalist patriarchy.

Sometimes I serve as their whipping boy. "You Americans this, that, and the other . . . ," they snarl, with no seeming awareness of whose British ancestors first taught Americans the wiles of empire-building.

I'm intrigued because I've never been accused of being an American before. I point out that just as England isn't London, so America isn't New York City or Hollywood. Just as the English have Cornwall and Yorkshire, so do Americans have Tennessee and Vermont. But when I mention having taken Sara to London's first McDonald's, they go into a group cardiac arrest that nearly ends the budding friendships.

Sometimes leaving a place behind lets you see it more clearly. As Sarah Orne Jewett once wrote Willa Cather, "One must know the world so well before one can know the parish." With three thousand miles between Tennessee and me, I start to remember things about my childhood that I've conveniently repressed — the iron staircase up the side of the State Theater, the water fountain at J.C. Penney's labeled "Colored," the ghetto of red-brick apartment buildings across the railroad tracks.

I remember my father's describing a Ku Klux Klan march up Broad Street when he was a boy during which he and his friends identified the marchers by their shoes. And I recall finding a tattered Ku Klux Klan manual in a box in our attic. When I brought it downstairs, my appalled mother said the box had been left there by one of my grandmother's cousins.

I also recall, before my wedding, a party at the house of some family friends at which one of the caterers turned out to be Henrietta. Henrietta was our cook until I was six. Cooks in those years also cleaned house and looked after children. Henrietta even went with us to New York to visit my mother's family. When Michael was born, she quit, saying four children were too many.

I hadn't seen Henrietta since, and I scarcely remembered her. But when I spotted her in her white uniform, setting a casserole of garlic grits on the buffet table, I rushed over and threw my arms around her. Her arms remained at her sides. I backed away, as shocked as she by my behavior. But my body must have stored up a record of her many kindnesses to me when I was small.

I explained who I was.

She replied, "It's nice to see you again, Miss Lisa."

She turned and walked back into the kitchen. I just stood there, wondering if there had been a hint of irony in her "Miss Lisa."

Looking back on this from London, I can certainly understand any irony. My family paid her the going rate of $20 per week to take care of us, while her own children stayed home alone. Ever since my Wellesley years I've been exempting Appalachia, and therefore myself, from racism, but I've been mistaken. Our town's pleasant life was made possible by the underpaid labor of our black citizens. The only roles in which I ever saw them were as maids, janitors, or yardmen.

I start a new novel to sort out these troubling memories, naming it *Original Sins*. But for me, unlike for my Puritan forebears, original sin isn't something that infects a baby at birth. It's imposed on him or her by the surrounding community insofar as they rank one another by superficial differences such as skin color, accents, possessions, or genitalia.

Gradually the politics of my new friends begin to seep into this novel about a small mill town in East Tennessee. I start regarding the Model City as a colony of Yankee industrialists, exploited for its cheap labor, abundant raw materials, and lack of environmental protection laws. These capitalists, fleeing the unions of immigrant workers up north, were lured to Kingsport by J. Fred Johnson's promise of a plentiful supply of "100 percent hardworking, God-fearing Anglo-Saxon workers," as promotional materials described the parents and grandparents of my friends and classmates.

By threatening the whites in town with the availability of the blacks, the benevolent plant managers on Watauga Street, with whom my grandmother played bridge and my grandfather played golf, kept wages low and profits high. Like Squanto, who taught the Pilgrims to grow corn, and Sacagawea, who guided Lewis and Clark to the Pacific, and Pocahontas, who saved Jamestown from starvation, my beloved grandparents were actually Uncle Tom Toms.

I reflect on the demented caricatures of these "100 percent Anglo-Saxon" mountaineers in the funny papers and on television — *Deliverance, Heehaw, The Beverly Hillbillies, Li'l Abner.* If you can dehumanize your victims, as American soldiers did the Vietnamese, you don't have to feel quite so guilty about exploiting or destroying them.

*Original Sins* features five characters who grow up together — two sons of a mill worker, two daughters of a mill manager, and a son of the manager's maid. Three leave town, and two stay. The question I struggle with in foggy Londontown is why those who leave a place leave and why those who stay, stay. Why did certain fish decide to crawl out on dry land? Why did my grandparents desert the coalfields of Virginia? Why did I abandon the beautiful Tennessee river valley they bequeathed me? After 592 pages I conclude that people leave a place because they don't fit in.

One of my new friends from London longs to see the American South, so she joins me on a visit to Kingsport. We meet my grandmother for lunch at the country club. I have to hand it to my grandmother: she doesn't even blink at my friend's spiky magenta hair and dangling labrys earrings.

We sit at a table by a window overlooking the Holston River. My grandmother points out her house on the opposite cliff. Then she asks my Marxist comrade if it's difficult to find reliable servants in London these days.

Back in London, I meet a family of Afghanis through mutual friends. The father has published several books of teaching stories taken from the Sufi tradition, and his sister has collected and recorded folktales from traditional cultures all over the world. The Sufi stories feature animals in the same role as do Cherokee tales — to illustrate the antics of an individual's psyche. The two sets of tales from opposite sides of the globe seem almost like branches of the same tree. A couple of stories are identical in both traditions, apart from adaptations to the local environments.

I consider staying permanently in London so that I don't have to be an American anymore. Although I've only officially been one since I arrived in England, shouldering the blame for everything that's wrong with the world has me already exhausted. I'd have preferred to remain a simple Appalachian peasant so that I could be a victim of American imperialism rather than its perpetrator. But if I could become an exile in England instead of just a tourist, I could disclaim responsibility for anything at all.

I also love living at the crossroads of the former British Empire. Every day I meet fascinating new people from South Africa, New Zealand, India. Each time I fly out of Heathrow, I stand in front of the departure board and savor the names of the destinations, just as I did with the boxcars back home: Athens, Barcelona, Lisbon, Moscow, Stockholm, Tangiers. . . .

On the other hand, after two years in London I still feel like a foreigner, despite the Tidewater land grants. My British friends are cool, witty, and urbane. Their most insulting epithet is "wet," meaning "earnest," which they often apply to Americans (despite the fact that it won't be Americans who will build an altar of teddy bears outside Kensington Palace after Princess

Di's death). If you lay dying among the strutting pigeons in Trafalgar Square, your charming rescuers would offer you a pun to undercut the gravity of your situation. The British lack the Christ-crazed hysteria of southerners and the somber fanaticism of Yankees, and I find myself homesick for both.

In the end, I conclude that it isn't healthy for me to live in a place where people hate me for eating hamburgers.

Back in Vermont, as I await publication of *Original Sins*, curiosity finally trumps inertia. For many years I wondered why my father or grandparents didn't take us to meet our Virginia relatives. But I've had my driver's license for over twenty years now, and I've never gone either. Now that I have a child of my own, I find myself more interested in the gossamer webs of kinship. So I decide to fly to Tennessee, leave Sara with my parents, and at last drive to southwest Virginia to meet some of these strangers who reputedly share my genes.

After I arrive at my parents' house, my grandmother's silver Cadillac materializes in the driveway like the coupe of Cruella De Vil. I go out to greet her. Her frosted perm is afrizzle, but she says nothing. She believes that cultivated people should communicate in ultrasonic squeaks, like bats. And she does get her point across: she doesn't want me to visit her childhood stomping grounds. But I don't know why.

She slides out of her car. As I hug her, I can tell that she's lost weight. Encased in mink, she feels like a bear emerging from hibernation after a long winter's nap. I've heard through the grapevine that the Virginia Club is appalled by my first novel, *Kinflicks*. It's bawdy and contains some vulgar language. It also implicitly criticizes Tennessee Eastman, Kingsport's sugar teat, for polluting the town's air and water. No one has uttered a word about the book to my grandmother, in keeping with the old southern dictum, "If you can't be kind, be vague."

Looking me up and down, my grandmother says, "You know, your father's a wonderful man."

"Yes, ma'am, he is." I glance at her quizzically.

"He never has a bad word to say about you!"

She sweeps inside to greet Sara, leaving me standing in the driveway feeling as though I've just been slapped.

My father's response to *Kinflicks* was, with an amused smile, "I ought to take you out to the woodshed."

But my friend Nellie reports that he's written on a slip of paper the amount of money for which the paperback rights sold and pinned it inside his suit jacket. Whenever people bring up the book at parties, he just opens his jacket and flashes the amount at them to shut them up.

I soak my corn bread in the liquid from my soup beans at a cafeteria in Clintwood, Virginia. Across from me sit my father's schoolteacher first cousins, Vonda and Zella. I'm trying to figure out why my grandmother has never introduced us. They seem delightful in every way.

I'm intrigued by their names, but they have no ancestral explanation for them. Their parents just liked the sounds. This isn't uncommon in our region. Some of my relatives I've never met are named Arbutus, Nicatie, Bluford, Darkus, Ordealy, Perlina, Orbra, Bureta, Ancil, Rebeal. One is even named Spicie Dewdrop. And I've heard of girls in Riverview called Formica Dinette and Placenta Sue.

Vonda tells me about a road trip another cousin took with my grandmother. Several hours from home my grandmother realized that she'd forgotten her glasses.

When they checked out of their hotel the next morning, my grandmother said to the desk clerk, "Sir, I know that your guests must sometimes leave their eyeglasses in their rooms?"

"Yes, ma'am," he said, "plenty do. We save them in a box in case they come back for them."

My grandmother explained her plight. She proposed borrowing an abandoned pair to use on her trip, which she'd return to him on the way home. He pulled out the box of glasses. She tried some on, picked a pair she liked, and continued down the road. Vonda marvels at my grandmother's resourcefulness, insisting there has never been a problem she couldn't solve. (*Kinflicks* may be the first.)

A jury arrives at the cafeteria from the courthouse across the street. Our waitress explains that the case they're hearing involves a football star at the local high school. The previous year he ran into a goalpost headfirst, scoring a winning touchdown and breaking his neck. He was buried in a church cemetery in town. The footballer's parents have divorced, and his mother is moving away. She's suing the father for custody. She wants to dig up their son and take him with her.

After lunch, I scale a steep hill on the edge of town. In the doorway of her attractive contemporary house I meet my grandmother's cousin Hetty Swindall Sutherland. A decade older than my father, she wears her gray hair in a braid coiled atop her head. Vonda and Zella have reported that she sprints up and down her bluff, into town and back, every day. She reminds me of an aging Heidi. After assuring me that the rumors of a Cherokee in the family are untrue, she gives me a huge volume of oral histories collected early in the twentieth century by her late lawyer husband from the original settlers of the county.

Back in the car I look up the references to my various ancestors. One concerns my four-times-great-grandmother Betty Reeves. Her great-granddaughter, a first cousin to both my grandparents, states that Betty was a Portuguese Indian. I sit in stunned silence. Is this what my grandmother doesn't want me to know? Some of the early Melungeons claimed they were Portuguese. . . .

I also find several accounts of Civil War skirmishes in that area. I learn that my grandmother's grandfather John Wesley Swindall (also my grandfather's great-uncle) was a sergeant in the Union army. There's a photo of him and his wife. He has straight black hair, a bushy gray beard that conceals his face, and small dark eyes. His wife, Polly Phipps, a granddaughter of the Portuguese Indian Betty Reeves, is a dark-eyed brunette. I read that John Wesley's mother, Betsy Swindall, never married and that John Wesley's father was named Solomon Tolliver.

I discover that my grandmother's great-uncle Eli Vanover injured an arm fighting for the Union in the battle of Cranesnest in 1864. Her great-grandfather George Howell also fought for the Union in that battle.

My grandfather Reed's parents, as well as some Vanover relatives of my grandmother, moved behind Union lines in Kentucky so as not to have to support the Confederacy. My grandfather's grandfather Robert Y. Haynes was taken prisoner by some Confederate soldiers, who slaughtered one of his cows. Ironic that my grandfather put himself through medical school by caring for Confederate veterans, some of whom might have fought against his own relatives.

Having at last accepted that Appalachians are as racist as other southerners, I now discover that most of my ancestors supported the Union. I'd revere my ancestors, whoever they are — but who the hell are they? No wonder my grandmother, self-proclaimed duchess of Dixie, doesn't want me prowling around over here. If she's a southerner, then Billy Graham is Jewish.

Next I drive to the town of Wise to meet a distant cousin named Greg. We sit over glasses of iced tea in a coffee shop. He has dark, shiny hair and ruddy coloring. A few years younger than I, he's writing a history of my grandmother's family, the Vanovers. He, too, is a schoolteacher, and he tells me about tracing the Vanovers back to Cornelys Van Hovgem, who emigrated in 1684 to Flatbush in Brooklyn from Zeeland in the Netherlands. His descendants moved to New Jersey and then to North Carolina, where the fifth Cornelius Vanover married a woman named Abby Easterd, who is Greg's and my four-times-great-grandmother. Greg says some of her earlier descendants applied for membership in the Cherokee Nation based on their claim that she was a full-blooded Cherokee.

He shows me the first photo I've ever seen of William

Vanover, my grandmother's grandfather, himself a grandson of Abby Easterd. He has high cheekbones and dark eyes set deep in their sockets. If the rumors about Abby are true, he'd have been a quarter Cherokee, and he does look it.

There are other nonwhites in the family, Greg says. When I press him, he replies that some Vanovers were described as Black Dutch by their neighbors. When I ask what this means, he hops in his car and speeds away. Later I write him several letters that he never answers.

My fourth stop on this Heritage Trail is the cabin of my grandfather's nephew Bob, the son of a man who drove a wagon from the lowlands loaded with merchandise for his father's store in the mountains. Bob was like a kid brother to my grandfather. My mother says I met him at my grandfather's funeral, but I don't remember him.

Banjo music drifts from his tiny cabin, which sits alone in a hilltop clearing in the middle of nowhere. Bob answers the door, holding the banjo by its neck. Well along in years, he looks like my grandfather's identical twin, tall and lean with a large beaked nose and ears with unusually long lobes. Put a headdress on him, and he'd be a dead ringer for a Shawnee warrior.

Nancy Skaggs, my grandfather's paternal grandmother and Bob's great-grandmother, was reputedly kidnapped by several renegade Shawnee from her family's homestead in the Virginia backwoods. The story goes that a man named George Reed tracked these Shawnee to their encampment and rescued Nancy as the Shawnee slept. George and Nancy hid overnight in a cave while the enraged Indians hunted for them.

Nine months later, Nancy, now Mrs. Reed, gave birth to my grandfather's father, also named George Reed. Everyone apparently pretended to believe that old George was, in fact, the father of little George. But they must have wondered if it were really possible to make love in a cave while angry Indians were searching for you. Could one of the Shawnee have actually fathered little George?

Every second family in the South claims descent from either a Cherokee princess or a European woman abducted by ravaging natives. Several volumes of Indian captivity narratives were published in the nineteenth century. Some of the kidnapped Europeans wanted to remain with their captors, saying that they found Indian society more congenial than the lives they'd left behind.

The card-carrying members of Native American tribes that have achieved recognition from the federal government call such Europeans who claim Indian ancestry "wannabes." I understand their scorn, stemming no doubt from an aversion to sharing their casino profits with those whose ancestors escaped the depredations heaped on others whose complexions left them no choice but to be labeled Indian.

I once talked in Boston with a couple of members of a small California tribe who ridiculed the Cherokee for accepting so many wannabes. I felt as though I were at a meeting of the membership committee for the Virginia Club. (Future DNA testing will show that federally recognized tribes exhibit an average of 61.1 percent Native American ancestry, whereas the unrecognized exhibit 47.6 percent.)

The function of such pervasive wannabe mythology may be to explain away darker-skinned family members. Also, if you can claim a few drops of native blood, perhaps you don't have to feel quite so guilty about the relentless atrocities committed on Indians by your European ancestors.

But in some cases wannabes could be actually-ares. Plenty of people with documented Indian heritage who were pale enough to dodge it didn't want their names on some official government watch list, where they'd be sitting ducks for any new form of discrimination that might come down the pike. Even now some descendants of these unrecorded Indians sneer at the "reservation Indians" for having been bought off by government subsidies.

As we sit down on Bob's cot, he tells me about having been a miner and then a car salesman. He says my grandfather owned one of the first autos in the county — a Model T Ford. He was thrilled at the prospect of putting his horses out to pasture. But when he tried to drive the car on his house calls, it got mired down in the rutted wagon paths that served as roads.

One day when he was creeping down a steep incline, his brakes failed. The car picked up speed. My grandfather jumped out just as the Ford careened off the track and bounced down a cliff on its hard rubber tires. At the foot of the cove it plunged into a creek. He decided to leave it there and bring his horses back from retirement.

When I mention having visited Hetty, Bob tells me about two of her husband's in-laws, brothers named Cage and Buck Ervin, who were arrested for passing counterfeit coins. While awaiting trial in a jail cell, Buck groaned, "Cage, I'm worried that we won't get justice."

"Shut up, you sorry fool," Cage hissed, "we don't *want* justice."

Then Bob tells me about my grandfather's uncle Caleb Haynes, who longed to be a preacher. At the end of his first sermon, as he exhorted his audience to come to the altar and be saved, he proclaimed, "The time which was to have arriven has arroven!" The congregation started giggling and couldn't stop.

Next Bob tells me about my grandfather's first love, Maggie Gibson. She married someone else and moved to Kentucky. I recognize Gibson as a Melungeon surname. Having failed to learn from experience, I ask Bob if Maggie was Melungeon.

Bob grabs his banjo and begins playing a reel, explaining that he often plays it for barn dances. I have to admire my relatives' powers of deflection. They've honed to a fine edge the ability to tell someone to get lost in the most charming ways possible.

As I drive away, I reflect on my grandfather's failed love. Did he not marry Maggie because she was Melungeon? Might his sister Evalyn have opposed such a union? Or did Maggie's family object to him because he was a landless, penniless orphan? Or was he too young? He ran away from his sister's farm in his early teens, hiking a hundred miles through the Cumberlands to join two brothers in Kentucky. Was he trailing woefully along after Maggie and her new husband? Or might he and Maggie have tried to run off together and been stopped? I'll never know now because my grandfather is dead. Although sad for him that this relationship didn't work out, I'm glad for myself. Otherwise, I wouldn't exist.

One after another I pass the church marquees on the outskirts of Kingsport, consulting their messages as earnestly as I would the slips in fortune cookies:

**JESUS IS MY ROCK AND MY NAME IS ON HIS ROLL.**
**A MIND IN THE GUTTER IS A LIFE DOWN THE DRAIN.**
**COME ON IN AND JOIN OUR PROPHET-SHARING PLAN.**
**AVOID TRUTH DECAY: BRUSH UP ON YOUR BIBLE.**

And today's winner is, I silently announce to my imaginary audience of enthralled Christians, the Bethel Presbyterians with

**NOTHING TO BE THANKFUL FOR? TRY TAKING YOUR OWN PULSE.**

Back at my parents' house I tell them about my encounters. We try to decide whether my grandmother is afraid I'll have learned about Maggie Gibson, Betty Reeves, Abby Easterd, Bob Artrip's low-rent living arrangements, John Wesley Swindall's having been in the Union army, or his illegitimacy. Or is there some other unsavory secret I haven't yet sniffed out?

My father tells us about Bob's father, Casander, the teamster who was also sheriff for his county. One afternoon when my father was a boy, Uncle Cas took him fishing. They sat on a hillside while Cas drank from a jar of home brew and tossed sticks of dynamite into the creek below. He sent my father down to collect the fish that landed on the shore.

Finally my father asked, "Uncle Cas, isn't this against the law?"

Cas replied, "Son, in these parts, I am the law."

22

My father speculates that this is why his parents left that area — to escape both the omnipresent moonshine and the casual violence. He said my grandfather carried a revolver when he lived there, not just as protection against drug addicts but also in response to a death threat from someone unhappy with his political affiliation.

My mother has just returned from church, where she's heard that my grandmother's aunt Ura Grizzle is ill. My mother suggests I go see Ura, since she's 104 and may not live much longer. Maybe she'll provide some of the information my grandmother has censored. My father has said that when he was a boy Aunt Ura told him there were Cherokee in her family. I've met Aunt Ura just once, even though she lives only a dozen blocks away with her daughter, Annette. For many years she was the truancy officer for the Kingsport schools.

"If 'twere well done," quotes my mother, "'twere well 'twere done quickly."

My mother is pleased I'm showing an interest in my ancestry. She's spent all her adult life in the South with her nearest relatives nine hundred miles away. Her own ancestors have been more real to her than her everyday acquaintances, not unlike the cast of *The Young and the Restless* for a soap opera addict. She's constantly struggling to decipher boxes full of their correspondence. She refers to them, in a phrase from the Episcopal prayer book, as her "cloud of witnesses."

My mother's favorite saying, no doubt handed down from Cotton Mather, is, "Use it up, wear it out, make it do, or do without." She prides herself on never having bought a mattress, having inherited them all. Every mattress in our house has been slept on by scores of her witnesses. They feel like it, too, each with a body-shaped crater in the center that it's impossible not to roll into at night, like an open grave. Lying there in these family foxholes, I always feel as though I'm cradled in the embrace of my Pilgrim fathers.

I phone my grandmother to convey greetings from Vonda,

Zella, Bob, and Hetty. But I censor news of Maggie Gibson, Abby Easterd, Betty Reeves, and John Wesley Swindall. She's so intent on her Tidewater ties to Confederate cavaliers that I don't have the heart to unknot them. But I do realize that it's through such cowardice that the great scams of history are perpetuated.

Although my evasions about my trip may have put her mind at ease, I can tell from her tone of voice that she's still suffering over *Kinflicks*. As a peace offering, I ask if we can go together to visit Aunt Ura.

She hesitates, then replies, "Well, we might could, but we hadn't ought."

There's a long silence. Every time she comes out with one of these anachronisms from the hills, I'm reduced to speechlessness, feeling myself in the presence of a flesh-and-blood fossil. She seems embarrassed, as though her dentures have just tumbled out on the dinner table.

"Why not?" I finally ask.

"Aunt Ura may be dying."

"Isn't that all the more reason to visit her?"

"Let her die in peace," murmurs my grandmother.

I say nothing, but I see no reason why Aunt Ura should get to die in peace when I'm coming unglued trying to figure out what these people are hiding from me. I've never been a fan of conspiracy theories, believing for example that Lee Harvey Oswald was likely a lone lunatic. But lately my grandmother has been behaving like Lady Macbeth in more than just her diction. Who are these shunned ancestors whose legacy she's strangled with her well-manicured hands?

I go see Aunt Ura anyway. After all, she's my twice-great-aunt. I find her lying on white sheets in a bedroom in Annette's house. Her face is dark and cracked like an old motorcycle jacket. Her sharp cheekbones form caves for her tightly shut eyes. She resembles a mummy. I reflect with wonder that her father John Wesley Swindall fought in the Civil War. As Faulkner said, "The past is never dead. It's not even past."

I sit down and chat with Annette, eventually describing my mission. I don't use the M-word, having finally understood that it's a deal-breaker for older people who haven't grown up in an era of ethnic chic. But I do use the C-word, asking Aunt Ura in her apparent coma if she knows whether we have any Cherokee ancestors.

She lies so still that I begin to suspect she's already dead. After a while she rolls over and turns her back to me. Annette looks at me, her dark eyebrows raised, and shrugs. I apologize to Aunt Ura for bothering her, and I wish her a speedy recovery.

As I head back to my parents' house, I reflect that someone who's guarded her secrets for 104 years isn't about to spill them now, deathbed or no, and certainly not to a published author. This is Kingsport, Tennessee, after all, not Hollywood, California.

## Blood Sport

FOR THE NEXT DECADE AND A HALF, I give scarcely a thought to my annoying ancestors. I'm too preoccupied with the present, having joined a feminist karate group. We've hired a brown belt from Florida to instruct us. But everyone is down on her because she acts as though she knows more than we do. Many are complaining that she's elitist. We spend our practice sessions sitting in a circle with her, processing our resentment. Those who feel a circle is too fascistic roam the room, offering their feedback from wherever they please.

I've also joined a basketball team called the Hot Flashes. We play in the Burlington city league against teams of former stars from the local colleges. Because of our antihierarchical policy of letting every member play an equal number of minutes, even those who can't dribble, we usually lose by at least a hundred points.

In addition to my athletic endeavors, I'm busy policing a teenager, writing novels and traveling to promote them, getting divorced, conducting romances, and attending therapy sessions to recover from them. A child of the sixties, I came of age believing that the human heart was just another muscle, one that could be strengthened by aerobics, the more the better. Always a slow learner, I prowled around a few too many campfires, trying to project an aura of louche glamour, before finally understanding that my heart is not a muscle. It's a mushmelon, unsuitable for use as a kickball on the playground of desire. I've also gradually come to understand that other people's hearts can be snapped as easily as chicken necks and must be handled with care, or not at all.

Never one to waste material I've paid good money to acquire, I write my third novel, *Other Women*, about the interaction between a therapist and her client, a lesbian mother and emergency room nurse who's trying to comprehend the violence in the world. It's set entirely in New England, the first time I've grappled fictionally with Yankees. But since I've by now lived longer in the North than in Tennessee, it seems about time. And therapists strike me as the Yankee equivalent to southern preachers — the often flawed mortals to whom you skulk once you finally admit that you don't have all the answers. For several hours each week for six months I've interviewed my ex-therapist, trying to gain some insight into the mechanics of the process.

Psychotherapy was nearly as popular as polio when I was growing up. We Kingsporters were supposed to pull ourselves up by our bootstraps while maintaining stiff upper lips. I start fretting that once this book about people who acknowledge problems and seek help for them is published, I'll undergo a public defrocking as both a southerner and an Appalachian.

To make matters worse, both southern and Appalachian women are known for standing by their men, single-handedly harvesting tobacco crops, sewing wardrobes from flour sacks, and planting petunias in diesel tires — even as their men drink, gamble away their paychecks, run around with honky-tonk whores, and knock their devoted wives senseless. I used to see the "accidents" resulting from this ethos while working as a candy striper at my father's hospital during high school. By featuring a heroine who prefers to stand by another woman, it seems likely that I'll not only get myself defrocked but may also be branded on the forehead with a large letter *L* in the middle of the church circle at the head of Broad Street.

\*

My father calls one night in the midst of all this personal growth to say that my grandmother has died. I'm unexpectedly grief-stricken — unexpectedly because she was ninety-nine years old and I thought I was prepared for her departure. Every time we parted during the past twenty-five years she told me, "Now, Lisa, this is the last time you'll see me alive."

She always seemed leery of death, which surprised me because she was such a staunch Baptist. I suspect she was worried about hell, though I can't imagine why, since I'm sure her most egregious act might have been to steal a recipe or two from a fellow Virginia Clubber.

In any case, you can't prepare for the loss of someone you've loved. My grandmother has loomed large in my life, and with her goes a whole chunk of my past. With her also goes my last chance to learn firsthand the truth about her mysterious family.

*Other Women* comes out, and nothing much happens. There are the usual nasty reviews that no one but me notices — and some nice reviews that I scarcely notice because I'm so upset by the bad ones. If anyone in Kingsport has even read the book, they don't mention it. (This means they hate it.) I get a few letters from disgruntled therapists, suggesting that I stick to my own profession. But the defrocking and branding don't occur. I'm almost disappointed. As any mother of a teen knows, most people prefer even negative attention to no attention at all.

One night I find myself in the basement of a Vermont church with several dozen recovering alcoholics. The therapist I interviewed for *Other Women* died of alcoholism as I sat at her bedside in the Burlington hospital. Although I thought I knew her well, I had no clue she was a closet drinker. Since I drink very little, and my parents and grandparents not at all, I didn't notice any warning signs. But I still blame myself for not having somehow intervened.

I'm also mad as hell at her for posing as an expert on human behavior while secretly drinking herself to death. I've been trying to convince myself that a creek can still convey water to the thirsty even if it absorbs none itself. But creeks don't charge $75 an hour for their services.

While sitting there listening to grim sagas of violence and despair, I glance at a woman who's cross-legged on the floor beside me. In her lap lies an open copy of *Other Women*. Many sentences are underlined in black ink or highlighted in yellow. I suppress a snort of laughter and decide not to tell her that the crackpot to her left is its author. It might be as demoralizing as learning that your priest abuses altar boys — or that your therapist is an alcoholic.

Fourteen of us are gathered at Richard's cottage on Lake Champlain — my parents from Tennessee plus all my siblings, their spouses, and children from North Carolina, Virginia, Pennsylvania, and California. It's twilight. The day has been a scorcher, and the lake surface is glassy. Most of us are eating inside when John and his wife Dale yell from the porch that something strange is going on in the lake. We all run out and stand along the bank, hearing waves crashing on the rocks farther down the point.

Suddenly, some twenty feet offshore we spot a snakelike creature the diameter of a truck tire slithering past us. At any one time three or four rolling humps break the surface. They're dark in color, but they glisten in the fading light. Speechless, we watch this creature, which appears to be about thirty feet long, as it parallels the shoreline. Its wake slaps the shelves of rock below us.

"Somebody get a camera," murmurs Michael. But no one moves.

The animal curves away from us and heads out to the middle of the lake.

My family has never even heard of Champ, as Vermonters call this legendary creature. I find it satisfying watching them struggle to fit it into their scientific worldview. In addition to my father, Bill, Michael, and Jane are physicians. John is a sociology professor. They've always been a sleeper cell of skeptics in a loony world. Every woolly concept that was ever voiced at our dinner table — astrology or UFOs, the Virgin Birth or the parting of the Red Sea — was always blown clean like a dandelion gone to seed.

I'm the black sheep, often agraze in the pastures of la-la land. I'll believe anything, at least for a while. I inherited this trait from my grandfather Reed, who once bought beachfront property in Florida sight unseen. When he visited it, it lay under three feet of water. He sold it for pennies on the dollar to a developer, who filled the area with sludge from the Gulf, built a gated community, and made millions.

My family members are speculating about floating logs, wakes from unseen boats, and schools of giant fish. But all reluctantly agree that none of these scenarios fits what we've just seen.

Richard phones the Champ hotline to report our sighting. The man on the other end, who's never seen Champ himself, despite having spent his vacations floating around the lake in an inflatable boat, nearly weeps as he adds ours to his list of 250 sightings. The first recorded one was by Samuel de Champlain in 1609, and several of the most recent were by Vermont's former governor Richard Snelling, an enthusiastic sailor.

Coincidentally or not, the cliff across the lake from this cottage was called Snake Mountain by the Iroquois, who had a legend of a horned serpent who lived in these waters. The lake at this point is over four hundred feet deep. Some believe it to be connected by underwater caverns and rivers to smaller lakes in Canada and the Adirondacks, where there have also been reports of Champ-like creatures over the centuries.

The handful of sane scientists who will openly endorse the possibility of the existence of a breeding colony of Champs in Lake Champlain propose that they're descended from marine reptiles called plesiosaurs, thought to have gone extinct along with the dinosaurs sixty-five million years ago. Their reasoning is that some survivors were trapped in Lake Champlain after the last ice age, when the glaciers melted to form the lake and the land crust, freed from their weight, rebounded to cut the lake off from the St. Lawrence seaway and the Atlantic.

The next morning John, the professor, comes downstairs looking frazzled. He has puffy bags under his eyes. He announces, "I've finally figured it out: that was no sea monster. It was a line of frogmen in wet suits doing the butterfly."

I begin to suspect that in my northward flight toward freedom, I haven't really left home. The house I'm living in, on farmland outside a Vermont village of 2,500 people, is an 1803 brick Georgian with a layout identical to that of the house in which I grew up. The foothills I used to hike, with Sara in a backpack, are similar to those I roamed as a child. The fields around me are full of Holsteins, just like our farm back home.

Vermonters, although more reticent than East Tennesseans, have the same droll affability. The accent is different, but the grammar "mistakes" are the same. I could just as easily hear "I ain't never seen nobody like you" in Vermont as in Tennessee. And I know a man up here who's called Snake Eye.

Vermont, I finally register, is merely the northern end of the Appalachians, which is why I feel so much at home here. The entire mountain range was settled by Anglo-Saxons and Celts — predominantly English Puritans in Vermont and Scots-Irish in the South. The settlers' ballads, clogging, and speech patterns were nearly identical all along its length, apart from contributions by the Cherokee in the South and the French Canadians in Vermont. I conclude that the Mason-Dixon line is an imaginary demarcation established for reasons of political manipulation. The reality is that Vermonters and Tennesseans are two of the Lost Tribes of Britain. I don't have to choose between them anymore because they're one and the same.

In the grip of this awareness I write my fourth novel, *Bedrock*, which features a Vermont village full of eccentrics, composites of people and situations I've known in both Tennessee and Vermont.

By now I've lived in Vermont for twenty-five years, and several of my mother's eighteenth-century ancestors lie buried in Rockingham, Vermont. Nonetheless, a Boston reviewer maintains that I have no right to satirize Vermonters since I'm a southerner.

I'm standing on a hillside overlooking Lake Champlain. The sun is setting in shades of salmon behind the Adirondacks on the opposite shore. In the field below me, several dozen buffalo are grazing. I'm surrounded by a hundred women in attractive cocktail attire. At the top of the hill perches a vast white pinnacled tent that resembles Camelot, where we'll soon dance, drink, and dine.

But meanwhile, we're watching two women dressed in white satin tuxedos wave feathers over a smudge pot so as to waft smoke toward the four poles. As the priestess in her embroidered robe reads lines from Kahlil Gibran, I realize that I'm wrong once again: this event would never ever occur at the Southern Baptist end of the Appalachians.

Once my daughter is grown and gone, I'm lonely in my farmhouse in the Vermont countryside, despite the amiable Holsteins all around me. So I buy an apartment on the Upper West Side of Manhattan near Central Park. When my parents come to visit, we walk down to the Roosevelt/St. Luke's Hospital, where my father was a resident. We study the dome of the old operating theater where he watched and performed hundreds of operations. They point out the apartment on West Fifty-eighth Street where they lived for four years. My mother tells about wheeling John twice a day to the playgrounds and zoo in Central Park even while pregnant with me.

I've unwittingly bought an apartment only nine blocks from the site of my conception. Like a salmon leaping upstream, I've returned to my spawning ground.

With a second jolt I comprehend that I'm not actually a southerner, an Appalachian, or a Yankee — I'm a New Yorker. (New Yorkers aren't Yankees. They're a breed apart.)

I spent my first seven months in utero on the Upper West Side and in Central Park. I no doubt absorbed through the wall of my mother's abdomen the honking horns and screeching brakes, the sirens of police cars and ambulances, the shrieks of children in the playgrounds, the clop of carriage horses' hooves, the scraping of skate blades on the ice rink, the melodies from the calliope at the merry-go-round, the calls of birds and animals at the zoo, the speech of shopkeepers and waiters, the tunes at the Broadway musicals about which my parents are reminiscing. The amniotic fluid in which I floated was composed of water from the New York taps, and my bones were formed of calcium from the milk and cheeses bought at New York delis.

After all these years of searching, I finally know who I am: I'm a cosmopolite, a creature of busy streets where darkness never falls. This city chicken has finally swooped home to her natal roost.

My apartment is located in a building near Central Park, one of half a dozen built in the early 1900s by European writers, painters, and musicians who wanted space in which they could work as well as live. Most apartments, including mine, have huge north-facing windows for the painters. Some have extra soundproofing for the musicians. The elegant front apartments have two-story living rooms and elaborate oak woodwork. The rear ones like mine, much smaller, were the working studios.

My building has a cage-style elevator. Every time I enter it, I expect to find Katharine Hepburn seated on its tapestry-covered banquette. The other owners are friendly, helpful, and interesting. Some are writers, publishers, and photographers. Others are involved with the Metropolitan Opera just down the street. There are lawyers and stockbrokers, businesspeople, filmmakers, and restaurateurs.

The only bad apple I'm aware of was murdered shortly after my arrival by a girl in his stable, according to one of my doormen. (Like a Greek chorus, the doormen of New York know all—

and tell all.) Slight and bespectacled, the murder victim played an oboe in an orchestra when he wasn't pimping. We used to chat about Mozart in the elevator.

I have several friends in the city from my publishing days, as well as some writer friends and a college roommate. I find my fellow New Yorkers quite stimulating. The only problem is that we're so busy that we rarely see one another. We work day and night, and on the weekends most go to country houses. Although I still own my house in Vermont, it's too far away for weekend excursions, so I often write on weekends as well. New York is my new orange crate.

I keep in touch with my New York friends via messages on our answering machines. Unless you impersonate the Dalai Lama, they can't make a date with you on their Palm Pilots in under three weeks. Once those weeks have expired, they cancel.

Canceling in New York is a spiritual discipline, like a Japanese tea ceremony. It's important to cancel, but not too soon. If you don't cancel, the other person may think that you have nothing more important to do than to see him, which will lessen his respect for you. But should you cancel too soon, he might have time to make other plans, rather than sitting at home alone thinking about how much more important you are than he.

The only way to be absolutely certain that you maintain the respect of your New York friends is never to call them at all, which will prove that, like them, you're too busy and important to have time for your friends. But this may incite them to call you for dates that they can cancel so as to regain your respect for them as people who are too busy to see you. Either that, or they'll forget all about you.

If you do get to lay eyes on the elusive New Yorker, it's often at very delightful dinner parties. During the conversations everyone lets it be known that not only is he or she a New Yorker, he's also Jewish or French or Chinese, African-American or Italian-American or Irish-American. Their confidence about exactly who they are gives me a severe case of genus envy.

One night I try to emulate their ethnic élan by mentioning that not only am I an authentic in utero New Yorker, I'm also an Appalachian-American. My dinner companions look at me pityingly and segue seamlessly to another topic.

I guess if you live in a city of eight million, you need to be very clear about who you are or you might lose yourself in the crowds. This possibility reminds me of a Sufi story I heard from my Afghan friends in London about a merchant in a crowded caravanserai who ties a gourd around his ankle before going to sleep so that he'll know which person he is when he wakes up. To tease him another merchant ties his gourd on to someone else's ankle while he's asleep. When he awakens, the first merchant looks at the gourd on the other man's ankle and says to him, "Excuse me, but if you're me, then who am I?"

I'm sitting in an office in midtown Manhattan speaking my pidgin French with a chunky man with dyed red hair that doesn't suit his weathered face. You very quickly run out of small talk with a stranger, especially in a language not your own, but since this immersion course lasts for two weeks, we have to keep talking no matter what. So our topics are becoming increasingly intimate.

I tell him that I've decided I'm too lazy to be a New Yorker. I like to hang out. My character was shaped by cruising Broad Street. I'd like to cruise Broadway, but I can't find anyone who isn't working to do it with me. (In fact, the only person I can find to hang out with me at all is this elderly Frenchman who's charging me eighty dollars an hour. He thinks he's running a language school, but he's actually running an escort service.)

My tutor is Jewish, and he tells me about his activities with the Resistance during World War II, employing his language skills and various disguises against the SS somewhere in the Alps. Four times he was captured and sent to camps from which he escaped. He complains that some Frenchmen who collaborated big-time with the Nazis have never been charged.

I tell him about my father's experiences in the field hospitals of France. He listens intently. Then he thanks me for having done without my father as a baby so that he and others like him could live. Once I figure out what he's said, I almost burst into tears. I've never thought about it like that before.

Then he asks me (in French), "Why do you want to go to Paris? New York is the greatest city in the world. Why not just stay here?"

I don't admit that what I'm actually interested in is the three-hour lunches and the early-evening assignations with paramours that I've read about in Belle Epoque novels. Instead I explain that some of my ancestors were French and that I want to experience their world.

"Their world!" he snorts. "The French! What are the French? I'll tell you what the French are: the French take an anorexic woman and drape her in fabric and call it haute couture. The French cover disgusting animal organs with a sauce and call it haute cuisine. The French don't bathe for a week and then douse themselves in scent and call it *eau de quelquechose.*"

Although alarmed by this tirade, I assure him that I still want to go there. My mother's father's grandfather, Phillip Grün, was a miller in Alsace. And some of the ancestors that Great-grandma Pealer edited out of her DAR application were French Huguenots named Sauvage. My mother and I have tracked them from Montpelier to Picardy to London to Massachusetts.

My teacher gives a Gallic shrug. "You notice they all left?"

Undaunted, I rent a sixth-floor walk-up atop the butte of Montmartre from Jan, a professor friend in Florida. The entire City of Light spreads out below me, the Eiffel Tower in the center. I sit by the open doors in the afternoon sun for hours, smoking miniature Dutch cigars and reading French history, transfixed by the view as the swallows swoop and the clouds drift, as the sunlight shifts and fades, as the stars pop out above the city and the Eiffel Tower illuminates.

As with London and the land grants, and my New York days in utero, I expect to feel right at home here in Paris because of my French ancestors. Also, I know some writers and publishers here, as well as some American professors who own flats in which they spend vacations and sabbaticals.

But instead I soon feel like a Hun hunkered down outside the gates of Rome — especially after a French friend confides that it's considered bad manners to use someone's bathroom at a party. She says foreigners are forgiven since they don't know any better, but that French children are trained to use the toilet before they leave home and to hold it until they get back. This sounds not unlike the instructions given Negro children in the South during segregation. I blush thinking about all the French toilets I've unwittingly defiled.

I start to see what my tutor in New York was trying to warn me about. Distaste for the natural has inspired the French to invent such elegant contortions as ballet, dressage, Versailles, and the espaliered fruit tree. Since my French ancestors' surname, Sauvage, means "savage," I realize that my siege of the battlements of Artifice may as well be lifted before it's even begun.

I continue to find my French companions delightful in every way, but I come to understand the genesis of their Hundred Years' War with the British. In fact, I'm amazed it didn't last longer. No two groups could be more different and still metabolize oxygen. The English specialize in understatement. If his house and entire family have been swept away in a flash flood, an Englishman might acknowledge having had a bit of bad luck.

Whereas the French specialize in inflation. They're not just pleased to meet you, they're *ravi* or *enchanté*. They're not just sorry to miss your phone call, they're *désolé*. (In reality, the emotional charge behind a French *ravi* and an English *pleased* are roughly similar.)

You can see more of these differences in their novels. *Pride and Prejudice* starts with courtship and ends in marriage. *Madame Bovary* starts with marriage and ends in death.

For the English, love is pleasant, and sex can be rather jolly. But for the French, to love is to suffer. And a French friend once admitted that for her the best parts of sex are the chase before-hand and the Gitane after. From my reading of Lacan I know that for any self-respecting Gaul, an attraction, once consum-mated, is finished because *le désir* can exist only when its object is unattainable. Even Napoleon was quoted as saying, "The only victory in love is flight." This may explain why Paris has more citizens who live alone than any other city in the world.

In the end, I'm forced to face the fact that the Catholic an-cestors of my French friends, if they knew the Sauvages, hated them. They wanted to kill them in especially painful ways. They invited some Huguenots to Paris for a royal wedding and then murdered somewhere between 10,000 and 70,000 of them all across France, tossing them into the rivers until the waters flowed red with Huguenot blood. That's why the Sauvages fled. And you can't happily go home again if the people you left be-hind ran you out in the first place.

My fifth novel, *Five Minutes in Heaven,* is written in front of that window overlooking the Eiffel Tower, with the Arc de Triomphe and Notre Dame, Les Invalides and the Pantheon, lying below me like miniatures in a child's toy village. The book turns into an attempt to unite my own scattered beads of mercury — urban and rural, northern and southern, American and European. My main character grows up in East Tennessee, lives in New York City, and then moves to Paris. Experiencing these cultural dif-ferences, she comes to understand that love in its highest sense is the only force that can override the conflicts and violence that such surface variations incite.

Once I finish it, I feel suffused with an unfamiliar peace. I don't have to try to choose among my warring heritages anymore. They are all me. My psyche is a Balkans, but I can establish my own Yugoslavia within. I can be my own Tito.

A couple of American reviewers demand to know why an American would want to write about France, and French pub-lishers want nothing to do with the book.

\*

I return to Kingsport to do a reading from *Five Minutes in Heaven*. In preparation, I drive to Hair Benders, where I've had my hair cut on recent trips home by an entertaining beautician named Diane. This time she tries, as usual, to convince me to let her dye my graying hair. With a tragic expression she lifts strands and lets them fall limply to my head. I explain that I spend much of my time in Vermont and New York, where many women don't dye their hair.

She replies, "You know, that's the truth? Those Yankee women don't make a lot of effort. Why, one time I went up at Baltimore, and I couldn't hardly find me a woman worth looking at."

As she trims my dreary hair, she informs me that her mother was once the girlfriend of Duke Means, a notorious local moonshiner. One weekend when Duke failed to phone, her mother retaliated by marrying a mortician at the funeral home where she styled the hair of the corpses (which Diane says beauticians call, among themselves, "deadheads").

One night a few weeks later, Duke appeared at her door with his bodyguards. Showing her a small revolver cradled in one hand, he said, "Either you can come with me right now, or I can drop you to the floor."

Not surprisingly, she went with him.

Their affair eventually ended on an airplane runway in Middle Tennessee. The flight in Duke's private plane had been a stormy one, the plane bobbing like a cork on an angry sea. They couldn't find the airport through the cloud cover, and the gas was about to run out. Diane's mother prayed to the Lord that if He'd let them land safely, she'd return to her husband. All at once the sun burst forth and the clouds parted to reveal the landing strip.

Finding herself on the ground in one piece, she realized she had no choice but to strip off the jewelry Duke had given her and tell him it was over.

"I still don't see why she thought she had to return the jewelry," muses Diane. "It wasn't like that was part of the deal."

I tell her that my father was on call years later when Duke was carried into the emergency room with a gunshot wound in his chest. (He refused to say who had shot him or why.) Duke's heart had been nicked, and his chest was filling with blood. His family arrived and gathered around his bedside with a hamper full of fried chicken and deviled eggs.

Despite having no pulse, Duke was still conscious. My father explained to him that he needed to take some stitches in the bullet hole in his heart.

Eyes closed, Duke replied, "I don't want nobody operating on me but Doc Taylor."

My father said, "But Duke, we can't find Dr. Taylor. He's out on the golf course somewhere. And if I don't operate right now, you'll die."

Duke said, "Well, Doc, if Taylor don't show, you can just take me on over to the graveyard."

He didn't — and they did.

During my reading at a bookstore in the Kingsport mall, my friend Jody spots a new book and buys it for me — it's called *The Melungeons: The Resurrection of a Proud People.* The author, Brent Kennedy, is a self-acknowledged Melungeon.

As I read it that night, I encounter all the familiar origin theories. In addition, Kennedy presents his own belief that the original Melungeons descended, in part, from Turks marooned on the Carolina coast in the sixteenth century. He maintains that the name Melungeon may come from the Turkish *melun can* or the Arabic *melun jinn*, both meaning something like "cursed soul," which is no doubt how people stranded in a strange land surrounded by surly natives might feel about their plight. Later, he theorizes, this sobriquet was adopted by Europeans as a term of opprobrium for the descendants of these early Turks.

Kennedy goes on to discuss the different branches of his own family. One branch turns out to be on my family tree as well — twice over, since my grandparents were cousins. His grandmother's grandmother and mine were the same person: Polly Phipps, a granddaughter of the alleged Portuguese Indian, Betty Reeves. Polly's sister Susan was my grandfather's grandmother. In the appendix, Kennedy lists 137 Melungeon-related surnames. Fourteen appear in my grandparents' families.

I hunt down Kennedy by phone. Explaining that I'm both his third and fourth cousin, I request a meeting, to which he agrees. I drive to his office at the University of Virginia in Wise, where he's vice chancellor. He's a slender, handsome man a few years younger than I. He has wavy dark hair, a very tanned face, and malamute blue eyes. We discuss our shared family members, and he explains why he believes them to be Melungeon.

He says his mother was so concerned about his non-Celtic looks when he was in high school that she tried to persuade him to dye his hair blond. I force myself not to ask if she's changed her name to Diane and gone to work at Hair Benders.

Brent says that he began his research after learning he had sarcoidosis, a debilitating inflammatory disease usually found in people with African or Mediterranean heritage. Yet he'd always been told he was Irish. One relative poured gasoline on her family photos and burned them up after he asked to see them. Another told him to rot in hell for suggesting that their family might be anything other than Irish. Someone bearing a Melungeon surname posted a fatwa against him on the Internet for proposing that Africans were among the Melungeon mélange.

He confesses bewilderment, having originally thought people would be as eager as he to know the truth about their backgrounds. Clearly, he never met my grandmother, for whom genealogy was a blood sport in more ways than one.

At the end of our visit, Brent shows me the scars from the removal of his extra thumbs. One of his remaining thumbs is disfigured. He tells me that his great-aunt and several other Melungeons he knows have been born with six fingers on each hand. He jokes that they're thinking of starting a Six Finger Support Group.

In a state of shock, I drive back to Kingsport and through the row of church signboards that loom like the placards of rival polit-ical candidates. But all these churches are stumping for Jesus.

The Presbyterians counsel,

**THE TEN COMMANDMENTS ARE NOT A MULTIPLE CHOICE EXAM.**

The Christian church across the intersection says,

**IF YOU STAND FOR NOTHING, YOU'LL FALL FOR ANYTHING.**

The Methodists' offering is

**GOD IS DEAD. —NIETZSCHE**
**NIETZSCHE IS DEAD. —GOD**

The Baptists:

**PRAY FOR A GOOD HARVEST BUT KEEP HOEING.**

And the Pentecostals:

**SEVEN DAYS WITHOUT PRAYER MAKE ONE WEAK.**

But I'm too overwhelmed by Brent's extra thumbs to choose a winner for today.

My father is intrigued by the notion of being a Melungeon, though he says he's glad my grandmother is no longer around to hear this. As a doctor he's often encountered diseases in his patients that aren't supposed to exist in mountain people of supposedly British ancestry, such as sarcoidosis and thalassemia, a form of anemia that, like sickle cell anemia, confers a partial immunity against malaria.

My father also says he's always wondered why his mother's grandfather, William Vanover, left a fertile farm in North Car-olina for hardscrabble land in the Virginia mountains. Abby Easterd, the alleged Cherokee, was William's grandmother. He left North Carolina not long after the 1838 Trail of Tears. Could he have been driven off his family's land in the aftermath of the Cherokee roundup? my father asks.

William's father, Cornelius VI, half Cherokee if the rumors are true, signed his will with an X. Might the Vanovers, unable to leave a written account, have been too ashamed to pass on orally what had happened? Might they have tried to spare their descendants further grief by concealing unpleasant facts? After the southeastern Indians were supposedly all marched off to Oklahoma, dark skin in the Southeast was equated to African ancestry. Mulatto and FPC meant the same thing, and those who insisted on being Indians were ridiculed for trying to escape their fate as Africans. Many hid their Indian ancestry from fear of being shipped west.

I've now read about some ancestors that Brent Kennedy and I share — the Sizemores. They're the laughing stock of wannabe genealogy. They claim Cherokee descent, but their paper trail shows them to be white.

In 1906, the U.S. Supreme Court set aside several million dollars and a large amount of land with which to compensate the descendants of Cherokee who lost land under the 1835 Treaty of New Echota just prior to the Trail of Tears. To qualify, applicants had to establish their kinship to a name on one of the official tribal censuses of 1835, 1848, or 1851. Exceptions were occasionally made for those who could prove that their ancestors visited and were visited by enrolled Indians.

The Sizemores filed two thousand applications for reparations, representing five thousand family members, many of whom belonged to a nonrecognized tribe in Virginia called the White Top band of Cherokee. In their interviews, several claimed that their ancestors didn't appear on the tribal rolls because they were afraid that if they registered, they'd be sent to Oklahoma. All these Sizemore claims were rejected. (Future DNA testing of Sizemore males will show nearly two-thirds have Native American Y chromosomes.)

If protecting their descendants from persecution was the Vanovers' reason for silence and subterfuge, I'm grateful. I ponder that water fountain at J. C. Penney's labeled "Colored" and the side steps up to the balcony at the State Theater. If my ancestors hadn't been so close-lipped, might I, too, have been barred from drinking chocolate ice cream sodas at Kress's lunch counter, along with so much else? Probably not, because my father likely wouldn't have gone north to college — or to college at all. He wouldn't have met my mother, so I wouldn't exist.

Back in Vermont I struggle to fill in the missing leaves on my father's family tree like a paint-by-number canvas, trying to determine whether or not they were Melungeon. Via various new cyber-cousins encountered on the Internet I sometimes learn another name. But unlike Greatgrandma Pealer, the national genealogist for the DAR, I can't link my father's ancestors to Europe. Most lines vanish in the mid-1700s, like creeks in desert sand, somewhere along the New River in the borderlands between Virginia and North Carolina. (Like the Pont Neuf, the New Bridge, which is the oldest bridge in Paris, some claim, based on the ages of the rocks through which it flows and rates of erosion, that the New River is the oldest river in the western hemisphere. Other geologists debunk this claim and posit various ages for the river between 3 and 220 million years.)

My brave entries on my charts start to have a hopeless feel to them, like the beads patients string in mental hospitals. So I put a couple of professional genealogists on the case. While I'm waiting, I look up Maggie Gibson, my grandfather's lost love, on the Mormon Web site. I find a Maggie Gibson born in southwest Virginia in the same year as my grandfather. But she's already died in Ohio.

Many months and dollars later the genealogists report that none of my father's ancestors except the Dutch Vanovers has made it out of the mountains and back to a seaport in an officially documented fashion.

I'm quite annoyed that my cousin Brent has opened this can of worms for me. By writing *Five Minutes in Heaven*, I thought I'd made peace with my crazy quilt of ancestors. But here I am face to face once again with those six-fingered peckerwoods who haunted my childhood. I feel deep nostalgia for the days when I was a Queen Teen and identity seemed a simple matter of not being a Devilish Deb.

Even though he's retired, my father is still very busy. He's entered every sweepstakes that exists. Stacks of mail arrive each day. He spends many hours filling out forms and pasting award stamps in boxes. He's made friends with the operators at the 1-800 numbers of the sponsoring companies. They give him tips for becoming a finalist. He wouldn't dream of being out of his house on Superbowl Sunday because he might miss the arrival of the Prize Patrol from the Publishers Clearing House.

Sometimes my father phones me in Vermont to ask what color I'd like the Jaguar he's about to win to be. I've planned the menus for more celebratory dinners at the Plaza Hotel than I can count on one five-fingered hand. Each Christmas we all receive nests of metal storage bowls decaled with violets, or sets of plastic coasters stenciled with Amish designs, which my father orders at the behest of the 1-800 operators to enhance his chances of becoming a finalist. What I enjoy most about my father's new hobby is finally finding someone as gullible as my grandfather Reed and myself — and right in our own family!

My father decides to take time out from his pursuit of sweepstakes triumphs to assist my ancestral research by attending some family reunions. He seems as eager as I am to uncover the truth about his elusive parents.

All over the South people with the same surname gather together on church lawns and in American Legion halls each summer. They catch up with one another, get to know new attendees, and eat some of the best potluck victuals ever invented, many of them involving miniature marshmallows.

My father drives my mother up to Hatfield-McCoy country in Kentucky for the Reed reunion. He phones me to report that it's uncanny to be surrounded by a hundred men who all look like his father — many well over my father's own six-four; with sky-blue eyes, noses like the beaks of hawks, and long earlobes. In my mind's eye, I picture an adult version of the children in *The Village of the Damned*.

My father's second reunion is held in a motel conference room in western North Carolina for the Reeves family. Betty Reeves, his three-times-great-grandmother, is the purported Portuguese Indian. My father is delighted with his newfound cousins. But they know nothing about Portuguese Indians, nor do they want to. Their main concern is to link their lineages to Christopher Reeve.

The woman who's organized this reunion arrives late in a new-model Cadillac, chauffeured by a black man in a uniform and cap. She bustles around greeting people and handing out name tags that link each Reeves to the various Reeves progenitors.

In her welcoming address, this woman offers to start a Reeves newsletter and organize another reunion for the following year. The grateful Reeves descendants take up a collection, each contributing $20 for postage and supplies. Thanking her "kissing cousins," the woman folds the bills and slips them into her Paloma Picasso handbag.

At the end of the afternoon the woman climbs into her Cadillac and waves good-bye to her assembled kinfolk, who wave gaily back, intoxicated by the hours of family reminiscences and by the platters of seafoam fudge divinity. They never hear from, or of, this woman again.

Dad returns glumly to his sweepstakes forms, muttering that his 1-800 operator friends would never behave so dishonorably.

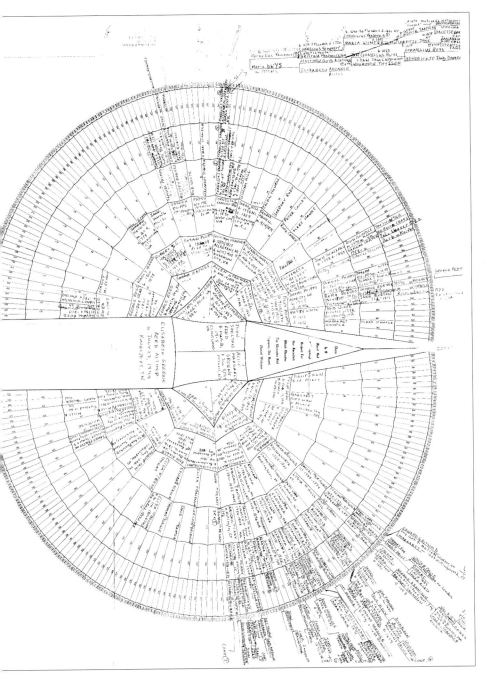

A work in progress: my family tree, in the form of a circle, tracing
my ancestors as far back as the sixteenth century

Polly Phipps, granddaughter of "Portuguese Indian" Betty Reeves,
and her husband, Union Army sergeant John Wesley Swindall
(the distaff grandparents of my grandmother Reed as well as
the great aunt and great uncle of my grandfather Reed)

Bob Artrip, one of my mysterious Virginia cousins

The lynching of
Murderous Mary in
Erwin, Tennessee

DORIS ULLMAN

Two Melungeon boys

My grandmother, Hattie Elizabeth Vanover Reed

My father, John Shelton Reed

My mother, Alice Greene Reed

Grandmother Reed (left) with my retired Latin teacher, Miss Elmore,
in Giza, Egypt, on a tour of the Holy Land

Climbing a family tree at one and a half years old

At age 14, in my band uniform, holding the family's
ancestral clarinet. Beside me stands my
best friend Martha, who will die in
a car accident several
months later.

At age 17, doing my best to impersonate
Scarlett O'Hara, before a night of
waltzing at the country club

At age 24 in Vermont, bearing the next generation

At age 41, water-skiing in the spot where we all spotted Champ,
Lake Champlain's camera-shy plesiosaur

In 2006, in front of the family cabin

# Wilderness Forts

M Y VERMONT FRIENDS SHAKE THEIR HEADS and murmur among themselves about the waste of a fine mind. They can't fathom my ancestor worship. They've meditated at ashrams, so they know that the past is dead and the future yet to come. That the key to contentment is to be here now, not there then. The only problem I have with the present moment is that it's so brief, whereas the past endures for as long as there's a single soul left to remember it, however distortedly.

A Swiss friend living in Vermont confesses that she doesn't get it. She'd thought America was the land of the future, freed from the European obsession with the past. Why do I want to gaze backward?

I try to explain that southerners, like Australian aboriginals, feel we scarcely exist except as an extension of our ancestors. We spend much of our lives in rapt contemplation of the Dreamtime. It's no wonder we lost the Civil War.

But secretly I'm beginning to agree that my preoccupation with the past is interfering with my participation in the present. I don't know whether my cousin Brent's belief that our shared ancestors are Melungeon is accurate or not. Are Melungeons just those from families with the traditional surnames who lived in the traditional strongholds? Our family includes several surnames that Brent maintains are Melungeon-related — Burton,

Fields, Hill, Martin, Phipps, Reeves, Sizemore, Swindall, Tolliver, Vanover, White. But only one of my ancestral surnames, Bolling, is found among the five that all researchers would agree are Melungeon — Mullins, Collins, Gibson, Goins, and Bolling. Of course, the daughters from those families would have taken their husbands' surnames, so the heritage would have spread. And although we don't live on Newman's Ridge, my grandparents grew up just over the border from it in Virginia. And I grew up just down the road in Kingsport.

Were you Melungeon only if your neighbors thought of you as such? I have no idea what my ancestors' neighbors called them behind their backs, any more than I know what my current neighbors may call me. My cousin Greg said that some Vanovers were labeled Black Dutch. Some say this term denotes the Dutch who, prior to immigration to America, mingled with the Spanish soldiers who invaded the Netherlands in the sixteenth century, or with Sephardic refugees in Amsterdam who fled the Spanish Inquisition during this same period. Others maintain that Roma (Gypsies) from Germany sometimes called themselves Black Dutch (Deutsche) to explain away their darker coloring, as did Germans from the Black Forest and the Danube region who were descended from African legionnaires stationed there by the Romans. Still others claim that the label Black Dutch, as well as Black Irish, was invented to disguise European families that had mixed with Africans and/or Indians on the early frontiers of this country.

If my ancestors were Melungeon, when did this mixing occur and among whom? It's like trying to unravel a sweater knitted by a homemaker hopped up on crystal meth. My current exit strategy from this quagmire is to examine each Melungeon myth in turn, anoint the least nonsensical, and then get on with my life. First, the Spanish explorers. Then the shipwrecked Portuguese. Finally, the Lost Colony. With a dollop of Pocahontas on the side.

Partly in order to facilitate this research, I accept a job teaching southern fiction at East Tennessee State University. I rent a condo in Johnson City, where the university is located, twelve miles southeast of Kingsport. I can't stay at the cabin on our farm because it's been rented out for a couple of decades to prevent vandalism. But I drive out there anyway, for old time's sake.

The dirt road down to the cabin has become deeply rutted and impassable without four-wheel drive. I park up top and descend the hill on foot. The renter has erected a couple of Quonset huts, which are crammed with collapsing VW bugs and corroded International Scouts. Two VW vans are decaying in the grass alongside the huts.

The metal roof of the cabin is rusting, and the shutters have fallen off. The white paint on the siding has faded and is peeling. Woodpeckers have excavated large holes through the siding down to the logs beneath in their quest for insects. The porch where we used to sit and watch the pond is stacked with debris, and the torn screens are flapping in the breeze. Mats of wild grapevines and kudzu entangled in the trees along the dam have blocked the view down the valley. The yard is mown, but everything else has run riot. Tattered black plastic covers piles of rotting firewood.

Peeping through the windows, I can see that the cabin itself is packed to the rafters with junk — furniture, piles of newspapers and magazines, who knows what. A pathway has been cleared from room to room.

My old friend Melancholy lays his gnarled hand on my shoulder. It was a mistake to come back to this farm. It was a mistake even to return to this area. Almost everyone I used to know is dead or gone. Our cabin is a wreck. My only companions down here will be ghosts — the ghosts of friends and playmates, the ghosts of my grandparents, the ghosts of ancestors I never even met. I plop down in the grass and consider crying.

Then I remember one of my mother's favorite sayings: "I'll but lie down and bleed awhile and then rise up to fight again."

Smiling reluctantly, I stand up and hike the hill to my car. From the top, this House of Usher doesn't look quite so dismal.

The valley is green and full of grazing Holsteins. The North Carolina mountains still roll away to the horizon in a palette of blues and grays. I decide to persuade my father to ask the renter to leave so we can restore the pond and cabin to how they used to be. Never let it be said that I desert old friends.

Once classes at the university begin, I discover that reinforcements have arrived in the Valley of the Dead. Although almost no one from my past is still around, the area is full of delightful new people. Some have come from far away — Birmingham, Florida, New Orleans, New York, Paris, Detroit. But others were here all along. We just ran in different circles and didn't know each other.

Hoping to start my Melungeon project off on the right foot, I revisit Ground Zero — Sneedville. A sea change has occurred since I visited twenty-five years ago. Apparently the shift was already under way then, although not evident to outsiders. The first stirrings of Melungeon Pride began with the various liberation movements of the 1960s. In 1965, the Kentucky author Jesse Stuart published a novel called *Daughter of the Legend* about a young lumberman from lowland Virginia who meets and marries a beautiful Melungeon woman from a fictionalized Newman's Ridge. (Stuart himself purportedly fell in love with a Melungeon woman in college but abandoned her because of opposition from his family. This novel may be his penance.)

Toward the end of that decade, advisers from the University of Tennessee in Knoxville and from Carson Newman College teamed up with some Sneedville citizens, including a school administrator and a Methodist minister, to explore ways to bring economic opportunities to Hancock County. They decided to stage an outdoor drama based on early Melungeon history called *Walk Toward the Sunset*.

Local workers built an amphitheater at the foot of Newman's Ridge. A specialist in such outdoor dramas was hired to write the script. Area Melungeons and college drama students enacted it under the direction of a theater professor. Despite opposition (including a bomb threat on opening night) from some residents who feared further ridicule, the drama was performed for six years. Although not ultimately a financial success due to lack of local lodging and dining facilities and a summer of gas rationing, the production did draw spectators from all over the United States. Most importantly, its version of Melungeon history instilled a new appreciation for their ancestry in Melungeon descendants themselves.

Atop Newman's Ridge, I discover a new church called the Goins Chapel built at the old cemetery containing the weathered tombstones of Mullinses, Gibsons, Collinses, and Goinses. I spot some attractive new houses along the main road. People appear to be returning to this ridge with its spectacular views. Or else those who never left have accrued enough money to upgrade their ancestral farmhouses.

Driving through Sneedville, I spot a young man on the main street wearing a T-shirt that reads "Proud to Be Melungeon." The local sheriff is parked by a curb in his cruiser. His graying hair is pulled back in a ponytail. Apparently he hasn't watched *Easy Rider* and doesn't realize that he's adopted the wrong persona. As I leave town, I notice on the marquee of the Baptist church an announcement that the Jews for Jesus will be presenting a program that Sunday on Christ's role in Yom Kippur. Although this sounds worth sticking around for, I have to teach the next day, so I head home.

When I get to Kingsport, a homecoming parade for Dobyns-Bennett is under way on Broad Street. Parking, I climb out of my car to watch the band march past. The music and the formations are much more sophisticated now than when I played my family clarinet in the fourth row. It was all we could do to blare out Sousa marches while tromping straight ahead in wavering rows. But this band with its jazzy tunes and elaborate interweavings has been invited three times to the Macy's Thanksgiving Day Parade in New York.

The flag swingers now wear diaphanous gowns instead of uniforms. Their flags are larger, the staffs longer, the fabric filmier, and the colors more vivid. Furthermore, their ranks have swollen from half a dozen to maybe forty or fifty. The builds of some flag swingers are closer to Miss Piggy's than to Farrah Fawcett's. Who says progress isn't possible? If only I weren't fifty-five years old, I might at last stand a chance in the auditions.

Another big difference is that some band members and flag swingers are African-American. The city schools were integrated shortly after I graduated. Among the crowds lining Broad Street are several young white women holding adorable babies with café au lait complexions. These infants are dressed in miniature Levis and Nikes or jumpers and Mary Janes. Everyone is admiring them and making faces at them to elicit smiles.

The social mixing that racists feared would accompany integration is happening. On the surface no one seems concerned. African-American students are included in all the school activities in at least a token fashion. But African-American boys dominate the sports teams and are charming and experienced in their dating behavior. Some choose white girlfriends, which can still incite resentment among the white boys and the black girls — and panic among some parents. A few of these girls end up having babies, whom the white grandparents sometimes raise (and dote on after their initial hysteria).

The parents of some students are also in mixed marriages — both white women with black men and vice versa. What was once a secret scandal has become unremarkable, if not yet commonplace.

I spot an open white BMW convertible next in line behind the band. Along the top of the back seat sit three attractive middle-aged women wearing cardboard Burger King crowns. A sign on the side of the car reads

**HAS-BEEN HOMECOMING QUEENS.**

D-B tradition allows one crasher per parade, and apparently this float of aging beauties is it for this year.

I recognize one of the queens as a new friend named Ina. She's a principal at D-B. We grew up five miles apart, but we never knew each other until recently because we attended different schools. She lived along the railroad tracks that passed my grandparents' house, and she, too, used to marvel over the names painted on the boxcars.

I feel as though she's stepped out of the pages of *Kinflicks* because she was head majorette at her high school, the one who twirled the fire baton at halftime. She was also homecoming queen in 1961 and an attendant to both Miss Burly Tobacco and Miss Holston Electric. The difference between her and Ginny Babcock, the main character of my novel, is that Ina has a brain and a sense of humor.

I wave and she waves back, twisting her hand as Queen Elizabeth does to the plebeians on her parade route.

I start reading in English translation the endless Spanish chronicles of de Soto's 1539 expedition through La Florida. The most florid and least reliable of the four versions was written by Garcilasco de la Vega, the son of an Incan woman and a Spanish conquistador. His 1591 account is based on interviews with participants conducted nearly half a century after the actual events. He may be the first published Melungeon author in history.

De Soto's route has been hotly debated by southern towns wanting to erect commemorative plaques that will draw tourists. But most historians agree in sending him through what is now western North Carolina and eastern Tennessee.

His four-year expedition started out with 200 mounted knights, 300 foot soldiers, 100 artisans and slaves, and 300 hogs. Like all conquistadors worthy of the name, they murdered, raped, and pillaged everywhere they went. They cut the noses and ears off Indians who objected, or they threw them to the war dogs for supper. They also seized native men as porters and native women as concubines and servants, chaining them together and forcing them onward.

By the time they reached the Mississippi River, they'd accumulated 500 native slaves, some no doubt pregnant, others toddlers sired by the soldiers. The Spaniards boarded rafts to descend the Mississippi to Mexico, abandoning most of these Indians and their half-Spanish progeny to the wilderness. An expedition that had departed from Spain as a sixteenth-century version of *Star Trek* degenerated into a Hispanic-American *Brady Bunch*.

En route to the Mississippi, some tried to escape from this dysfunctional caravan. As I read, I count ten deserters, half African slaves and half soldiers. Two were hunted down and dragged back. The motive for desertion in one case was depression; in another, illness. The rest were in love with native women.

Contrary to their bad press, natives often didn't mutilate and kill strangers. If the tribe needed a captive's skills, or if a family had lost a member and wanted a replacement, a captive could be adopted into a tribe with full rights.

Or a captive might be enslaved, as was a Spaniard named Cabeza de Vaca, who was seized by Indians on the Texas coast when his exploring fleet sank. He escaped, and it took him seven years to hike to Mexico, during which time he collected an escort of several hundred Indians who revered him for the Catholic rituals he performed for them like an itinerant magician.

Another Spaniard named Juan Ortiz was captured by a tribe in what's now the Florida Panhandle when he was separated from a party that was searching for de Vaca's expedition. In what may have been the original for the fable of Pocahontas rescuing Captain John Smith from death at the hands of her tribe, Ortiz was being barbecued over a welcome fire when the chief's daughter pleaded successfully for his release. After twelve years, part slave and part free, Ortiz joined de Soto as a translator when the Spaniards passed near his village.

Around eight soldiers and slaves who escaped from de

Soto's expedition weren't caught. It's possible some fathered children with the Indian women for whom they'd deserted. In addition, the swath cut through the southeast by de Soto's marauding troops would have been crawling with half-Spanish babies. To say nothing of the five hundred natives and their half-breed babies abandoned on the banks of the Mississippi.

Would the tribes have accepted these mixed children and their defiled mothers, or driven them out, or killed them? Would some of these children have survived to gang together and form their own tribe, either because they were outcasts (like the children with Vietnamese mothers and American soldier fathers) or because they'd inherited their Spanish fathers' sense of racial superiority?

Who can say? Not me, that's for sure. Historians of the Southeast have called the period from 1570 to 1670 both the Silent Century and the Great Black Hole because almost no written records exist of what was going on then. In any case, I can see no conclusive way to link de Soto's depredations to the Melungeons, whose historical stomping grounds were some sixty miles northwest of his nearest possible approach.

A requirement of my new teaching job is that I give four public lectures on topics of my choosing. One concerns the Melungeons. I go to get my hair done the afternoon before the evening lecture.

Diane shows me her new Chinese fighting fish, which is a vivid scarlet. He lives in a glass vase on her counter amid some floating greenery. She warms the side of the vase with her hairdryer to show me how he rubs up against the glass to feel the warmth. Then she holds a hand mirror up to the fish to show me how he bashes himself against the glass, trying to fight his own reflection. Although this seems an apt metaphor, I decide not to pursue it.

Once she settles down to her trimming, Diane starts complaining about her weight.

"You look fine to me," I tell her. And she does. She's tall and lean with long legs.

"I used to be as big around as Twiggy," she moans. "Now when I'm sitting, I look down and I think, 'What's all this crap in my lap?' "

I suggest the Pizza Diet. I explain that you follow a standard diet like Atkins or Scarsdale, but you substitute a slice of pizza for any item on the recommended menus.

"Does it really work?" Diane asks hopefully.

"No. But neither do the others, and at least you're happy as the pounds accumulate."

I tell her about my upcoming talk on the Melungeons, and she says her ancestors in southwest Virginia claimed Indian heritage. She wonders if they were Melungeons. She's about the fiftieth person in town to respond like this to my mentioning Melungeons.

Brent Kennedy also gives talks on the Melungeons around the area, and the venues are always jammed. He has a Ph.D. in mass communications from the University of Tennessee and is a charismatic and entertaining speaker. If he wanted, he could probably start a cult. Instead, he begs his audiences to do their own research and draw their own conclusions and add them to his, in hopes that synergy can yield some answers to this Melungeon mystery. He's assembled an academic advisory committee of archaeologists, linguists, historians, etc., who are researching related topics.

When I arrive at the Kingsport library for my talk, I'm flabbergasted. All the seats in the auditorium are taken. People are standing in back and sitting up front on the floor. After my remarks, people pose many questions, most of which I can't answer. I do my best to clarify the issues, but I'm the blind leading the blind.

The endless discussion is conducted with the urgency of a lynch mob. Many of these people have been told by their elders that their ancestors were fugitive cavaliers seeking safe haven in Virginia after the beheading of Charles I by Oliver Cromwell's cohorts. The notion that they might have been gypsies jailed for vagrancy or indentured Armenian textile workers instead is both titillating and unsettling. But for all I know, the latter could be as far-fetched as the former.

One warm weekend I drive down to Beaufort, South Carolina, and head out to the marine training base on Parris Island. (This was before 9/11. Now, a potential terrorist such as myself can't get anywhere near the marines.)

Alongside the eighth fairway of the course on which marines are trained to play golf, an archaeological dig is underway. Spoonful by spoonful, the dirt that has buried the Spanish town of Santa Elena is being removed. At this rate, it will take as many years to unbury the town as it did for the silt to cover it.

Built in 1566, twenty-three years after the conclusion of de Soto's expedition, Santa Elena was intended to be the Spanish capital of La Florida. At its height, it hosted close to four hundred soldiers and settlers, who lived in sixty houses with thatched roofs and walls of wattle and daub. Following repeated Indian attacks, the town was abandoned in 1587. Some citizens withdrew to St. Augustine. Others may have headed north into the wilderness in search of farmland.

I stroll out onto a point that protrudes into a marsh. A blue heron is flapping away, a struggling fish hanging from his beak. Spanish moss drapes everywhere like the hair of a hag. I feel as though I'm in a Halloween house of horrors.

As hooked and spliced golf balls whiz past me to plunk into the marsh, I read on a plaque that I'm standing on the site of Charlesfort. In 1562, four years before Santa Elena was built, some French Huguenots, fleeing Catholic persecution, built Charlesfort. But the soil was poor, so their crops didn't grow. Their captain returned to France in their only ship for more settlers and supplies.

Back at Charlesfort a hurricane blew down their huts. A fire destroyed their storehouse and their remaining supplies. Their acting leader hanged one disobedient soldier and marooned a second without food on a remote island.

Since the Charlesforters were soldiers, they had no idea how to hunt or fish, so they relied on the local Indians to provide them with game and corn. The Indians, eventually exhausted by the soldiers' unrelenting needs and faced with survival problems of their own, adopted a policy of tough love. The soldiers were soon reduced to collecting shellfish and wild greens — an early and unwelcome version of the South Beach Diet.

The hungry soldiers mutinied and killed their cruel commander. Somehow they managed to build a watertight boat, caulking it with Spanish moss and tar. Then they stitched their linen shirts and sheets into sails and embarked for France.

Becalmed in the middle of the ocean for three weeks, these bad-luck boys again ran out of food. So they cast lots to determine who would be sacrificed for supper. The unfortunate fellow who'd been marooned on the island lost. Finally, an English patrol ship picked up the survivors.

Meanwhile, back on the Carolina coast, the Spaniards marched north from St. Augustine and slaughtered several hundred other Huguenots at a second fort called Fort Caroline. Then they continued to Charlesfort where, like dogs peeing to mark their territory, they constructed Santa Elena atop the ruins of the abandoned Huguenot fort.

Following an Indian attack, the Spaniards temporarily quit Santa Elena. While they were gone, yet another shipload of hapless Huguenot settlers ran aground in the Santa Elena sound. Since the Indians had as much trouble differentiating among the various European tribes as the Europeans did among the native tribes, they mistook these Frenchmen for Spaniards and attacked them. But once the French established their true identity, the Indians escorted them to their villages and insisted they remain as guests, illustrating the different receptions the various European tribes inspired in indigenous people.

When Spaniards colonized, they first read the natives an official *requerimiento*, which stated that the natives were now obliged to give obedience to the emperor and king of Castile and to the supreme pontiff and vicar of God in Rome. Should they refuse, the commander in charge would continue, "I will seize your wives and children, and I will make them slaves, and I will sell them or dispose of them as His Highness might command. And I will seize you and your goods and do you all the hurt and harm which I can. And I declare that the deaths and damage which might grow out of it will be your fault, not that of His Highness, nor mine, nor of these cavalrymen who accompany me."

This must have seemed insane to people who didn't speak Spanish and knew nothing about Christianity. Yet any who objected were branded on the forehead with the Spanish king's seal to indicate that they were now legally enslaved. The unbranded were often illegally enslaved as well and were forced to serve as porters and concubines. Or they were shipped as laborers to mines and plantations in the Caribbean.

In contrast, the French, upon encountering a new tribe, gave the headmen shirts embroidered with fleurs-de-lis and organized parades that showcased the native leaders. Amid carefully orchestrated pageants, they planted decorative stone posts, claiming the land for the French king. They donned native outfits and learned their languages. They ate the local cuisine and charmed the women with kind words in their own tongue. They fought shoulder to shoulder with the warriors against their enemies.

The English, meanwhile, tried their best to set up replicas of the green and pleasant land they'd left behind — hence, New England, New York, New Jersey, New Hampshire, New London, and so on. When they couldn't resist contact with the native women, they pretended it hadn't occurred and regarded any children that resulted as inexplicably pale natives.

In other words, the Spaniards raped, the French seduced, and the English denied. The results are mestizos in Latin and South America, *métis* in Canada — and, perhaps, Melungeons and related groups in the United States. Forty percent of French

Canadians now claim *méti* ancestry. Latin and South America count 40 million Indians and 60 million mestizos. But few outside the Appalachians have ever even heard of the Melungeons, and by 1900 only 250,000 Americans were willing to identify themselves as Indian on the U.S. census.

I drive north from Santa Elena, crawling along roads that more or less trace the estimated route of Captain Juan Pardo. Pardo was sent north from Santa Elena in 1567 with around 120 troops to establish a series of six forts along a pathway meant eventually to extend to the Spanish silver mines in Mexico. (At that time no one had a clear idea of just how broad our continent really is. Explorers in eastern Canada kept thinking they'd found a passage to the Pacific.)

Pardo's route followed Indian paths, which in turn followed animal trails. The buffalo and deer had eons earlier located the least steep passages through the mountains, the driest paths through the swamps, the most direct routes to the salt licks and springs, and the most fordable spots along the rivers.

After several hours of wandering through the tidal swamps and sandy coastal plains of South Carolina, the road begins its rise to the Piedmont. I pass through some sand hills left by an ancient ocean and arrive at the Mulberry archaeological site on the Wateree River near Camden, South Carolina. It's thought to be the location of Talimeco, the main town of the chiefdom of Cofitachequi, through which both de Soto and Pardo passed. When de Soto arrived here from the southwest, he was greeted by a young woman (the niece of the queen) wearing a robe made from the hide of an albino deer and riding in a litter shaded by the wings of white swans. She hung three strands of river pearls around de Soto's neck in welcome.

Her aunt's sway extended over an area the size of the Netherlands. Because many of their warriors had recently died of smallpox brought from the coast by natives who'd traded with Spaniards, this queen and her subjects had little choice but to feign hospitality and wait for the Spaniards to leave. After receiving reports about the conquistadors in action, the queen decided to remain in hiding. When de Soto tried to force a young warrior to guide him to her, the warrior impaled himself on an arrow and died rather than betray her.

De Soto insisted the queen's courageous niece accompany him, correctly believing that her people wouldn't attack him so long as she was his captive. This woman and an attendant, aided by an African slave and several soldiers, managed to escape and vanish near present-day Asheville.

The University of South Carolina is excavating this town, which is located on private property. The local people conceal its whereabouts from me as diligently as the Indians did that of their queen, several assuring me that you can't get there from here, etc. I finally locate the road into the site, but I decide that death by gunshot is too high a price to pay simply to view a field surrounded by pine forests. I know from photos and from correspondence with the head archaeologist that only two of the ten mounds found here in the nineteenth century still remain, the others having been leveled by farmers' plows and by natural erosion. One of these two is now crumbling into the river, and the other is only two feet high.

I cross the river and station myself opposite the site. All I can see is a tangle of vegetation reminiscent of *The African Queen*. I try to picture the town with its five hundred lodges spread out before me. In de Soto's day, a temple sat atop the highest mound. It was roofed with conch shells, and its sides were covered with painted mats. Six pairs of armed wooden warriors with grimacing faces guarded the entrance. Inside, de Soto's troops found several boxes of river pearls, but none of the promised gold and silver that had lured them into signing on for this grueling expedition. Nearby were four longhouses full of native corpses, victims of the smallpox epidemic. The entire town would likely have been surrounded by a high palisade of tree trunks plastered with clay.

Twenty-six years later, Captain Pardo arrived from the southeast at a much smaller and less prosperous Talimeco, where he met with area *caciques* (Spanish for "chiefs"). His soldiers constructed his second garrison here — Fort Santo Tomas.

The road continues to rise as it winds through endless pine forests across the state line into North Carolina. When I first began reading road maps as a child, I believed that whenever we drove uphill, we were headed north. But on this particular trip this misapprehension is quite accurate: As you drive north from Parris Island through the coastal swamps, the road does rise continuously until you reach the piney forests of the Piedmont. This ascent continues into the foothills of the Smokies, and from there to the mountain passes.

Reaching the foothills, I enter stands of oak and hickory trees with leaves tinged gold and rust. Hazy blue mountains scallop the western horizon. In Pardo's day, chestnut trees would also have been common, but a blight decimated them early in the twentieth century. The journals of the southeastern explorers marvel over the height and girth of the trees. Vast herds of deer grazed on grassy hillsides, burned over for that purpose by the Indians, as though the deer had been semidomesticated.

Each of Pardo's forts was manned by ten to thirty soldiers. These men took a formal pledge to hold the fort for their king until instructed otherwise. They swore to do so "under pain of perjury and of infamy and of falling into less value." After further Indian attacks, the Spaniards finally departed from Santa Elena for good, withdrawing to St. Augustine and abandoning these soldiers in their wilderness forts. They were never heard from again. One Spanish record suggests that the forts were destroyed by the local Indians soon after they were built.

At the base of the Blue Ridge escarpment, I stop at an archaeological dig called the Berry site, which sits along a peaceful creek that flows into the upper Catawba River. A town that

Pardo knew as Joara, and de Soto as Xuala, was located here, as was Pardo's Fort San Juan. Burned beams notched by metal axes and pottery shattered by fallen timbers indicate to archaeologists that this fort was destroyed in some catastrophic way. But no skeletons have been found.

I bend over to pick up a chunk of quartz lying amid the excavations. One side is smooth and the other jagged. Holding it in my palm, I reflect that it was a silent witness to whatever happened here. If only it could speak, it could tell me whether Indians burned the fort and killed the soldiers. Or did they enslave the soldiers? Did they adopt them? Did the soldiers, realizing they'd been abandoned by their commanders and no longer had to honor their pledges, burn the fort themselves and join a native tribe? Did they abduct native wives and start their own tribe? Did they meet up with those settlers thought to have headed north from the deserted Santa Elena? I study the crystalline spikes expectantly, but they aren't talking.

A Spanish exploring party in north Georgia in 1597 was told by Indians at a town called Ocute "that across a sierra . . . four days journey north from there were people who wear short hair, and that the pines were found cut with axes, and that it seemed that similar signs could not be but from Spanish people."

In 1653, an exploring party financed by a Virginian trader named Francis Yeardley reported meeting a Tuscaroran chief at his hunting camp in North Carolina. He told them of a wealthy Spaniard who'd lived in his home village for seven years, along with his family of thirty, among whom were seven Negroes.

John Lederer, a German explorer born in Hamburg in 1644, traveled from Virginia into the North Carolina wilderness on three occasions. He wrote in his journal in 1670 that "two days journey and a half from hence to the Southwest a powerful Nation of bearded men were seated, which I suppose to be the Spaniards." He decided not to advance farther into the Carolina Piedmont because he "thought it not safe to venture myself

amongst the Spaniards, lest taking me for a spy, they would either make me away, or condemn me to a perpetual Slavery in
their mines."

In 1674 Abraham Wood, another Virginian trader, wrote that
an employee of his named Needham (who was later murdered
by an Indian) was told by some Indians in Cherokee territory
that "eight days' journey down this river lives a white people
which have long beardes and whiskers and weares clothing, and
on some of ye other rivers lives a hairey people." (Indian males
had sparse facial hair, which they usually plucked.)

Could any of these hairy people have been descendants
of Pardo's abandoned soldiers? All would have been within a
couple of weeks' walk from Newman's Ridge. Could they have
been the progenitors of the Melungeons? And if they weren't
connected to either Pardo or the Melungeons, who were they,
and what became of them?

I arrive at a town called Old Fort, which sits near the foot of the
Swannanoa Gap into the Blue Ridge Mountains. Believing it to
be connected to the Berry site's Fort San Juan because of its
name, I stop. There's a small museum, built of ocher river rocks
by the WPA. It sits alongside a rushing stream.

Inside, the docent, a small, neat, elderly woman, informs
me that the town is named not for Fort San Juan but for
Davidson's Fort, which was built there around 1770 as a refuge
for European settlers heading into Cherokee territory via the
Swannanoa Gap. The Piedmont tribes had already been shoved
off their land. The Catawba, earlier known as the Ushery, had
lived in several large towns on the Catawba River. Their population had been reduced by war, slavery, rum, starvation, and disease from an estimated 10,000 at the time of their first contact
with Europeans to some 400.

The Cherokee were the next target, despite a 1763 treaty
that barred Europeans from crossing the crest of the Blue Ridge

into their territory. However, when some Cherokee sided with the British during the Revolution, American patriots claimed this as an excuse to launch a scorched-earth assault against Cherokee towns and to open up their homeland to European squatters.

The curator says that in 1690 James Moore, secretary of the colony of South Carolina, came to the Old Fort area with an exploring party. Some local Indians told him that Spaniards were operating silver mines some twenty miles from there. The remains of Fort San Juan are twenty miles northeast of Old Fort.

I mention how unpleasant the conquistadors' lives must have been — worse than backpacking along the Appalachian Trail with the Girl Scouts (as I'd spent much of my youth doing) — because you had either to kill or be killed every time you turned around.

She says, "Well, they were all running either toward something — like the gold and silver that Cortez found in Mexico and Pizarro found in Peru — or they were running away from something."

She explains that some of de Soto's and Pardo's soldiers were conversos desperate to escape the Spanish Inquisition. (Conversos were the Spanish and Portuguese Jews and Muslims who converted to Christianity to evade persecution. But many continued to practice their original faiths in secret, which left them vulnerable to charges of heresy.)

In 1492, Jews were expelled from Spain by King Ferdinand and Queen Isabella. One hundred fifty thousand fled to Portugal, which was already 20 percent Jewish. But after an earthquake in Portugal in 1531, for which the Jews were inexplicably blamed, the Inquisition began there, too. Thirty-two thousand heretics (which included Protestants and Muslims as well as Jews) were burned in Spain. In Portugal, 40,000 were tried and 1,800 were burned. Muslims were persecuted throughout the sixteenth century and were finally expelled in 1609.

An estimated one to three million Jews and Muslims left Iberia altogether, many hiking through the Pyrenees to France.

Others hopped any ship they could find. Some were thrown into the sea or dumped on desolate coasts or sold as slaves or murdered for the gold in their teeth. The lucky ones found refuge in London, Amsterdam, Sicily, North Africa, Constantinople, China.

"So you can see," the curator concludes, "why those who could join an expedition to the New World would do so. Unfortunately, the Inquisition followed them to Mexico. But that might explain the willingness of some to remain up here in wilderness forts, surrounded by annoyed Indians."

"Are you a schoolteacher?" I ask.

She laughs. "Law, no, honey, I'm just an old woman."

We also discuss the various Melungeon origin theories. I point out that the most common Melungeon surnames sound English, not Spanish. But some of the given names are more ambiguous. One is Navarrh, harking back to the ancient Basque kingdom of Navarre in what is now northern Spain and southern France.

Another such name is Mahala. Mahala Mullins was a well-known Melungeon moonshiner in the last half of the nineteenth century who was reputed to weigh around four hundred pounds. One tale maintains that her cabin straddled the Tennessee-Virginia state line. When the Tennessee revenuers arrived to arrest her, she merely waddled to the Virginia side of her house, and vice versa. Another tale claims that she was never arrested because she was too obese for the revenuers to get her out the door. One deputy explained that she was "catchable but not fetchable." When she died, her kin had to remove one side of her cabin so she could attend her own funeral.

A third potentially Hispanic given name is Canara, which was passed down to the men in Brent Kennedy's family for generations. The elderly woman opens an atlas and points out Canara, a district just south of Goa, the Portuguese part of India, and Caneiro, a Portuguese village near Coimbra. For good measure, she also points out the Canary Islands, which provided the Americas with many immigrants.

I muse that even if some of de Soto's deserters and Pardo's soldiers were Portuguese or Spanish conversos, even if they survived the destruction of their forts, even if they lived happily ever after with native wives and mixed children, even if they were murdered and their offspring withdrew to form their own tribe — there's still nothing to link them to the Melungeons.

She nods agreement and says, "Well, honey, no one's figured out the Melungeons for three hundred years now. So I don't reckon we'll do it this afternoon. But it sure is fun trying!"

She may be having fun, but I'm slowly losing what's left of my mind. As we part, she says, "Thank you for coming. It's not often I get to talk with someone as smart as I am."

"Not even half," I reply.

Passing through the Swannanoa Gap, I descend into the mountain-rimmed bowl in which Asheville now sits. In Pardo's time, an Indian village called Tocae was located here. I cross the town and exit from this bowl along a road that parallels the French Broad River, which flows northwest into Tennessee. Before the Civil War this road was a trail of packed earth called the Buncombe Turnpike. Drovers used to conduct vast herds of hogs down from the mountain forests, where they'd fattened on the rich mast of acorns and chestnuts. Their destination was the South Carolina plantations too addicted to cotton culture to raise their own food. The towns along this turnpike had huge pens on their outskirts to house the visiting hogs and cattle. Farmers came down from the hills with wagonloads of corn to feed them, while the drovers roamed the towns looking for food, liquor, women, or just a hot bath.

Some of these hogs may have been descended from de Soto's original drove of three hundred, since he left pigs in the Indian towns as a future food supply for visiting Spaniards. Many no doubt escaped from the bewildered Indians and also from the expedition itself as it wandered through the southern wilderness for four years.

This is the land of the balds, the grassy mountaintops that remain mysteriously bare despite being below the tree line. When viewed from a high spot along the Appalachian Trail, they stretch into the distance like a string of tawny pearls. On misty mornings they float like islands on a sea of pale pink clouds. Farmers used to herd their cattle to the balds to graze in the summertime. General Lee sent exhausted cavalry horses from the Virginia battlefields to these coves and balds to recuperate.

This is also the land of the "pilots," the courageous mountain guides who led escaped slaves northward before the Civil War. During the war, they conducted some of the estimated one thousand fugitives who hid out in the caves in these mountains — Confederate draft dodgers and deserters and escaped Yankee prisoners — across East Tennessee to the Union lines in Kentucky. They were the South's unheralded equivalent to the French Resistance during World War II.

The French Broad alternates between slow-swirling pools and rapids that run white with foam. I reach one dark, shadowy stretch that used to be a sacred site to the Cherokee. It was said to be home to the Uktena, a horned serpent with a third eye in its forehead that hypnotized and destroyed anyone who gazed upon it. The queen's niece from Cofitachequi made her escape from de Soto near here, along with the African slave who reportedly loved her.

It was also in this area that Captain Pardo's astonished troops encountered a bare-chested Indian man who, wearing the long hair and short skirt of a woman, was walking alongside the women. Prior to being introduced to homophobia by Europeans, many native tribes were said to revere such men (as well as women who fought as warriors). They believed that the Great Spirit had fashioned these people specially, giving them the strengths of both sexes. Some served as priests and medicine men. The Spaniards labeled them sodomites and used their mere existence as an excuse to murder or enslave their entire tribes.

I reach the little town of Marshall, twenty-five miles north-west of Asheville, which some believe to be built near or atop the ruins of an Indian town called Cauchi, where Pardo's troops constructed Fort San Pablo. (Others place Cauchi farther south near the town of Canton.) The French Broad races past Marshall, picking up speed as it descends toward the Tennessee Valley, where the ruins of Pardo's Fort San Pedro and the Indian town of Olamico are said to lie beneath Douglas Lake.

Now Marshall is just a sleepy county seat with a courthouse and a train station renovated for bluegrass concerts. I stop at a restaurant run by a Moroccan. His couscous is the best I've ever eaten.

Heading back to Kingsport, I wind along a narrow road above a placid creek. In the tree branches overhead, I spot scraps of clothing, a bald tire, and a rusted tricycle, testimony to the power of this quiet little stream when it's engorged with flood waters.

I pull over at a sign announcing the site of the Shelton Laurel Massacre, a Civil War My Lai. The story goes that some Union sympathizers were denied their share of salt at hog-killing season by the Confederates who ran the store in Marshall. This was a death sentence, since farm families relied on preserved pork products to get them through the winter. Some versions maintain that the store had no salt to sell because Union troops had closed the route to Saltville, the Virginia town that supplied that area.

The Union men rode to town, broke into the store, and took some sacks of salt. The store owner's wife caught pneumonia while protesting this midnight raid and died. The distraught store owner led some Confederate soldiers from Knoxville to ex-act vengeance.

Unable to locate the perpetrators, they tortured their wives and mothers, hanging them by their necks until they were almost strangled and then cutting them down. One young mother was tied to a tree overnight in the freezing cold while her naked baby lay screaming in the doorway.

Finally wringing the whereabouts of their menfolk out of the women, the soldiers tracked them down and marched them toward Knoxville. A short way along the road, they ordered them to kneel in the snow. Then they shot all thirteen, including several old men and young boys.

I arrive at the outskirts of Kingsport and pass the His Grace Is Sufficient Mobile Home Park. On down the road I discover that the Quality Body Shop has erected a signboard like those at the churches. It reads,

**YOU THINK IT'S HOT HERE?**

This need for public testimonials seems to be spreading around town like fleas on hounds.

As I pass the Christ the King Motel, I realize that I'm harmonizing at the top of my lungs with a gospel quartet on the radio: "Are your garments spotless? Are they white as snow? ARE YOU WASHED IN THE BLOOD OF THE LAMB?"

It occurs to me that I may be spending too much time in Tennessee. Everything I've fled is starting to seem normal again. The problem with not knowing who you are is that you become an empty vessel. Any charming charlatan can fill you with his own brand of hemlock. That's probably why most people cling so desperately to the identity that's been handed them, even when it's false.

I pull into my parents' driveway. Walking in the back door, I find my father in his recliner, talking on the phone. Because of his back he can no longer ski or play golf or tennis. Mostly he sits in his chair in a lovely, sunlit room he's had built onto one side of the house, where he reads or watches TV or listens to classical music or talks on the phone. He's been known to chat for half an hour to a wrong number.

Sometimes he rides his motorized chair to the den to organize his sweepstakes forms or to work on his computer. Occasionally he rides his chair around the block or careens across the backyard spraying dandelions with weed killer.

His back troubles began many years ago. He used to have so much pain that he'd kneel and rest his elbows on the operating table between operations. The nurses spread the word around town that Dr. Reed prayed between operations. Soon he was swamped with every ailing Christian in town.

I listen to him explain to some unsuspecting fund-raiser that if his organization wouldn't spend so much money on phone calls and mailings, they'd have that much more to devote to their charitable activities. My father sends small contributions to many charities, hoping they'll call him so that he can explain this.

Smiling, he waves to me. Meanwhile, he's telling the fund-raiser that 12 percent of his foundation's solicitations goes for administrative expenses. In contrast, the Salvation Army spends only 2 percent on administration. He says regretfully that this is why he'll be giving to the Salvation Army, rather than to the poor sap on the other end of the phone.

# The Bermuda Triangle

WHILE DIANE TRIMS MY HAIR in preparation for a Melungeon conference at Brent Kennedy's college, she tells me about all the women we know in common whose undyed hair makes them look so much older.

I reply that my gray gives me a credibility I lacked when dark-haired.

Diane says nothing, but I can feel her thinking that although she's blond, there's never been any question of her credibility. She'd no doubt agree with Dolly Parton who, when asked if she minded "dumb blond" jokes, replied, "Law, no. I know I'm not dumb, and I know I'm not blond."

Diane sighs. But she cheers up once we start discussing recent plane crashes — one off Long Island, another off Nova Scotia.

"You know what's happened?" she asks.

I make the mistake of shaking my head, nearly losing a lobe to her snipping shears.

"El Niño has blown the Bermuda Triangle north."

As I digest this, I'm alarmed to find myself wondering if it might not be true. Once you've seen the Lake Champlain monster, anything seems possible.

One allure to life in Kingsport is that my haircuts cost half what they do in Vermont, which is in turn half of what they cost in New York City. Of course, New York stylists pass along tidbits about the stars whose locks they tend as an incentive for their favorite nobody clients to return. This is how I know things I've promised never to reveal about several celebrities foolish enough to impart their darkest secrets to unethical hairdressers. However, no New York hairdresser has ever shown me the antics of a Chinese fighting fish or explained the symbiosis between El Niño and the Bermuda Triangle.

Armed with clipped but undyed hair, I head for Wise with my brother Bill, who's visiting my parents from California. He's tall, lean, and muscular. Probably because John and I tortured his teddy bear when he was a toddler, he's become a karate master who could kill either of us with a flick of his wrist.

We find two thousand people gathered beneath a large tent. For two days we listen to reports on and energetic discussions of Melungeon-related topics. Although some participants look like escapees from a NASCAR race, almost everyone amazes me with his or her knowledge of world history and personal ancestry. I'm so outgunned here that my pistol doesn't even leave its holster.

Bill seems interested in the data, but he's a true scientist. From the distracted, dreamy expression on his face I suspect that he's ingesting the information but reserving judgment on its accuracy and implications.

On the second afternoon, a Turkish professor from George Washington University named Turker Ozdagan takes the podium to discuss the similarities between kilim carpets and Native American blankets. He points out that both Turks and Native Americans came from the Altai Mountains of Central Asia. Some went northeast across the Bering Strait to America, while their cousins headed southwest to eastern Europe and the Aegean. He maintains that if Turks did come to America in the sixteenth century, as Brent Kennedy proposes, they'd have assimilated into Native American tribes with ease because of the cultural similarities that already existed.

"It would have been a natural marriage," he says, "one in

fact that would have gone largely unnoticed by most Europeans arriving in the New World over the ensuing centuries."

Every shade of skin, eye, and hair is represented beneath this tent, but as I listen to Dr. Ozdagan, I start to become aware of a certain distinctive combination: Many attendees have, like my cousin Brent, wavy dark hair, faces that appear tawnily tanned, and deep blue eyes. Once I zero in on this look, I see it everywhere. It's like a reunion of failed Elvis impersonators.

But I'm baffled. If Melungeon heritage is Hispanic or Turkish or African, plus Native American, where do the blue eyes come from? I'd thought blue eyes represented a recessive trait that genes for darker eye color overwhelm. Who are these bizarre-looking people?

I study Bill. I realize that he and I look equally bizarre. I've met my childhood bogeyman, and he is me.

One speaker discusses physical traits associated with non-Caucasian heritage. Afterward, audience members tug at the corners of one another's inner eyes and stick their fingers into each other's mouths, checking for East Asian eyefolds and Native American shovel teeth. They also stroke the backs of one another's heads like primates grooming for lice, trying to determine who has the Anatolian lumps indicative of East Asian or Native American ancestry.

Bill observes, but I join in. I'm downcast to discover that the backs of my teeth are smooth and my eyelids are single-folded, albeit drooping with age. There's a lump on my head, but it's probably an old football injury. Once again I'm an Episcopalian watching the Baptist Youth depart on their hayride without me. I'm beginning to suspect that I'm wasting my time. If Melungeons actually exist, it's unlikely that their ranks include my family, or surely we'd have heard about it before now.

Ina and Nellie have volunteered to accompany me to my next station along the Melungeon Via Dolorosa — Roanoke Island at the northern end of the Outer Banks of North Carolina. Ina

believes her family to be Melungeon. Her paternal grandmother's maiden name was Freeman, a common Melungeon surname, and these Freemans lived near the base of Newman's
Ridge. Her maternal grandmother always claimed to be half
Cherokee.

Nellie is just along for the ride. She grew up on eleven thousand acres in Alabama that she calls the "planation" (for reasons
that escape me). She's an English teacher at Dobyns-Bennett
and a columnist for the *Kingsport Times News*. Her columns alternate among community service stories, tales of life on the planation, and pieces that support abortion and gay marriage and
attack fundamentalist preachers and right-wing politicians. Yet
sometimes she drives her Mercedes to St. Paul's Episcopal
Church to attend services in her ankle-length mink coat. She's
such a moving target that her enemies can't figure out how to attack her. The most they can do is write outraged letters to the
editor offering to take up donations to send her to Cuba. But this
doesn't bother her because she never reads the paper, any more
than she reads the hate mail that arrives at her house, which she
tosses unopened into the trash.

In any case, she'd love to go to Cuba. Nellie has cruised into
the fjords of Norway, around Cape Horn, and along the ice
shelves of Antarctica. I've never met anyone as interested in
everything as she. She's even interested in the Melungeons.

As we drive across North Carolina from the Blue Ridge
through the piney Piedmont to the swampy coastal plains, Ina
and Nellie regale me with tales of Dobyns-Bennett. Some of my
old teachers are still there, including my nemesis, Mrs. Hawke,
who turns out to be Ina's cousin. Ina has thirty-eight aunts and
uncles, forty-five first cousins, nine double first cousins, and God
knows how many second and third cousins. This is one of the
many challenges of Appalachian genealogy. The families are
huge and interconnected, and many people share the same
names generation after generation. One of my ancestors had
eighteen children, and many of them had at least a dozen.

Nellie tells about Ina's sleuthing skills at school. Students are no longer allowed to leave campus for lunch, but one day Ina saw some entering the building who, instinct told her, were returning from McDonald's. When she confronted them, they denied it. So she invited them out to the parking lot. Once there, she asked the most nervous-seeming to take her to his vehicle, a white truck. She requested that he unlock the door. He did so. She reached in and pulled out a McDonald's cup.

"That's left over from breakfast," he said quickly.

"Then why is it full of unmelted ice?" she asked.

He remained silent, so she asked him to pop his hood.

When he'd done so, she said, "Well, Clint, you've failed the Ice Test. And now we'll do the Engine Test. If you didn't go out to lunch, it will be cool."

As she reached out her hand to touch the block, he pushed it aside and said, "You don't want to do that, ma'am. You'll burn yourself."

As we approach Roanoke Island, they request my lecture on Sir Walter Raleigh's Lost Colony. I obligingly explain that in the sixteenth century England, Holland, France, Spain, and Portugal were locked in a struggle to rule the world. It was like a giant video game, each country trying to establish a foothold in the New World, while simultaneously destroying everyone else's. The Spaniards appeared on the verge of victory because the pope had granted them most of North and South America. (I confess to not knowing why the pope thought it was his to give.) Spain was now looting those continents of their gold and silver in order to finance its conquest of Protestant northern Europe and its defense of Christendom against the Muslim Ottoman Empire, which was encroaching from the east via the Balkans and the Mediterranean and from the south via North Africa.

These New World colonies were a double blessing: they allowed the various nations to stake their territorial claims, and they were also a dumping ground for troublemakers — criminals, debtors, prostitutes, and religious and political heretics. No one in his right mind would have chosen to join a colony bound for the Americas, but most weren't in their right minds. They were the madmen, the dreamers, the paupers, the fugitives, and the fanatics. Many believed right up until they were slaughtered or starved to death that their god would keep them safe.

We check out the reconstruction of the Lost Colonists' fort, trying to imagine cowering behind those flimsy palisaded posts as enraged Indians tried to scalp us.

"It definitely isn't how I'd have chosen to spend my time," I confess.

"Not unless the alternative were the gallows," Nellie says.

In the harbor bobs a replica of their ship. It's scarcely larger than Dolly Parton's tour bus.

"I'm amazed they didn't murder each other on the voyage over," says Ina.

"Once they got here, they probably wished the ship had sunk. At least sharks kill you quickly," I reply.

I tell them about Sir Walter Raleigh's three attempts to people this small green island. The first, commanded by Sir Richard Grenville in 1585, involved around a hundred settlers. While Grenville returned to England for supplies, the colonists antagonized some Indian neighbors by burning down their village because they claimed an Indian had stolen one of their silver cups.

Being mostly city dwellers, the colonists were unable to hunt, fish, or farm. Like everyone's worst nightmare relatives, they constantly demanded corn from the Indians and stole fish from their traps. But there'd been several years of drought, and the Indians were barely able to feed themselves. When they moved inland to their winter camp, as they did every year, the colonists became convinced that the Indians were trying to avoid feeding them (likely) and were plotting an attack against them (also likely).

As the situation deteriorated, the English privateer Sir Francis Drake arrived off the coast, en route to England from the Caribbean, where he'd sacked the Spanish town of Cartagena in what is now Colombia. Cartegena was the main port at which gold and silver looted from Incan mines were loaded onto Spanish ships, which sailed back to Spain in large fleets, in an effort to avoid being plundered by privateers from other countries. The loading on the docks was done by slaves — South American Indians, Africans, Protestants, Turks, and Moors. The Turks and Moors were routinely captured during Spanish sea battles with the Ottoman fleets on the Mediterranean, the most notable being the battle of Lepanto in 1571.

After raiding Cartagena, Drake had spare room on his ships because yellow fever had killed some of his soldiers and sailors. So he rounded up several hundred slaves who'd assisted his attack against their Spanish captors. Originally he intended to take them to Cuba to set up a colony from which to harass the Spanish treasure fleets. But a storm drove Drake off course toward eastern Florida, so he decided to sack St. Augustine instead and then head back to England, stopping off at Roanoke Island to see how Sir Richard Grenville's colony was faring.

In fact, the colonists were now cold and hungry, sick and scared. Drake offered to leave them some supplies and slaves or to take them back to England. After a dreadful storm demoralized them even further, they decided to go home, even though it meant abandoning three absent colonists who were delivering a message to a neighboring Indian village.

At this point, what happened becomes speculation. Some historians believe that Drake, having lost some ships from his fleet in the storm and not having enough room for the colonists, dumped some of the freed slaves from Cartagena on Roanoke Island. (This is the basis for Brent Kennedy's belief in a Turkish component for the early Melungeons, in addition to some Turkish and Armenian textile workers later brought to Jamestown as indentured servants.) In any case, Drake left Cartagena with

135

several hundred slaves of various ethnicities, but he arrived in England with only one hundred Turks. Either the others were dumped on some coast while still alive, or they died on the voyage and were heaved overboard. It wasn't unusual for ship captains to unload sick, unruly, or otherwise unwanted passengers on some desolate shore.

Meanwhile, Sir Richard Grenville returned from England to Roanoke Island with new recruits, only to find neither his colonists nor freed slaves of any nationality. He left a dozen soldiers, some German miners, and a Jewish mineral expert from Prague named Joachim Ganz to guard the island until a new expedition could be launched.

When this new expedition arrived in 1587, they found no soldiers, slaves, miners, or colonists — only one skeleton. Soon, a new settler who'd gone crabbing alone was found dead. The colonists under their watercolor-painting governor, John White, accused their long-suffering Indian neighbors of having murdered him (probably true). As punishment, they killed the chief of the Roanoke Indians whom they held responsible. Then they burned down a Roanoke town. Unfortunately, the hostile Roanoke who'd lived there had left, and some of the few Indians who still liked the English had moved in.

As usual, the colonists ran out of food, and by now all the Indians were hiding when they saw them coming with their empty baskets. These Indians must have felt a mix of exasperation, pity, and contempt for the colonists with their greed, incompetence, and capricious violence. At least the Pilgrims took Squanto's fish and learned to plant them so as to fertilize their corn crops, proving the wisdom of the old saw that if you give a man a fish, it feeds him for a day — but if you teach him how to plant a fish, he won't raid your traps.

By now the Indians were dying left and right from European diseases, as well as from war with the English and starvation caused by feeding the invaders winter stores already depleted by an ongoing drought.

John White sailed to England for more supplies. The arrival of the Spanish Armada off the English coast delayed his return. When White finally made it back to Roanoke Island three years later (on the third birthday of his granddaughter, Virginia Dare, supposedly the first English child born in America), the island was once again empty. The word CROATOAN was carved on a tree, minus the Maltese cross the colonists had been instructed to carve if they were in danger. Though how they thought they'd have time to carve anything at all while being attacked by Indians remains a mystery.

A tribe called the Croatan lived about halfway down Cape Hatteras and were probably the colonists' last remaining Indian fans. Some historians believe the Croatan may have already absorbed Grenville's soldiers and/or the three original missing colonists, and perhaps some of the dumped slaves as well.

"Why would the Croatan have wanted such a sorry bunch?" Ina interjects.

I explain that one named Manteo, the son of the Croatan *weroansqua* ("female ruler," and perhaps the origin of the word *squaw*), had traveled to England in 1584 with Captain Edward Barlowe, who scouted Roanoke Island in preparation for the first colony there. Manteo learned English and adopted English dress. With him went an adviser to the chief of the Roanoke named Wanchese. When both returned to Virginia, Wanchese immediately defected and warned his tribe about the threat posed by the English. But Manteo remained loyal to the English and persuaded his mother's tribe to assist them.

One North Carolinian historian maintains that the Croatan were originally named the Hatteras and that the members of the Lost Colony started calling them Croatan because they had evidence of Croatian ancestry for them. Although this may sound like one of Diane's theories, it's not as far-fetched as it first sounds. In the sixteenth century, the Croatian republic of Dubrovnik (earlier known as Ragusa) produced ships that were the largest and sturdiest in the world. Spain chartered some of them and their Croatian crews for its treasure fleets. Croatian sailors also sailed with Columbus, the Cabots, and Verrazano. Various place names along their routes are thought to be of Croatian origin.

In addition to the possibility of Croatian sailors being shipwrecked on the Carolina coast, one Croatian historian has found evidence in the Ragusan archives of Croatian emigrants to America in 1510–20. Another claims that ringleaders of a failed peasant revolt in Croatia in 1573 established a settlement in America.

A researcher named Charles Prazak has listed a number of ostensibly Croatian words found among the Algonquin tribes of coastal Virginia and North Carolina. For example, the head of the Powhatan Nation was himself called Powhatan, and the Croatian *pohotan* means "cruel leader." Pocahontas's real name was Matoaka, and the Croatian *matorka* means "big little girl."

Captain Barlowe said of some local Indians he encountered on his scouting mission in 1584, "They were of color Yellowish and their hair black for the most part, and yet we saw children that had very fine auburn and chestnut-colored hair." He himself assumed they were descended from stranded Europeans. He also reported that some coastal Indians spoke of "at least two Spanish ships wrecked within living memory," from which they had salvaged some iron spikes.

In 1709, an explorer named John Lawson (killed by the Tuscarora two years later) visited a tribe on the Outer Banks whom he called the Hatteras, who claimed descent from the Croatan. Lawson believed them to be descendants of the Lost Colonists and said they reported that "several of their ancestors were white people and could talk in a book as we do, the truth of which is confirmed by gray eyes being frequently found among these Indians and no others. They value themselves extremely for their affinity to the English and are ready to do them all friendly offices."

Lawson also reported that "the ship which brought the first colonists does often appear amongst them, under sail, in a gallant posture, which they call Sir Walter Raleigh's ship."

Other historians believe that at least some of the Lost Colonists headed north to live with the Chesapeake tribe on the southern shore of Chesapeake Bay. This tribe was slaughtered twenty years later by the Powhatan from the northern side of the bay. Chief Powhatan showed Captain John Smith of Jamestown a musket barrel, a brass mortar, and some chunks of iron he claimed were seized during this raid.

Reports later reached Jamestown that four Englishmen, two boys, and a young girl had survived this attack and were "living to the south with Indians who had stone houses of more than one story." Several search parties were launched from Jamestown, but these survivors were never located. However, a Jamestown colonist named George Percy reported seeing an Indian boy of about ten with "a reasonable white skinne" whose hair was "a perfect yellow."

"But the oddest part of this whole thing," I tell Ina and Nellie, "is that John White, the governor who went back to England for supplies and was delayed in returning by the Spanish Armada, had a daughter and granddaughter among the Lost Colonists. When he finally arrived at Roanoke Island and found them missing, he had good reason to suspect that they were living nearby with the Croatan. Yet he never dropped by to check on them. He had various excuses — a storm that drove his ship southward, a need to pick up fresh water, a leak in his ship, etc. But he went back to England and never returned."

"No one could accuse him of being an overprotective parent," Nellie agrees.

After a lunch of taco salads at Wendy's, we head down the Outer Banks, passing through the beach town of Nags Head. I mention having once vacationed nearby with my family. Nellie knows my parents and knew my grandmother from socializing with them for years. Ina knows them, too, from playing tennis with my sister and watching the town tennis tournaments with my parents. She never met my grandmother, but she reports seeing her almost daily while driving into town. She says my grandmother would nose her silver Cadillac into the road from her driveway without looking in either direction. She assumed the other cars would stop to make way for her, which they did.

I explain where Nags Head got its name: in the nineteenth century, town residents reportedly hung lanterns around the necks of their mules and led them up and down the dunes on stormy nights so that ships at sea, struggling amid the swells, would mistake the bobbing lights for those of another ship and would believe themselves in open water — until their ships ran aground on the reefs, where the locals could plunder them.

The Outer Banks are hardly more than spits of sand thrown up from the maw of the ocean, but they provide a barrier behind which stretch quiet bays. According to John White's lovely watercolors, the various Algonquin tribes speared fish from dugout canoes in these estuaries. The existence of these dunes and shoals explains why North Carolina developed more slowly than Virginia or South Carolina. Islands appear and disappear under the pounding surf, and inlets open and close like the shells of oysters. This coast offered no real deepwater ports such as Newport News or Charleston.

The trade winds and currents in the Atlantic carry ships in a giant clockwise oval from Portugal, past the Canary Islands to the Caribbean, then up the eastern coast of Florida. Veering eastward above Bermuda, the currents continue to the Azores and back to Europe. If a storm hits a ship off the Florida or South Carolina coast, it can be driven northward onto the Outer Banks, which are nicknamed the Graveyard of the Atlantic. An estimated 10,000 people have been shipwrecked there over the centuries, and nearby houses from colonial days are said to be framed with beams salvaged from wrecked ships.

As for the fate of the passengers, who knows? No doubt many drowned. Of those who crawled ashore, some may have been killed by natives. Others were most likely saved for slavery or adoption.

Some old-time Melungeons reportedly insisted they were descended from stranded Portuguese sailors. The Portuguese were the world champion sailors of the fifteenth and sixteenth centuries, and some undoubtedly ran aground along this coast. It would have been a long, hard four-hundred-mile trek from the Outer Banks to Newman's Ridge. Early exploring parties could cover as much as twenty miles per day on good days, so a drive that had just taken us seven hours might have taken them a month. Or Melungeon progenitors could have moved inland more gradually — a few dozen miles farther west with each generation.

"The only thing that's clear anymore," I tell Ina and Nellie, "is that most of what we learned in school was garbage. The Southeast wasn't an empty wilderness when Europeans 'discovered' it. It was crawling with nearly two million Indians and an unknown number of Europeans, Middle Easterners, and Africans. I'm quite annoyed to have been the innocent repository of so much misinformation."

I glare at them, since they're both teachers. Then I tell them about a hundred Huguenots in South Carolina who survived Spanish attacks by fleeing to Indian villages. About a group of African slaves who escaped inland from a colony established in 1526 south of the Outer Banks by a Spaniard named Ayllon. About a dozen more examples of people roaming the Southeast who weren't supposed to be here at all, according to my history texts.

Ina glances at Nellie in the backseat. "Sorry," she says to me with a shrug. "But we've got our hands full chasing down drug dealers."

We drive two hundred miles southwest to Lumberton, the main town for the Lumbee Indians, whose name is said to have originated from the Lumber River on which many now live. A nearby settlement of French Huguenots encountered them at their present location in 1709. The Lumbee claim descent from the Croatan, the Hatteras, and the Lost Colonists. Many researchers scoff at this notion.

The approach to the town is bleak. Down-at-the-heels trailers dot the fields. Pawnshops and deserted flea markets alternate with defunct car dealerships. Many signs are in Spanish, reflecting the recent influx of Hispanic migrants into the Southeast. The customers in a supermarket parking lot appear as ethnically varied as pedestrians in midtown Manhattan.

We park near a courthouse with huge white pillars out front. While Ina and Nellie stroll around town, I grab some books from the back of my car, which has begun to resemble the Bookmobile that used to creep along the roads near our farm when I was a kid, the way the ice cream truck did in town.

I look up a list of the most common Lumbee surnames and compare them to the roster from the Lost Colony. Thirty-seven of forty-eight Lumbee surnames appear on the Lost Colony list. Some are so common that they'd be found anywhere in the South — White, Jones, Johnson, Smith, etc. But others are more unusual — Bridger, Berry, Sampson, Viccars, Dare. A few of the most distinctive Lumbee names — Oxendine, Locklear, Chavis, Lowry — aren't on the Lost Colony roster, suggesting that those families may be more recent arrivals.

But for me the Lost Colony has just been found. Like any sane settlers who were starving and under attack, they joined a friendly tribe and had babies with Indian spouses. Eventually their descendants moved inland, no doubt hoping to escape the depredations of advancing settlers. And the current generations are now farmers and tradesmen in and around this small North Carolina town that appears to be a cross between *Gone with the Wind* and *The Grapes of Wrath*.

But clearly the concept of lily-white throats brutally slashed by tawny savages suited the xenophobic English sensibility better than the notion of cheerful miscegenation. When Englishman John Lawson concluded in 1709 that the Hatteras were descended from the Lost Colonists, he said darkly, "Thus we see how apt Human Nature is to degenerate."

However, none of the Lumbee surnames corresponds to the

five traditional Melungeon ones. And, again, it would have been a difficult slog into the unknown, along a route densely populated by other Indian tribes, to reach Newman's Ridge. It's possible, I guess, but it seems a long way to go just to find bad farmland.

On the journey back home, somewhere near Hickory, we pass a truck that has painted on its sides

**DIXIE COFFINS: MEETING THE DYING NEEDS OF THE SOUTH FOR 50 YEARS.**

Ina tells about her sister-in-law's sister, who loved Coca-Cola so much that her family laid her out in her coffin with one waxen hand clutching a Coke can. I suppose it's no different from ancient burials in which warriors were armed for the afterlife with their finest weapons, or pharaohs with their favorite concubines.

Ina also tells about the death of her sister's mother-in-law. Her sister's husband was himself already dead (shot by his mentally ill brother), and he'd been buried alongside his father. When his mother's will was read, it was revealed that she'd left all her assets to her daughters and nothing to the three children of her dead son. So Ina's sister hired a backhoe operator to dig up her husband's coffin and move it to her own family's graveyard in another town. When the bereaved daughters arrived to place flowers on their mother's new grave, they found only an empty crater where their brother used to be.

As we cross the Blue Ridge toward home, we start seeing reminders of that most famous death of them all. On several hilltops, surrounded by drifts of redbud and dogwood blossoms, looms a large cross flanked by two smaller ones. Wooden crosses have also been erected outside many of the country churches. Some are draped with purple shawls and have a crown of briars encircling the upright.

These churches have their best Easter quips posted on their marquees:

**JESUS DIED ON THE CROSS SO THAT YOU MIGHT GET A LIFE.**
**1 CROSS + 3 NAILS = 4 GIVEN.**
**BODY PIERCING SAVED OUR SOULS.**
**GOD GRADES ON THE CROSS, NOT THE CURVE.**
**THE RABBIT'S FOOT DIDN'T WORK FOR THE RABBIT EITHER.**

On our return, I tell my parents about Ina's sister's moving her husband's coffin for spite. My father announces that he's decided to be cremated. This is big news because the Southern Baptist church in which he was raised doesn't approve of cremation. Since they interpret the Bible literally, some Baptists expect to leap into heaven with their earthly bodies intact. If you've been cremated or have donated your organs, you'll have a problem. Although my father is not a literalist himself, his childhood conditioning by Baptist preachers used to be strong enough to make him prefer burial just in case.

When we ask him what's changed his mind, he says that in the first place, he's put on weight and outgrown his only decent suit. If he's cremated, he won't have to buy a new one. And he's just learned that urns from two cremations can be buried in one plot. So if he and my mother are both cremated, not only can he inhabit the same plot as she for all eternity, he can also sell the extra plot — and prices have tripled since he bought it.

# Sea Cruise

I'M SITTING ON THE PORCH OF OUR RENOVATED CABIN, watching Len, who's wearing a baseball cap over his flowing locks, assist the one-armed turtle man from North Carolina. They're trying to drag a struggling turtle the width of a serving platter out of the pond. Last night they stretched a trot line baited with chicken necks across the pond. This morning fourteen forty-pound snapping turtles were thrashing from the hooks. I shudder, thinking about my recent laps in those waters.

The trick is to grab the tail, which Len has just accomplished. The turtle's scaly legs are clawing at thin air as his jaws chomp wildly, longing for a hunk of Len's leg. Len hauls the writhing creature up the bank to the dam, lays him on the ground, steps on the front of the shell to pin his neck, and pounds in his head with the edge of a board. Then he drops the twitching reptile into a gunnysack and ties it shut.

The turtle man will make big bucks selling these monsters to fancy restaurants for savory soups and stews (which I'll never eat again). If he ever gets out of the mud, that is. He's mired in it to his knees. Having just one arm, he can't pull himself out. I haven't had the nerve to ask him if he lost his arm to a snapping turtle, but I admire his determination. It's like Demosthenes trying to be an orator with a speech impediment.

Grabbing the man's arm, Len drags him up the face of the

dam on his belly. But his boots remain behind, buried in three feet of sticky clay. In some future century, an archaeologist will unearth them and speculate about an ancient cult that worshipped a boot-wearing god named Red Wing.

I wonder if I can ask the turtle man to return the empty shells. The Cherokee used to paint them and use them for bowls. I can already picture one piled high with taco chips at my next Superbowl party.

As Len and the now-barefoot turtle man attack their next victim, I pick up my banjo and pluck out a new melody that's been running through my head. My teaching job has ended, but I'm still in Tennessee. I haven't written fiction in a couple of years. I'm writing country songs instead. The working title for my latest is "When a Blueblood Lady Loves a Redneck Man." It's about a swanky woman who sells her Cadillac and mink to hit the road with a long-distance trucker. Watching Len, I've finally discovered a rhyme for Cadillac: gunnysack.

It may be the proximity to Nashville, or it could be the air pollution from Tennessee Eastman. Everyone I know is writing country songs. My brother John has written one called "My Tears Spoiled My Aim" about a man in prison for shooting at his wayward wife. His only regret is that he missed her because he was crying.

Those not writing songs are playing or singing them. I attended a dinner party hosted by the dean who arranged my teaching job. It was held at his handsome eighteenth-century log house on the historic Watauga River. He's a former college football star and a gifted poet. After dinner, he pulled out a guitar and began playing "Me and Bobby McGee." Then an English professor sang a Scottish ballad a cappella in a beautiful tenor. A couple of fiddles, a bass, a dulcimer, a mandolin, and a dobro materialized. Soon all the guests were belting out country classics.

You can't escape music down here. It's piped into gas stations as you pump your gas and into fast food restaurants as you gobble a quick burger. Once when I was at Wal-Mart, a live gospel band began playing "How Great Thou Art" at the front of the store. Some of the shoppers, greeters, and checkout clerks stopped in their tracks to harmonize on the chorus:

*Then sings my soul,*
*My Savior God, to Thee,*
*HOW GREAT THOU ART,*
*HOW GREAT THOU ART!*

Afterward, everyone cheered and applauded. My humble errand at Wal-Mart had been incorporated into a Christian operetta.

As I drive up the hill, I can see Len and the turtle man cutting another turtle loose from the trot line. The cabin down below looks better than it ever did. Once the renter finally carted away his junk, two master carpenters named Bobby and Allen worked on it for months, removing the siding and replacing the chinking between the logs. They added a modern bathroom and renovated the kitchen. Paul bulldozed the jungle that had overtaken the yard and the dam.

I drive to Kingsport to see if either of my parents wants to go to a Melungeon meeting in Wise. When I get to their house, I find that John is visiting from Chapel Hill. I invite him to come socialize with his six-fingered cousins, but he declines. The Melungeons annoy him. As an academic, he dislikes untutored enthusiasm and overactive imagination parading as fact. Besides, as a Britophile he wants to be Scottish. He's bought a tie in the hunting tartan of Clan Donnachaidh, to which the Scottish Reids belong. (Even so, John is popular in Melungeon circles because he was the first to propose that Melungeons greet one another with high fives and the phrase "Gimme six!")

I accuse him of cherry-picking his ancestors, just as our grandmother did. He replies that since everyone has 1,024 ancestors ten generations back, we may as well concentrate on the ones we already know about and not worry about the rest. After all, life is short and the grave is deep.

I see his point, but I still want to know who the 1,000 non-Scots were. So I drive to the meeting alone, up the expressway into the coal fields, a route my grandparents and three-year-old father took in reverse in 1918 in a Clinchfield, Carolina, and Ohio passenger car.

Arriving at the tent on the University of Virginia campus, I find several hundred people listening intently to Wayne Winkler, the head of public radio for East Tennessee, as he talks about growing up in Pennsylvania with a Jewish mother and a Cherokee father from Sneedville. He, too, has wavy dark hair, blue eyes, and olive skin.

While visiting his father's relatives near Sneedville in 1968, he read a newspaper article about Melungeons. When he asked where he could see one, his relatives fell silent. Finally his mother told him that his father's family was Melungeon, and so was he. He soon discovered that the term was considered an insult in that area because it implied African ancestry. But he himself, having grown up in a northern city during the civil rights era, was delighted with his new heritage. He composed an essay on the topic, which he submitted every time he was assigned a paper. He always got an A because his teachers were so startled by his material. When he told his future wife he was a Melungeon, she looked at him as though he'd said he was a leprechaun.

Wayne summarizes the various academic studies on Melungeons, the first in 1946 by William Gilbert in a survey of the ten largest tri-racial groups in the United States. In the early 1950s Edward Price, a professor of geography at the University of Cincinnati and at Los Angeles State College, traced the migrations of Melungeons from Newman's Ridge to neighboring regions and explored their ancestral connections to the other tri-racial groups. Calvin Beale, a demographer at the U.S. Department of Agriculture, coined the term *tri-racial isolate* for these groups in 1957, estimating their population at 77,000 in seventeen states.

In 1969 William Pollitzer and William Brown, anthropologists from the University of North Carolina, released the results of a gene frequency study on 177 Melungeons from Hancock County, which indicated that they were "about 90 percent white, almost 10 percent Indian, and relatively very little Negro."

A reanalysis of this data in 1990 by James Guthrie using newly available techniques confirmed these findings. But Guthrie stated that they supported either an English and African heritage or Portuguese heritage, since Mediterranean populations very early incorporated an African component. He cited similarities between the genetic makeup of Melungeons and that of populations in the Canary Islands, Portugal, Spain, Libya, Malta, Italy, and Cyprus, speculating that Melungeons are primarily Portuguese with about 5 percent each of "Black and Cherokee."

After this talk Brent Kennedy, who will be mobbed all day long by people who've read his book and discovered they're related to him, comes over to greet me, smiling and calling me "cousin," a word that means less than it used to now that I've seen how many cousins he has. Brent has just enough time to hand me a sheet of paper before a new group of cousins swamps him. It's like a family reunion from hell.

I sit down and study the paper. It's an archival list of settlers who came from Barbados to South Carolina around the time of Charleston's founding in 1670. The surnames of several of his and my ancestors appear on it. Sizemore appears under the heading "Portuguese Jews," Phipps under "Freedmen," and Reeves in the "Prisoners" category.

Toward the end of the day, Brent takes the podium to announce that a British geneticist named Kevin Jones, a professor at the University of Virginia at Wise, will be conducting a DNA study that may finally give some definitive answers about Melungeon origins. He explains that he'll be collecting hair samples from members of the traditional Melungeon lineages. Although this will take two years to complete, the audience heaves a col-lective sigh of relief. Science is riding to our rescue. Certainty will one day be ours. We depart, smiling and hopeful.

The ship motors out of the port in Barbados in the dark with the theme from the movie *1492* blaring over a loudspeaker. I stand on deck, watching the cane fields on the shore blaze, sending up swirling shrouds of sweet-smelling smoke. When I first saw these raging conflagrations on the trip from the airport to the boat, I was reminded of the nineteenth-century slave revolts. But the taxi driver assured me it was just the easiest method for clearing the fields after the harvest.

Barbados is a smoking gun in more ways than one. After re-ceiving Brent's list of South Carolina settlers from Barbados, I read some histories of the place and discovered that it was a seventeenth-century British dumping ground for what one his-torian termed "whores, rogues, drunks, and others who made civil life unpleasant for the upper classes." These people worked shoulder to shoulder with African and Indian slaves in the tobacco fields. I found accounts of prominent Creole families named Reeves and Haynes, both surnames in my father's family. But since I didn't know about this Barbadian connection while planning my trip, I didn't allow time to follow up on it in the li-braries and courthouses. In any case, so many smoking guns sur-round me that it feels as though I'm trapped in the Mekong Delta awaiting a medevac helicopter.

I've decided that to get into the heads of my early ancestors, I need to cross the Atlantic on a sailing ship, a trip all European and African immigrants would have taken at some point. It's a tough job, but somebody's got to do it.

Luckily our ship, the *Wind Song*, has six sails made from 21,000 square feet of Dacron, which are computerized to make maximum use of the winds. It also has a gasoline motor as a backup. Hence, we'll arrive in Lisbon in two weeks rather than the six to eight weeks it would have taken my ancestors.

If their ships blew off course, they could languish for days in the Sargasso Sea at the center of the clockwise circuit of winds and currents that help propel sailing vessels from Europe to America and back again. There are accounts of becalmed ships overrun by rats, which attacked the chickens, devoured the grain, gnawed the passengers' ears as they slept, and drowned in the drinking water. This may be the actual location of Diane's legendary Bermuda Triangle, which purportedly swallows errant ships and airplanes whole, like Jonah's whale.

Sailors called our projected path the Horse Latitudes because if the journey were taking too long and the grain and water were running out, they hoisted their horses from the hold and lowered them overboard, where they were ripped apart by sharks. And then there are the French Huguenots from Charlesfort, with sails stitched from their linen shirts, who were reduced to dining on one another. As we line the decks to watch the harbor lights fade, flicker, and vanish, I eye my fellow passengers, speculating as to who would yield the most tender steaks.

The next morning the old salts among us swallow hardboiled eggs as whole as possible. At the end of the day, they skip happy hour. Amused by their fussiness, I swill frozen strawberry daiquiris.

By the second morning, I'm as nauseated as a poisoned pup. As I strap on pressure-point wristbands and paste a Dramamine patch behind my ear, I feel like a failure, knowing my ancestors would have had neither. But vomiting all the way to Lisbon is more research than I care to undertake.

Once my stomach has settled, I sally forth to meet my fellow passengers. Several have made this crossing many times, loving the silence, the billowing sails, and the absence of phones and fax machines. One older man named Truman, a sailor, is headed to Lisbon to walk in the footsteps of Prince Henry the Navigator.

Although the *Wind Song* has stabilizers, this marvel of modern nautical engineering fails to impress me. As we merry passengers struggle to dance the night away, we resemble drunk drivers walking a patrolman's line. In the gym, I pedal a bike like a crazed church organist. But with the tossing of the waves, it feels more like riding a mechanical bull. I go to the beauty shop for a manicure and end up with nail polish all over my hands.

The captain invites me to dine at his table one evening. This is less impressive than it sounds, since every passenger is invited to do this at least once during the crossing. As he's infelicitously describing a voyage off Normandy during which his ship capsized and he nearly drowned, I see a rogue wave the height of a two-story house out the window. I point speechlessly with my fork.

The next thing I know, I'm flying across the dining room amid airborne bottles of Pouilly-Fuissé. I land, miraculously unharmed, and slide across the wooden floor like a baseball player headed for home plate. I pick myself up and dust off my gold lamé Nehru jacket, thinking about how much worse my ancestors must have had it in their tiny ships that would have bounced and bobbed like waterlogged corks throughout their entire two-month journey.

The other problem I haven't foreseen is the boredom. I read, watch videos, and eat endless platters of gourmet food, none of which would have been available to my ancestors. They counted themselves lucky if their drinking water didn't turn green. Often a lookout could tell that another ship was approaching by the stench wafting on the salty breezes. Seawater seeped into the bottom holds of all the ships, where it mixed with human and animal waste from above to form stinking cesspools.

In an effort to entertain myself, I lose all my spending money in the slot machines. Sailors and passengers in the old days reportedly played endless betting games with dice and small disks of clay, though some pious captains didn't allow gambling on their ships. Slaves, yes, but no gambling. They also danced jigs on deck to stay fit. Whereas my forty-five shipmates and I speed-walk in a circuit around and around the railings, trying to burn off the calories acquired from the overflowing buffet tables that we've paid thousands of dollars to access.

After day upon day with only different shades of blue, with no distinct dividing line between sea and sky, I become disoriented, as though I'm flying an airplane at night with no instruments. In my sleep, I dream of Vermont autumns, the mountains ablaze with flaming maples. I find myself rising early for the sunrises so I can greedily drink in the faint splotches of red, orange, and yellow above the putative horizon. The green of the trees as we approach the Portuguese coast is almost blinding.

We motor up the Tagus River, our sails furled, past the quays where slaves from Africa would have been unloaded and auctioned off starting in the fifteenth century. Trendy bars and discos have replaced the holding sheds. After disembarking, I stagger across the dock like a sailor on shore leave.

I drive north through Portugal to Galicia, the homeland of some of the soldiers who manned Captain Juan Pardo's lost forts. The first thing I notice is granaries on tall stilts. In John White's watercolors, identical cribs on eight-foot posts are found all over the villages of his Indian neighbors along the Carolina coast. Explorers reported such storehouses throughout the Southeast. Natives sat in their shade during the summer heat and kindled fires beneath them on chilly days to smoke out insects and rodents. Lovers in search of privacy trysted inside them. It's possible either that Galicians brought such granaries to America, or that they were introduced to Galicia from America at the same time that corn was. However, this does seem an obvious solution for keeping varmints out of your grain, one that could well have developed independently on both continents.

Northern Spain was the epicenter for the Christian reconquest of Spain from the Moors. It took seven hundred years. "Santiago" was the battle cry of the Christian warriors, in commemoration of the vast Catholic cathedral on the Galician coast, the destination of countless pilgrims who trekked along the Via

Compostela from all over Europe for centuries — and who still do. I pay my respects to this magnificent structure.

Then I head inland to the Picos de Europa. Some of the 200,000 Berber soldiers who fought the Christians on behalf of the invading Moors were rewarded with land in these mountains. Jewish and Muslim conversos hid out here during the ravages of the Inquisition in the sixteenth and seventeenth centuries. Like all mountains everywhere, they provided concealment for desperados of every stripe. As I wind along the narrow roads through the dense forests, I reflect that I might just as well have stayed in Appalachia, so similar are the two regions, apart from the Galician rains that never cease.

After returning my rental car in Madrid, I hop a plane to Istanbul. A press corps meets me at the airport. They snap my photo and ask me questions about the plight of the Melungeon writer in America. Mental note: disinherit Brent when I get home for no doubt setting this up. He's visited Turkey several times with contingents of Melungeons. They're always received like rock stars. They meet with government officials and are interviewed extensively in the newspapers and on radio and television. Apparently some Turks hope that this discovery of a group of Americans perhaps descended from early Turkish soldiers and sailors will encourage the American government to treat Turkey with more respect. Brent clearly hasn't told them that Melungeons don't have much impact on American foreign policy.

My friend Steve, a publisher from New York, is standing off to one side, pretending he doesn't know me. He and I discovered we were ideal traveling companions a few years earlier when he had a business trip to New Zealand at the same time I was doing a reading tour there. We drove around the South Island for a week, passing much of our time in small towns in which the only attraction was the Christian bookstores that featured such titles as *Why God Hates Women*. We spent the rest of our time in our rental car, stalled amid seas of sheep that stretched to the horizon in every direction. We sang along with Joni Mitchell tapes while I eyed all the legs-of-lamb on the hoof and Steve eyed the handsome shepherds tending them.

Steve and I visit the Uniform Room at the Istanbul Naval Museum to inspect the outfit worn by Turkish sailors from the fourteenth to the eighteenth centuries. Just as various speakers at the Melungeon conferences have maintained, the turban and the colorful sashes and vest are surprisingly similar to the garb worn by early Cherokee and Seminole warriors.

Afterward, we wander around Istanbul, dazzled by the calls to prayer intoned from minarets and by the fragrances of a thousand spices emanating from the markets. We pass a clock shop where I discover that it's true that the Turkish word for a timepiece is *saat*. In discussing possible Turkish origins for the Melungeons, Brent has pointed out that a man who met some isolated Melungeons at the turn of the twentieth century said they called a watch a "satz."

Some Turkish linguists have listed hundreds of such coincidences. For Alabama, for instance, they've proposed the Turkish *Allah bamya* — "Allah's graveyard." For Shenandoah, *sen doga* — "pleasant natural setting." A Cherokee chief was named Attaculacula. The Turkish *atta-kula-kul* means "spiritual father of the red men." The Cherokee term for themselves, which meant "principal people," was *ani-yun-wiya*. *Ana-youn* in Turkish means "primary people."

Leaders among the Creek and Seminole were given the title *hadjo*. *Hadja* in Ottoman Turkish meant "wise leader" or "one who has been on the Hajj" (the pilgrimage to Mecca). The honorific for the second tier of leaders in southeastern Indian tribes when Europeans first encountered them was *Mico*, tacked on to their town name, as, for instance, Joara Mico. Mico was a title applied to an officer on an Ottoman galley.

I'm no linguist, and I can't speak Turkish, so I can only listen to these arguments with interest. But I'm reminded of a church sign back home:

**COINCIDENCES ARE GOD'S WAY OF REMAINING ANONYMOUS.**

Driving southeast toward Capadoccia, Steve and I reach the sugar beet belt. Women in long dresses and headscarves labor all day in the sunstruck fields while the men sit in the shade at tire shops, smoking and chatting. At the end of the day, each man climbs onto his tractor, drives to his field, and waits while his women load his cart with sugar beets. Then he drives his tractor to the sugar beet mill. Steve and I discuss fomenting an uprising among these women, but we conclude that they're beyond hope. (However, I reflect that in southeastern Indian tribes men cleared the land and helped harvest the corn, but women did the planting and weeding. It had something to do with female fertility. This sounds to me like a Native American manifestation of that old line, "Men put women on a pedestal and then use it as a footstool.")

We stop at the underground city of Derinkuyu, which was carved into the tufa floor of a plateau by Christians trying to escape Arab raiders in the seventh century. (Tufa is compressed volcanic ash.) It extends eighteen stories downward and hosted twenty thousand people. There are a church, a marketplace, stables, and communal kitchens, as well as living quarters. A huge circular stone slab was rolled across the entry tunnel when enemies were approaching. At the very bottom of the town, there's reputedly a second exit tunnel though which fleeing citizens could pop back up to the surface like prairie dogs.

The area contains forty such underground cities, the largest of which housed sixty thousand people. Their function was the same as that performed in Appalachia and Galicia by mountain caves: to provide sanctuary for the pursued.

Our hotel that night is carved into a tufa cliff. As we drive to dinner, we pass through forests of towering rock phalluses. Erosion has eaten away the surrounding tufa, leaving only these massive open-air stalagmites, which are topped with slabs of less porous stone that have prevented the erosion of their supporting tufa pillars.

The entertainment at the hall where we dine is a dance called the sema, performed by a troupe of whirling dervishes. They're dressed in white robes, which symbolize shrouds for their egos, according to the printed program. And their conical hats represent tombstones. They spin interminably with outstretched arms, heads resting on their shoulders, eyes and mouths half open.

The program informs us that even as we eat, the dervishes will be achieving union with the Divine. But my Sufi friends in London told me that Jalaluddin Rumi, the Sufi teacher and poet who invented this dance, claimed he did so simply because his disciples were so lazy that he wanted to get them moving. In any case, it's safe to assume that these rituals are being performed tonight for tourist dollars rather than for spiritual enlightenment.

After the dervishes whirl offstage, another robed group comes out. Each places his left arm on his neighbor's shoulder, and they circle in sedate single steps, turning their heads sharply from side to side and exhaling "hu" and "ha" in unison. The program explains that *hu* means Him, "the divine presence which is beyond definition." *Ha* represents the last syllable of Allah.

This is startling. Some southeastern Indian tribes addressed their chiefs and their chief's relatives by crying "hu." Adults knelt and placed their hands on the ground as they did so. Children were trained to kneel and rest their foreheads on the ground in a posture that sounds suspiciously similar to the Muslim prayer posture. The chiefs in turn greeted the rising sun, their female deity, by shouting "hu."

At the end of a traditional dance that purified Cherokee ballplayers for an upcoming game (a circle dance that involved lots of twirling), they'd rush over to the spectators, who'd bless them by calling out "hu." Before the game, the players would surround the goalpost, holding hands and chanting "hu" three times. Cherokee priests recited their secret formulas in a low murmur, punctuated rhythmically by loud "ha"s. Some evangelists in the southern Appalachians still do the same. The word *hoo-ha* is currently used in the southern Appalachians to designate a pretentious person or event, or a ruckus. I don't know what, if anything, to make of these titillating coincidences.

Following these dancers, a man and woman in fashionable evening clothes perform a very erotic belly dance. I feel like a voyeur at a Times Square peep show. At the climax, the woman reaches into the man's jacket pocket, withdraws a bottle of raki (Turkish brandy), and dashes it to the floor, where it shatters into hundreds of skittering shards.

Steve and I watch openmouthed. The contrast between this haughty hottie and those babushka-ed sugar-beet slaves — between the robed dervishes and this gyrating gigolo in his double-breasted tux — sums up the schizophrenia we've sensed all over modern Turkey.

The next day we drive to Konya, the capital of the Seljuk Turks in the eleventh century and the target of thirteenth-century European crusaders (the forebears of the conquistadors). Prior to the Turks, Konya was occupied by the Byzantines, Romans, Persians, Lydians, Phrygians, and Hittites, all the way back to 7000 B.C. In A.D. 50, Saint Paul preached here and so offended his audience that they ran him out of town. Now Konya is best known as the site of the mausoleum of Rumi, whose masterwork *The Mathnawi* contains 25,000 rhyming couplets. His sarcophagus lies in a former Sufi monastery that features two domes, three minarets, and a tiled turquoise silolike structure. This monastery also houses a casket said to contain a hair from Muhammad's beard.

The fundamentalist Islamic guards at the tomb, looking like Aladdins who've lost their lamps, welcome Steve. But they eye me with distaste, despite the long sleeves and scarf I've donned for their benefit. Clearly they think I should be out hoeing sugar beets. They remind me of the scowling men who line the parade route during prochoice marches in Washington, seething with hatred for women who refuse to conform to their demented rules.

I recall a bracing quote from Rumi himself: "Don't let your throat tighten with fear. Take sips of breath all day and night before death closes your mouth."

Drawing a deep breath, I summon the image of Inez Milholland on her white horse, leading Greatgrandma Pealer through the deranged mobs in her fruit- and flower-bedecked bonnet. I march past the surly guards right up to Rumi's coffin, which is shrouded with a stiff velvet cloth heavily embroidered with gold.

One reason I like Rumi is that his poetry seems to flow from the same source as Cherokee beliefs. For instance, he says, "What strikes the oyster shell does not damage the pearl." Ever since Dr. Ozdagan pointed out at a Melungeon conference that Turks and Native Americans are cousins from the Altai Mountains of Central Asia, I've been doubly intrigued, wondering if the two systems might be streams from the same river. Many researchers describe Sufism as Islamic mysticism. But my Sufi friends in London assured me that its roots are much more ancient than Islam. But could they be fourteen thousand years ancient, so that the belief system crossed the Bering Strait with those who became Native Americans? Or is Dr. Ozdagan correct to entertain the possibility of a more recent infusion of Muslims into American Indian tribes? Or both?

Scarfless, I watch Steve insert his cash card into an ATM slot. Our cards work at some banks and not others. When they do work, they yield the equivalent of only about five dollars. So we play every ATM we find as though it were a slot machine.

A woman shrouded in black with only her eyes showing glares at me from across the street. She, too, thinks I should be hoeing sugar beets rather than hanging out bareheaded at an ATM kiosk with a good-looking blond infidel.

Steve shrugs at me sympathetically. Then the machine starts spitting out cash. After he collects it, we high-five one another as our somber chaperone shoots daggers at me with her contemptuous eyes. Although I've never been an especially fun person, I feel like Lucille Ball alongside this woman. Her grim gaze makes it clear that we should be gone from Konya by sundown.

Driving toward the Aegean, Steve and I pass through a town where Brent reported giving a talk and afterward meeting a young Turkish man. Having learned in the talk about Brent's extra fingers, the Turk explained that he, too, had six fingers on each hand, as do many Anatolians. He told Brent that they're called *alti parmak* — six-fingered ones.

I've become an expert on polydactylism (as we experts refer to extra digits). A recessive trait, it tends to appear in inbred populations. But it's more common in some such communities than others. Ina saw it in several children when she taught special education in rural East Tennessee. Researchers have found it in the Jackson Whites of New Jersey and the Wesorts of Maryland, both "tri-racial isolate" groups similar to the Melungeons.

Native Americans are four times more likely to have extra thumbs than Europeans or Africans. The trait is more common in males and more often found on the right hand. The *alti parmak* of Anatolia seem to provide yet more evidence of some genetic link between Turks and Native Americans.

Evolutionarily speaking, five fingers are thought to have won out over six because those with six fingers would have been clumsier and therefore less likely to survive to pass on their six-fingered genes. I've often wondered if extra fingers might not explain why so many Appalachians are such good banjo pickers.

The earliest mention of six fingers that I've come across is in the Bible at 2 Samuel 21:20, "And there was yet a battle in Gath, where was a man of great stature, that had on every hand six fingers, and on every foot six toes, four and twenty in all, and he also was born to the giant." This giant father was Goliath, and his polydactyl son was killed by the brother of David, the slayer of Goliath.

In India, people with six fingers are sometimes recruited as holy men. On the other hand (so to speak), Anne Boleyn had six fingers on one hand, and Marilyn Monroe was rumored to have six toes on one foot, and things didn't go too well for either of them.

Steve and I arrive at a small fishing port on the Aegean called Cesme. A sign identifies its main street as Wise Caddesi. As a result of Brent Kennedy's efforts, Cesme has become a sister city to Wise, Virginia, and the two towns have won a Sister Cities International Award.

Many men from this Anatolian coastal region fought for the Ottoman sultan in his sixteenth-century sea battles with Spain and its allies. Some never returned and are believed to have been either killed or captured by the Spaniards and turned into galley slaves. Some of these slaves would have served in the Mediterranean, and others would have been transported to colonies in the New World such as Cartagena.

An assistant to the mayor of Cesme takes us to lunch, during which he introduces us to some of his fellow citizens. Many have "the look" that I've noticed at the Melungeon conferences: they're lean, wiry men with wavy dark hair, tawny complexions, and bright blue eyes. When I ask my host about the omnipresent blue eyes, he mentions Alexander the Great, and I get a sinking feeling that I've just located a Turkish cell of the Virginia Club.

As we tour Cesme, our guide tells us that his hobby is designing and sewing dresses. Steve raises his eyebrows at me.

We arrive at an ancient stone warehouse on the wharf, from which hangs a sign that reads in English "Melungeon House." My guide explains that men from Cesme were no doubt among the slaves freed by Sir Francis Drake at Cartagena and then dumped on Roanoke Island, from which they headed inland to become the Melungeons. At Melungeon House, they would have boarded the boats that carried them to their destiny in

America. He asks if we think this landmark will attract American tourists. Despite misgivings, I assure him it will.

On a hill above Cesme, we come to lovely rolling woods. A signpost reads in Turkish and in English translation, "This forest area is arranged in memory of the people of Cesme; later named Melungeon, who were taken away to America by the Portuguese people in the sixteenth century." I can see that once handed a ball, the citizens of Cesme really run with it.

My guide explains that the masts for the ships that carried the soldiers and sailors from Cesme to their destiny in America might have been cut from this very forest. I try to think of a synonym for *destiny* to suggest for his use in future presentations. But all I can come up with is *fate*, which sounds so much more dreary.

Our guide drives us back to his house for coffee. A comfortable stuccoed villa with a yard full of flowers, it's located in a neighborhood that resembles a modest American suburb. From a trellis above his garage hang beautiful clusters of purple grapes. While he cuts us some, I notice a stack of cassettes alongside his tape player. Sorting idly through them, I discover that they're all by Barbra Streisand. This time, I raise my eyebrows at Steve.

Upon reaching New York, I continue to Tennessee, jet-lagged and discouraged. I don't know what I hoped to uncover on my journey. Certainly I observed some hints of possible Portuguese and Turkish connections to Melungeons. But there are so many hints, and they're all so distant in time and space and so impossible to prove. The DNA study offers the only glimmer of hope, but the results won't be reported for a couple of years.

As I drive to my parents' house, I discover that Kroger's, our neighborhood supermarket when I was growing up, has been transformed into a Christian nightclub called the Fire Escape. This makes me feel even more hopeless. Islamic fundamentalists have occupied Rumi's tomb in Konya, and now Christian fundamentalists have occupied Kroger's in Kingsport. Where will it all end?

"What in God's name do Christians do in a nightclub?" I ask my father as I enter his room.

He's sitting in his recliner before the TV. He shrugs. "Drink Virgin Marys?" He clicks off the set with his remote.

I plop down in a chair.

"Brent stopped by and plucked some of my hairs for that DNA study," he says, diverting me from the depressing topic of Christians at play.

"That must have been a challenge." My father is almost bald. He takes pride in this, attributing it to excess testosterone.

"Imagine that," he says, shaking his head. "I'm eighty-five years old, and I don't know who I am. And I'm not sure that I care."

"Me either," I mutter.

As I head out to the farm, I'm almost too demoralized even to notice the church signs. But I look up in time to read:

**GOD LOVES YOU WHETHER YOU LIKE IT OR NOT.**
**WHEN DOWN IN THE MOUTH, REMEMBER JONAH.**
**HE CAME OUT ALL RIGHT.**
**IF THE GOING GETS EASY, YOU'RE HEADED DOWNHILL.**
**GO OUT ON A LIMB. THAT'S WHERE YOU'LL FIND THE FRUIT.**
**NEVER GIVE UP, EVEN MOSES WAS ONCE A BASKET CASE.**

These messages seem designed especially for me as I wander in this Melungeon wasteland. Then I really start to worry, because only schizophrenics are megalomaniacal enough to believe that they're receiving personalized billets-doux from the cosmos.

## Forebear Fatigue

I'M HELPING SARA LEAN FORWARD in the hospital bed so she can push harder when the baby suddenly slides into the waiting hands of the doctor. This may be old hat to the medical professionals in the room, but I'm still awestruck by the whole thing. I've been having flashbacks — to my grandfather holding me after my father's departure for boot camp, to my mother displaying Michael in the hospital window, to that snowy night during deer season when Sara herself was born.

The nurse hands Brett the scissors, and he clips his son's umbilical cord with an unsteady hand.

While sponging Sara's face, I realize that I'm studying the baby's hands from the corner of my eye. But an extra digit or two would no longer alarm me. To the contrary, they might qualify him to become a shaman.

As the doctor carries him over to the infrared lamp, the baby gasps the first of what I hope will be several hundred million breaths. Brett follows to watch the nurse clean up his son.

"Is he okay?" Sara whispers, exhausted.

"He's wonderful," I assure her.

I'm looking out at Lake Champlain through the window of my new condo. In my arms is my grandson, Zachary, wrapped in a mint-green flannel blanket. His harried mother is showering upstairs. I've moved to Burlington, and Zachary and his parents are now living in the farmhouse in which Sara grew up. Our family recycles houses the way others recycle outgrown clothing. My grandparents gave their house to my parents, and my parents gave their cabin to us kids. All our dwellings are crammed to the rafters with ancestral furniture, artwork, and tableware. Each generation serves as curator to all previous ones.

Although it's still cool, the traffic on Lake Champlain has picked up, and I watch a parade of windsurfers, canoers, kayakers, and sailors. Yankees are very busy and fit people, especially in contrast to Tennesseans, whose idea of a cardiovascular workout is to carry a cooler filled with Budweiser to the top row of the NASCAR bleachers.

I once attended a NASCAR race at the track near Kingsport. The BMIs (body mass index) of most spectators probably exceeded their SATs. Many men were shirtless, their bellies hanging out over the waistbands of shorts that rode so low that their butt cracks showed. The women wore halter tops and short shorts several sizes too small.

The incessant whine of the circling cars would have driven mad anyone who wasn't drunk. The only moment of relief was when one car crashed into the wall. The crowd went wild, like a bullfight audience when the matador is gored, or Romans in the Colosseum when the lions brought down a Christian. As the fans exited after sizzling for hours on the aluminum benches in the hot sun, they resembled a clan of Tomato People, with toothpick arms and legs poking out from round red globes.

I glance at Zachary, who's sleeping peacefully, his pursed lips making sucking movements, like a slumbering pup whose legs twitch as he dreams of the chase. I study his fine, fair hair and tiny perfect features.

I've been reading up on genetics in hopes of understanding the results of the Melungeon DNA study once they're announced. I've learned that we humans share 60 percent of our protein-coding genes with chickens, from which we diverged

310 million years ago. Chickens descend directly from dinosaurs. Humans also share 96 percent of our genes with chimpanzees. And we share 99 percent of our DNA with one another. A handful of the genes that differ governs our visible physical characteristics such as skin, hair and eye color, and body type. Which version we end up with is determined by interconnected processes that aren't yet fully understood.

Some older texts, with the racism characteristic of their era, maintain that a nonwhite family can "bleach" in four generations. More recent textbooks confirm this basic idea in more scientific jargon. In theory, should a 100 percent non-European mate with a 100 percent European, their child would possess approximately 50 percent non-European ancestry. Should this child, in turn, mate with another 100 percent European, their child would be around 25 percent non-European, genetically speaking. After another such mating, offspring would exhibit roughly one-eighth non-European ancestry. Racists used to insist that such "octoroons" were sterile, like mules (hence the word *mulatto*). In reality, many children born to octoroons disappeared into the white community. It only appeared that octoroons didn't reproduce.

But these percentages are only averages. In practice, a child can inherit all, some, or none of an ethnically mixed parent's minority ancestry, depending on how minor that ancestry is. Two siblings share only 50 percent of their DNA on average, some pairs more and others less. This explains the very different physical appearances of siblings in some families.

Studies have shown that the vast majority of the 35,000 to 50,000 African-Americans who switch their census designations to white or Hispanic each year have 12.5 percent or less African heritage. Some with up to 25 percent are still able to "pass." But those with more than 40 percent of a non-European heritage normally resemble the phenotype for that heritage so strongly that they don't attempt to switch to another ethnicity, assuming that they'd even want to.

The average African-American has almost 20 percent European ancestry, and one quarter have Native American ancestry as well. A third of African-American males have European Y chromosomes. (I will later encounter several European-identified men who have African Y chromosomes.) Geneticists have calculated that nearly 40 percent of the Native American gene pool represents other ethnicities. One-third of white Americans have some African ancestry, white Texans possessing on average 5 percent (in addition to what all *Homo sapiens* share as heirs to our genetic Adam and Eve, who were African). White, after all, is a description not of race but of skin color — and not a very good one at that. Most people with albinism have some pigmentation and, thus, some hint of coloring to their skin. And only mass delusion allows human beings to imagine that exclusive races exist.

If my grandparents were both partly Melungeon, whatever mixture that entailed at the end of the nineteenth century, my father would be about as Melungeon as each of them. Since he married a Yankee, I myself would be half as Melungeon as my father and my grandparents. Since I also married a Yankee, Sara would be around a quarter as Melungeon as her great-grandparents. She, too, married a Yankee, so Zachary would be one-eighth as Melungeon as his twice-great-grandparents.

I study the slumbering baby. I would do anything to make his upcoming life easier and more pleasant. If that entailed falsifying records, changing my name, fabricating new ancestors, and never admitting this to a single soul, would I do it? I certainly would. I'd order a fake British coat of arms off the Internet and join the DAR. And I'd kneecap anyone who tried to rip off my mask.

But would it make Zachary's life easier not to be taught to honor all the ancestors to whom he owes his existence? Not knowing who I am hasn't worked that well for me. I've wasted a lot of time trying to wedge my psyche into borrowed shoes that have pinched and chafed and rubbed it raw.

The Melungeons, whoever they might once have been, are

ceasing to exist through outmarriage. Ironically, it's only during these last twilight years that their putative descendants are discovering and celebrating this complex legacy. I vow to make sure that they don't vanish before their story is told — if only I can figure out what that story is. I've already started writing about a young boy in Galicia, as sweet and innocent as Zachary, who joins a sixteenth-century Spanish expedition to La Florida, where he's forced to confront the truth about how badly many human beings treat those who appear unlike themselves.

Strolling to the bank of mailboxes outside my condo, I wave to Sara as she drives away with her precious human cargo. On the bumper of a parked car, I spot a sticker that reads

**I SUPPORT THE RIGHT TO ARM BEARS.**

Smiling, I reflect on what might happen to my car if I pasted such a sticker on its bumper in Tennessee, where a man's choice of firearms is as important to him as his wife's choice of hair color is to her.

Bumper stickers are Vermont's equivalent to Tennessee's church signboards, although they usually have a political rather than a religious drum to beat. When civil unions were being debated in Vermont, opponents' cars sported stickers reading

**TAKE BACK VERMONT.**

Supporters countered with stickers saying,

**TAKE VERMONT FORWARD.**

Some comedian posted on his bumper the message

**TAKE VERMONT FROM BEHIND.**

Another sticker I saw recently read

**VEGETARIANS DO IT WITH RELISH,
AND THEY ALWAYS USE CONDIMENTS.**

Inside my mailbox, I discover a postcard from a London friend named Ramsay, who's traveling in Pakistan. On the front is the word *Malangs* and photos of three bearded, disheveled old men in multicolored clothing, one draped in chains. The explanation on the back is that Malangs are Muslim mendicants who embrace poverty in order to detach themselves from the chains of materialism.

Ramsay's message reads, "Does that name sound familiar? Thought you'd be interested."

I'm very interested. It's one more brick for my Great Wall of Bewilderment. Earlier in the week my brother John forwarded me an e-mail from a woman named Joanne Pezzullo laying out her theory that the word *Melungeon* comes from the Old English *malengin* — "guile, deceit." She quoted a verse from Edmund Spenser's 1589 *Fairie Queen:*

> *For he so crafty was to forge and face,*
> *So light of hand, and nymble of his pace,*
> *So smooth of tongue, and subtile in his tale,*
> *That could deceive one looking in his face;*
> *Therefore by name Malengin they him call.*

This unflattering description fits right in with Nashville journalist Will Allen Dromgoole's 1891 description of Melungeons as sneaky rogues. It seems unlikely the largely illiterate settlers of Appalachia would have known *The Fairie Queen,* but it does illustrate that the word *malengin* was in common usage in the Elizabethan era to describe an undesirable. And as I observed in my own grandmother, archaic words and speech patterns have survived longer in the Appalachians than in less remote settings. One spring day near our farm, as an older man in overalls was filling my gas tank, the sun went behind a cloud and a sharp breeze blasted down the valley. The man looked up and said, "Hit's kindly airy, ain't it?"

Other researchers have discovered that Portuguese plantations in Brazil employed Moors who called themselves "mulangos" or "melungos." Tim Hashaw claims this term came from *malungu*, used by Kimbundu-speaking Angolan slaves in both Brazil and Virginia to designate a watercraft and, by extension, a shipmate or comrade.

James Guthrie discusses some residents of the Anatolian maritime empire of Miletus, who fled a Persian invasion in 494 B.C. to settle on the island of Melun in the Seine. In 52 B.C., Julius Caesar reported driving these "Melungeons" from the island, some of whom were last seen sailing west into the sunset.

C. S. Everett maintains that *Melungeon* came from the Italian *melongena*, meaning "eggplant." He claims it's an epithet still used by Italian Americans to describe someone of African heritage because of an eggplant's dark skin. And he points out that there were Italian settlements in central Virginia in the late eighteenth century.

A genealogist named Pat Elder has proposed the Old French *melanjan*, which also means "eggplant," as the origin of *Melungeon*, explaining that Baron François de Tubeuf tried to establish a French colony on the Clinch River in southwestern Virginia near a large Melungeon settlement in 1793. Elder also suggests "malinjun" as a possible source for the term, hinting at the hilarity to which the whole topic eventually reduces those of us who explore it. It's a certifiable syndrome known as Forebear Fatigue.

Returning to my office, I log on to the Internet and discover that the contemporary Melungeons are restless. Brutal battles are being waged at the various chat sites. A girl gang of professional genealogists is attacking Brent, claiming he's not a real Melungeon because his ancestors aren't listed as FPCs on the censuses. Brent has pointed out that censuses were conducted by local people, who'd have given the neighbors they liked or feared the benefit of the doubt since the consequences of being designated an FPC were so dire. He's also presented them with citations from records earlier than those they've consulted that do list some of his ancestors as FPCs. And he's explained that much of the Melungeon mixing presumably occurred before record-keeping, or even literacy, existed on this continent.

These belligerent genealogists are also insisting that the Melungeons weren't in fact the "white Indians" found living in East Tennessee by John Sevier in 1784, and that no one claimed Portuguese ancestry for the Melungeons until 1848, when it was fabricated to explain away their dark complexions in an attempt to avoid classification as FPCs. They maintain that there's nothing mysterious about Melungeon origins, that they're descended from a group of mulattos who migrated west from Louisa County, Virginia — and they've got the paper trail to prove it.

They also chide Brent for broadening the definition of Melungeon to include every mixed-race wannabe in America. And they ridicule the idea of a Turkish component in the Melungeon makeup, portraying Brent and those pursuing similar connections as cultists, cranks, and crackpots.

Their hostile tone baffles me. There's something about the Internet that turns perfectly nice people into harridans. It may be the absence of facial expressions and tones of voice. Unsure of whether they've made their point, people shriek it into cyberspace.

I discover that several more splinter groups have split off from the Melungeon totem pole. One wants to apply for state recognition of individual Melungeons as Indians so they can qualify for various scholarships and grants. The mainline Melungeons are opposing this, preferring to emphasize the multiethnic nature of Melungeon heritage.

Another group is accusing those who champion the Portuguese and Turkish origin theories of racism for trying to explain away their darker coloring as something other than African. Yet most Melungeons I know are scouring the census records and throwing cocktail parties whenever they locate ancestors designated "mulatto." In fact, a baffled African-American reporter for a Washington, D.C., newspaper has recently confessed in print that she's never before encountered white people so eager to be African.

Yet it's clear from the Internet chat sites that not everyone with a Melungeon surname is eager to be African. Some are downright appalled. Others are furious about the DNA study. Since we don't know who the Melungeons are in the first place, they point out, who's to say that those sampled for the study are representative? And in a fit of I'm-more-Melungeon-than-thou, some with documented ancestry back to those who bore the traditional Melungeon names and who lived on Newman's Ridge in the nineteenth century are raging that Melungeon wannabes are trying to abduct their hard-won heritage. Still others are furious that certain diseases like sarcoidosis and thalassemia have been labeled Melungeon, fearful of what this might do to employment prospects and insurance coverage.

Everybody's mad about something, and I'm no exception: I'm mad at my grandparents for dying without telling me what they know about this mess. My head is reeling from the strain of trying to sort out all the old information and fit in the new.

But Brent keeps trying to levitate above the fray. He always acknowledges everyone's point of view, however demented, often referring to the Middle Eastern tale of the elephant. Each of us is exploring an ear or a leg, but it's all part of the same elephant, he insists in a voice that usually goes unheard above the din of clashing opinions.

It's an elephant, all right, the elephant in the room that our grandparents wouldn't discuss. But now nobody will shut up about it. In the 1990s, captive elephants killed 65 people and injured 130. Before this flap is over, our Melungeon Murderous Mary is going to trample us all to pulp.

I find myself unable to renounce either lesbian weddings on Lake Champlain buffalo farms or mud-wrestling matches between monster turtles and one-armed trappers. So in the autumn I now head south to Tennessee with the ducks and the snow geese, to the land where men in their personals ads say that they're seeking a girl who can bait her own fishing hooks. And

when the ice breaks up so that Lake Champlain resembles a giant frozen margarita, I shoot back up the Shenandoah Valley to
Vermont, land of the silent sunset sailors and the solo skiers who
vanish into the darkening woods. If some of my ancestors were
Native American, I've reclaimed their nomadic ways. I'm like a
dog that turns around and around before lying down, but that
never actually lies down.

Consequently, I don't have a lot of friends. People tend to
want others to pick one team and play on it to the death. Most of
my pals are misfits like myself, standing with each foot firmly
planted in canoes headed in opposite directions. I used to think
that a real friend was someone who, had I been Jewish in Germany, would have hidden me from the Gestapo. Now that I'm a
senior citizen, I know that a real friend is someone who will drive
you home from your colonoscopy.

Upon my return to Kingsport, I borrow my parents' new car
for the next leg of my disjointed journey. And when I reach
Jamestown, I'm newly amazed by human tenacity. I can imagine
few less appealing sites for a settlement. The point on which the
triangular fort was built in 1607 is low and swampy, promising
bad water, soggy gardens, humidity, insects, and disease. Most
Jamestowners were as devoid of survival skills as were the Lost
Colonists. During one especially bad winter that they christened
the Starving Time, they ate rats, saddlebags, and each other. In
three years the population declined from 500 to 60.

The other problem was the Powhatan Indians, thirty-two
Algonquin tribes with an estimated 14,000 to 22,000 members,
the most powerful being the Pamunkey, Nansemond, Matta-
poni, Rappahannock, Chickahominy, and Appomattock. Like
the tribes around Roanoke Island, they took pity on the inept
colonists and tried to help. At first. Pocahontas (my grandmother's alleged cousin), a daughter of the chief of the Powhatan
Nation, even married a Jamestown man named John Rolfe, organizing her tribe to carry food to the starving Englishmen.

But as usual, the English soon wore out their welcome by

ignoring Pascal's sage observation that all the troubles of mankind could be avoided if only everyone would sit quietly in his own room. The Powhatan eventually attacked the English in 1622 and 1644, and the English attacked back, razing their villages. As with all conquistadors, what tipped the balance in favor of the English were horses, metal breast plates, muskets, germs — and the initial hospitality of their victims. By 1670, there were 40,000 Englishmen in the Tidewater and only 4,000 Indians.

And by the end of the seventeenth century, only 1,800 Powhatan remained. If they failed to wear striped coats in territory the English had claimed, the English were encouraged to shoot them. Many Powhatan had already fled west to the mountains. Throughout human history, those threatened with extinction have always headed for the hills.

Driving around the Northern Neck of Virginia, I'm intrigued finally to lay eyes on my grandmother's Mecca — the Tidewater. So often did we face east and worship it that I'm a little disappointed. It's just pleasant, rolling farmland drained by several tidal rivers that probe inland from the Chesapeake Bay, like the fingers of an outstretched hand.

In the early years in Virginia, manual labor was performed by indentured servants shipped from Britain, an estimated 30,000 to 50,000 of them convicted felons. After a fixed period of four to seven years, they were set free to make their own way. Or not. Of every ten indentured servants, one became a farmer and one an artisan. The other eight either died or became day laborers or vagrants. Many headed west to "unoccupied" land. Because Indian hunting grounds weren't under cultivation, they were regarded as unoccupied, despite the fact that the game in those forests provided Indians with much of their sustenance.

In the beginning, some Africans were also manumitted after fixed terms of service. Or their masters freed them in their wills and left them land. Or the slaves raised and sold crops and livestock on the side and bought their freedom.

In his study of 280 families that comprised 80 percent of the free African-Americans in seventeenth- and eighteenth-century Virginia and North Carolina, Paul Heinegg found that all these families but one originated from unions of white women with black men, both slaves and free. The one exception resulted from a white master and his black slave woman — an arrangement that became the rule rather than the exception later on.

The first boatload of African slaves arrived at Jamestown in 1619, and the situation for blacks began gradually to deteriorate. Plantation owners preferred slaves to indentured servants because they didn't have to free them just as they were getting the hang of hoeing tobacco. In addition, a bout of plague in London diminished the supply of white servants.

Over the course of world history, slaves hadn't necessarily been dark-skinned. They were simply those defeated in war or seized in raids. But an act of the Virginia General Assembly in 1639 prohibited Negroes from bearing arms. In 1662, another act proclaimed that all children were free or bound according to their mother's condition. In other words, if a child had a free mother, he himself was free, even if his father were enslaved. If he had a slave mother, he was a slave, even if his father were free (and even if his father were white). This act also imposed a large fine on any Christian who fornicated with a Negro.

By 1680, the term *white* had come into common usage as a racial category. A law prohibiting white-black marriages was passed in 1691. In 1723, more laws passed banning manumission and denying Africans the vote. Dark skin increasingly became a badge of slavery — dark skin of any origin. The annals of Jamestown list East Indian, Turkish, and Moorish servants and slaves, in addition to Native Americans. The free descendants of the early unions between Africans and Europeans, between natives and Europeans, became vulnerable to seizure and sale. Many headed for the hills.

A Melungeon origin tale concerns two men, Vardy Collins and Buck Gibson, said to be Cherokee from Virginia who borrowed white men's names. Vardy darkened Buck's skin with charcoal and sold him to a farmer. Buck ran away, washed off the charcoal in a creek, and caught up with Vardy. Then they headed for the hills with the farmer's money.

In a Best Western hotel near Richmond that night, while reading a biography of Pocahontas, I first realize that receiving a land grant was not the Big Deal the Virginia Club used to make of it. It was simply the way governments persuaded citizens to move to dangerous territories they wanted to annex. If you planned to farm in America, you either bought land from another farmer or from a speculator, or you received a grant from some government for performing a task like fighting in a war. Or you paid the passage for an indentured servant and received a chunk of land as a bonus. If you had no money and had performed no worthy deed, you either hired yourself out as a tenant or a laborer, or you squatted on seemingly unoccupied land, paid the taxes or not, and hoped for the best.

I also learn that as of 1976 Pocahontas had an estimated two million living descendants, with more being born every day. Studying her family tree, I start twitching. With growing dread, I pull out my own ancestral charts. Normal people carry laptops when they travel. Southerners carry their family trees.

Checking and rechecking, I reach the appalled conclusion that my grandmother was — in fact — descended from Pocahontas. And so was my grandfather, since they share an ancestor named Jane Bolling. Jane Rolfe, Pocahontas's granddaughter, married Robert Bolling, the grandfather of Jane Bolling.

Jane Rolfe died after giving birth to Jane Bolling's father, John. Her husband, Robert Bolling, then married an Englishwoman. Those Bollings descended from Pocahontas through Jane Rolfe and her son John are called Red Bollings. Those descended from Robert's English wife are called White Bollings. So my grandparents were Red Bollings. That makes my father a double Red Bolling. It also makes him a fourth cousin to his own mother, as well as a fourth cousin, once removed, to himself. In addition, it makes Brent Kennedy, who's also descended from John Bolling, my double ninth as well as my third and fourth cousin. Scribbling on a pad, I calculate that thirteen generations back I had 8,192 ancestors. Two were Pocahontas. I'm finally going mad.

I stumble into the bathroom and stare into the mirror. If some of my genes are from Pocahontas, they've left no trace, except for a complexion that makes me look embarrassed, which I often am, particularly by this new discovery. I'm starting to feel like the lunatic I once encountered at a genealogical chat site on the Internet who traced his ancestry back to Romulus, one of the twins sired by Mars and suckled by a she-wolf, who grew up to found Rome.

Returning to my biography, I discover that Pocahontas had a cousin named Nicketti, an alleged daughter or granddaughter of Opechancanough, Chief Powhatan's brother. Opechancanough, chief of the Pamunkey, organized the massacres of the British in 1622 and 1644. Nicketti married a Scotsman referred to only as Trader Hughes. Around 1720, they opened a trading post in Monacan Indian territory on the Otter Creek, which flows into the James River near present-day Lynchburg, Virginia.

A faint bell rings in my addled brain. I drag out my charts again. My worst suspicions are confirmed: one of my grandfather's older brothers was named Robert Hughes Reed. And several Vanovers married Hugheses in southwest Virginia. My grandmother had four cousins named Nicatie and a second cousin named Pocahontas Phipps. According to the biography, *nicketti* means "dewdrop" in Pamunkey, and my grandmother also had a second cousin named Spicie Dewdrop Vanover.

Full of remorse for mocking my grandmother behind her back for so many years, I lie awake much of the night. If the six-finger rumor is true, if the Pocahontas rumor is also true, if the Lake Champlain monster actually exists, what other myths are true? Is the one about the Vanovers being Black Dutch true? Was

Abby Easterd Vanover actually a Cherokee? Could Betty Reeves have really been a Portuguese Indian? Maybe they weren't trying to explain away darker skin after all. Maybe they were simply passing on what had been handed down through the generations.

On the theory that where there's smoke, there are mirrors, I assemble what I've learned about the Portuguese — apart from Betty Reeves; apart from the Sizemores, the Portuguese Jews from Barbados; apart from Brent's family name Canara, found in Portugal and Goa; apart from Juan Pardo's converso soldiers; apart from the 1990 gene-frequency study proclaiming the Melungeons Portuguese; apart from the theory that the word *Melungeon* came from the Portuguese "melungo."

One of de Soto's four chroniclers was Portuguese. He was referred to only as the Gentleman from Elvas, a town in Portugal. (Elvis also being . . . oh, never mind.)

A traditional Melungeon surname is Goins. In some old records, it's spelled Goans, which various researchers have connected to Goa, the Portuguese colony in India. Some maintain that when the early Melungeons said they were Portuguese Indians, they meant East Indians, not Native Americans.

Two Virginian explorers named Batts and Fallam found a "Portugal" living among the Saponi Indians in 1671.

Refugees from a group of tribally mixed Indians who lived at a British fort in Virginia called Christanna around 1714 later settled in North Carolina, where they were referred to as the Portuguese community.

A man named William Mallory Johns, who was born in 1765 of a white father and a Monacan mother, was nicknamed "Portugue."

Among the early slaves brought to Virginia were Creoles descended from Portuguese slave traders who'd mated with African women in the West Indies and at the slave factories on the African coast. Some referred to themselves as Portuguese and were known by such names as Antonio, Bashaw Farnando,

Emanuel Driggus (from Rodriggus), John Francisco, Domingo Matthews, Anthony Longo. Some slaves converted to Christianity and anglicized their names on board slave ships because prior to 1667 Christianized slaves were freed. Others anglicized their names after otherwise gaining their freedom. Antonio, for example, became Anthony Johnson, and John Francisco became Francis Payne.

During this period, even Spaniards in America were claiming to be Portuguese (if not English) because Portugal was a sometime ally of England, whereas Spain was her nemesis. The victorious do write the history, erasing the vanquished. And sometimes the vanquished help them do it.

These are all the Portuguese clues I can summon, and I can't see that they add up to much of anything, except for proving that a lot of people who were Portuguese, or who claimed to be Portuguese, or who others claimed were Portuguese, were running around the Tidewater in colonial days.

I fall into an exhausted stupor around dawn.

I drive slowly westward across Virginia, through rolling pastures and dense forests that were occupied by ten thousand Monacan Indians in the mid-eighteenth century, the largest tribes being the Saponi, Tutelo, and Manahoac. Unlike their archenemies the Powhatan, the Monacan didn't usually fight the Europeans. They just kept dodging out of the path of the ever-advancing English juggernaut like wandering war refugees.

In 1714, a few hundred of them lived at the above mentioned British fort, near present-day Lawrenceville. By this time most Indians who dealt with Europeans had taken European names. Many adopted the names of neighbors they liked or officials who had helped them. Those who'd been enslaved sometimes used their masters' names, as did African slaves. Three surnames at Fort Christanna were Collins, Goins, and Bowling, all traditionally Melungeon, Bowling perhaps connected to the Red Bollings and perhaps not.

A Virginian surveyor named William Byrd stopped off at Fort Christanna in 1728 and hired a Saponi named Bearskin as a hunter for his party. During the trip, Byrd interviewed Bearskin, reporting that his tribe believed in a supreme being who created the world, protected the good, and punished the evil. They also believed in a heaven and a hell. Bearskin's lengthy description of heaven, recorded in Byrd's journal, sounds identical to the paradise of Islam, with beautiful and obliging women, plentiful game and corn, and a mild climate. This offers another vague hint of a possible connection between southeastern Indians and Muslim Turks or Moors.

The road I'm meandering along was built atop an old trading trail called the Occaneechi Path that extended from the Tidewater to the North Carolina Piedmont tribes. In the seventeenth century, traders trekked along it with trains of as many as one hundred horses, bearing trade goods (beads, cloth, rum, iron tools, rifles, and ammunition) on the way over, and furs and hides on the trip back. Bear, beaver, bobcat, deer, fox, mink, muskrat, panther, raccoon, squirrel — those bales of skins represented an entire Noah's ark of southeastern animals. The returning trains also included Indians captured from enemy tribes by Indians friendly to the British. These captives were consigned to slave markets on the coast.

The men who handled the traders' horses on these trips were welcomed at the native villages by young women who wore their hair short to indicate that they were "trading girls," available to the men in exchange for beads, cloth, and ribbon. The tribes encouraged these women because their presence was a lure. Since these Indians were matriarchal, any babies from such matings would likely have been accepted by their mothers' clans. Some became guides, interpreters, and hunters for the traders. Others no doubt identified with their English fathers, leaving their native villages behind and trying to pass for Englishmen.

The Virginia traders competed with other English traders

who traveled north from Charleston, South Carolina, and with French traders who came east from their trading posts along the Mississippi. The natives played them against each other. The most successful traders were those who married native women and lived at least part-time in their villages, even though some deserted these wives and their half-breed children when their trading days ended. The explorer John Lawson explained that the Charleston traders fared better than the Virginians because more had taken Indian wives "whereby they soon learn the Indian tongue, and keep a Friendship with the Savages."

By late afternoon, I reach the banks of the New River in southwestern Virginia near the North Carolina border. Before a treaty ceded this area to Europeans in 1768, it belonged to the Cherokee, who used it primarily as a hunting ground. By then it was also occupied by some of my grandmother's ancestors — the Bryants, Cooleys, Hanks, Howells, and Rudys.

A battle erupted between some Indians who owned peach orchards here and some European squatters. But which side were my ancestors on? Or were they on both sides? This was a wilderness with no towns. Since many Europeans were living illegally on Indian land, they were in no hurry to travel to distant county seats to register deeds they didn't have. Births, marriages, and deaths during these years were usually recorded in churches, but church here consisted of a circuit rider's occasionally preaching in a private home and then moving on. A few families recorded such information in their Bibles, but many settlers were illiterate.

At dusk, I park my car alongside a road that runs down into a wide flat valley with a creek along the far boundary. Forested hills rise up on every hand. Some Black Angus are grazing alongside the creek. At the end of the valley sits a farmhouse lit by a few dim lights. A dog by a barn barks and then stops.

I stand there in the soft twilight, letting the fact sink in that ancestors of mine, whatever their ethnicity, once farmed this rich bottomland. One might have stood right where I'm now standing to enjoy this peaceful view. Or some might have fought in these pastures for the right to remain on this beautiful land.

I spot an old log structure well back in the woods behind me. Hoping to snare a souvenir of this spot, I walk over, unlatch the wooden door, and wrench it open.

I find myself face-to-face with half a dozen wooden shelves, all of them stacked with bulging black plastic garbage bags. Their necks are twisted shut and tied with twine. Failing to heed the warning that curiosity killed the cat, I slide a bag off its shelf. It's quite light. I poke it like a child trying to guess a Christmas gift. The contents feel like shoe boxes.

Despite having learned in charm class at J. Fred's not to rifle the possessions of others, I untie the twine, open the bag, and pull out what does turn out to be an empty cardboard box. On its cover in large black letters is printed

## LIVE LOBSTER: DO NOT OPEN!

The box looks brand-new, as though it's never contained anything at all, much less a lobster. The entire bag is filled with these boxes, as are, presumably, all the other identical black plastic bags.

All of a sudden I realize that if I don't get back to the main road in about thirty seconds, I'm a dead woman. I stuff the box into the bag and the bag onto the shelf. I close and latch the door. Glancing around in every direction, I dash to my parents' car, climb in, slam and lock the door, turn the car around, and race back to the highway.

Appalachia used to be known for its moonshine. Someone who came too close to a still, even if he didn't realize it, might get shot. Most farmers grew lots of corn, and one way to preserve it was to turn it into white lightning. When Prohibition ended, a new cash crop was needed, and marijuana filled the bill. Some grew it in the national forests so that their own land wouldn't be confiscated if the DEA discovered their plots. Others retrieved bales from Central America tossed from private planes, chopped and repackaged the leaves, and distributed them.

More recently, Appalachia has become a haven for methamphetamine labs. All you need is a stove, some saucepans, neighbors with no sense of smell, and a list of ingredients you can buy at Wal-Mart. I don't know whether those lobster boxes were intended for marijuana or crystal meth, but I do know that the nearest ocean is three hundred miles away.

I spend a nervous night in a Motel 6 in Galax, Virginia, thanking my lucky stars that I haven't been chopped into tiny pieces, packed in lobster boxes, and FedExed around the country like some modern-day Osiris.

Two teens in Johnson City were less fortunate. According to the prosecution, a trucker shot them, perhaps in a drug deal gone wrong. He cut off the boy's head and hands and dumped them into a lake so that no one could identify his corpse. He failed to take into account that a hand would float to the surface for a trolling bass fisherman to hook.

Meanwhile, the trucker allegedly moved the bodies from his mother's house into a self-storage shed. Then he split for New York in his diesel rig, assigning his aged mother and aunt the job of cutting up the girl's body and the rest of the boy's with a hacksaw and a chain saw. This chore took the frail old women a long time — too long. The corpses began to stink. Another alert self-storer noticed the stench and phoned the police. The trucker was charged with murder, and his mother with corpse abuse.

I fall asleep and dream of dismembering a boiled lobster and dipping its meat in melted butter.

After an artery-stupefying breakfast of biscuits and sausage gravy, I head south. The ancestors of both my paternal grandparents had one thing in common: they were all living near the New River, on both sides of the Virginia–North Carolina border, by the last decades of the eighteenth century. And half a century later most had moved northwest into the foothills of the Cumberland Mountains along the Kentucky-Virginia border.

Because of conflicting charters, a thirty-mile strip from the Atlantic coast to the Blue Ridge was claimed by both Virginia and North Carolina, which were granting and taxing the same plots of land. The region gradually filled up with people the governor of Virginia characterized as "loose and disorderly." They settled wherever they found vacant land and often refused to pay taxes to either state. Nor did they consider themselves subject to the laws of either regarding firearms, fornication, manumission, miscegenation, or voting rights.

When the boundary survey was finally completed in 1779, the resulting state line was crooked. A sliver nearly two miles wide at the inland end was again claimed by both states. In addition, the territory across the Blue Ridge (where Kingsport would be built 150 years later) was variously claimed by the Cherokee, North Carolina, Virginia, the State of Franklin, and also by Tennessee once it gained statehood in 1796. A similar free-for-all atmosphere lured droves of the "loose and disorderly" from farther east to join the de-tribalized Indians already living there. This entire area was, understandably, called the Squabble State. Some court cases over land disputes weren't settled until the end of the nineteenth century. These, then, were my ancestors and their fabled land grants.

I arrive in West Jefferson, North Carolina, the seat for Ashe County. It's a thriving mountain town nestled in the foothills of the Blue Ridge. I drive to a handsome, crumbling old brick courthouse on a hill and consult various deed books. Except in the will of her husband Cornelius Vanover, I find no whisper of Abby Easterd, my supposedly Cherokee four-times-great-grandmother, nor of any Easterds at all. But I do notice that a Phipps ancestor of both my grandparents lists a young woman as a tithable slave in a 1782 tax list. Five years later he has a white wife the same age, a small child, and no slave. It may be a coincidence, or it may be an example of how people doctored documents to suit their shifting circumstances.

The area that is now Ashe County belonged to the Cherokee

until a 1777 treaty ceded it to North Carolina and/or Virginia. My ancestors named Easterd, White, Stamper, Hill, and Phipps were living here by 1777. Were they Cherokee? Were they refugees from displaced Virginia or North Carolina tribes? Were they the mixed descendants of English and/or French traders? Were they European squatters, formerly indentured servants who'd fled the coast in search of land? Were they slaves escaped from the Tidewater, or free descendants of the early unions between indentured Englishwomen and African men? I don't know, and I don't see any way to find out, short of a DNA study on my father. But the Melungeon study for which he's already a subject is a blind one. The participants won't be told their individual results.

After leaving West Jefferson, I drive along a valley that winds among some steep hills. I pass a sign reading

## MULATTO HILL ROAD

Braking, I turn off and follow the road to the top of a ridge, from which I spot the ruins of a couple of cabins and wide expanses of pastureland rimmed with forest.

I'm surprised this word is still in use. *Mulatto* sounds cruel to the modern ear. The term ceased to be used on Virginia censuses in 1920 because that state was by then coming to recognize only black or white, no shades of brown that might imply interracial mixing.

Eventually I reach the Blue Ridge Parkway. I amble a hundred miles down it, through some of the most breathtaking scenery on earth, to the reservation for the eastern branch of the Cherokee Nation, located near the most precipitous part of the Smokies. The town of Cherokee is like any other mountain town with a Holiday Inn and Burger King. The only differences are the complexions of some of its citizens and the museum and traditional Cherokee village set up for tourists.

The Cherokee are an Iroquoian tribe, thought to have been driven to the southern Appalachians in the mid-fifteenth century by warfare. When de Soto encountered them in these mountains in 1540, they appeared less prosperous and more egalitarian than their lowland neighbors, who were living in villages that featured elevated mounds on which only priests and chiefs lived. But by the eighteenth century, the Cherokee had absorbed so many refugees from the Virginia and Carolina tribes and had so prospered from the fur trade with Europeans that they'd become the largest and strongest tribe in the Southeast.

More than any other tribe, the Cherokee attempted to adapt to English ways. Many wore European clothing, learned to speak English, and converted to Christianity. They developed a Cherokee alphabet and published their own newspaper. Most Cherokee became literate in their own language. Some Cherokee planters lived in plantation houses and owned slaves. Others operated gristmills and river ferries.

A few sent their sons north to an interdenominational Foreign Mission boarding school in Cornwall, Connecticut. In a grim comedy of Christian hypocrisy, two young Cherokee, John Ridge and Elias Boudinot (whose Cherokee name was Buck Watie), sons of prominent tribal leaders, fell in love with white women, one the daughter of a school administrator and the other a daughter of the town physician. After a huge ruckus, these couples married. The agents of the school called these marriages "criminal" and complained that the doctor's daughter, Harriet Gold, had "made herself a squaw." Livid, they shut down the school. European men had raped Indian women for centuries, but an Indian man's marrying a European woman for love sparked outrage.

Meanwhile, white settlers wanted Cherokee land and wouldn't take no for an answer. Many simply settled on it and fought off any Cherokee who objected, as did those who originally settled around my family farm. The Cherokee resistance to this land grab was led by a chief named John Ross, himself only one-eighth Cherokee by blood. After countless political manipulations, 16,000 Cherokee were rounded up at gunpoint and put on barges, or marched on foot, to Oklahoma — past the roadside graves of those who had gone before them. Some 4,000 died en route. In Oklahoma, the survivors were soon joined by 44,000 Creek, Choctaw, Chickasaw, and Seminole who'd been deported from other southern states.

But the forebears of those living today on the Cherokee reservation in the Smokies stayed behind, most legally through arrangements made with the North Carolina government prior to the Removal. Many others subject to removal refused to leave. Some were hunted down by federal soldiers and marched off to stockades, as gangs of white men swarmed down from the woods to loot their belongings, steal their livestock, dig up their ancestral graves for buried jewelry, and burn down their cabins.

Many Cherokee women married to European men also stayed behind in North Carolina and Tennessee with their mixed children. This category may have included my four-times-great-grandmother Abby Easterd, her son Cornelius Vanover, and his son William.

I go into a bookstore and buy a paperback that gives the various government rolls of members of the Cherokee Nation. You must prove a family connection to a name on one of these lists in order to be a card-carrying Cherokee. Flipping through it, I don't find any Easterds or Vanovers. I do find a family called Eas-tuh. But the similarity of sounds may be just a coincidence. I also find some Hanks, Hills, and Howells, and one family called Coo Lee, but I don't know if they have any connection to my grandmother's ancestors with those surnames, and I don't know how to find out.

This road appears to be another cul-de-sac. I'm starting to loathe that rogue babysitter who first croaked the word *Melungeon* at me. If she weren't already dead, I'd charge her with child abuse. This project, undertaken with such enthusiasm, is proving as never-ending as Cher's farewell tour.

I drive over to the flashy new Cherokee casino that looks as though it belongs in Atlantic City, not in the heart of the Smokies. The only Cherokee I spot are parking cars. Within, the banks of slot machines are as swathed in clouds of cigarette smoke as the mountain peaks outside are in mist. I sit down at a machine with a cup of quarters and wind up donating them all to the Cherokee Nation. It's the least I can do, since my ancestors, if any were Cherokee, managed to sidestep the Trail of Tears.

Like patients on life support, the other players are hooked to their whirring slot machines by cords around their necks, from which hang cash cards that are inserted into the machines. As they draw deeply on their cigarettes, these white folks stare at the spinning wheels of fortune with glazed eyes. Many will die from lung cancer, completely broke. Their money is paying for schools and clinics for the Cherokee. It's also paying for land. The Cherokee are slowly buying back some of what was taken from their ancestors by the ancestors of those who are now losing their 401(k)s in the one-armed bandits. Perhaps there is a God after all — one with an antic sense of humor.

When Spaniards first arrived in what is now the United States, an estimated five to twenty million natives were already living here. By 1700, over 90 percent had died from alcohol, slavery, starvation, war, and disease. In one of history's grim ironies, many survivors survived because of European genes that gave them immunity. Yet on the 1900 federal census, only 250,000 were willing to identify themselves as Indian.

However, on the 2000 U.S. census, some 4,119,301 people defined themselves as Indian, either alone or in combination with one or more other races. The Cherokee are the largest tribe listed, with 281,069 members. An additional 448,464 people checked "Cherokee" as well as some other category or categories. Wannabes or not, reinforcements have arrived. Some are most likely descended from tribes in Virginia and the Carolinas whose remnants were absorbed by the Cherokee, but there's no way to prove this. Even DNA testing can't yet distinguish among the different tribes and may never be able to do so, since so much amalgamation has occurred.

*

Quarterless and in the parking lot, I can't remember where I've parked my parents' new car. I think it was blue. I rarely notice brands or styles. My only concern is that a car get me where I want to go. I wander through rows of vehicles with plates from all across the nation, feeling increasingly frantic. How in the hell can I find this car when I don't even know what I'm looking for? I realize that this is an apt metaphor for my search for my wretched ancestors.

I force myself to stand completely still. Taking a deep breath, I ask myself what Ina with her ice test or my grandmother with her eyeglasses scam would do in my place. They might wait until 4:00 A.M. when everyone else will have departed, leaving my parents' car sitting alone in the lot. They might phone home and ask my parents for the make and color of the car they've been driving for three days. This seems too humiliating for a grown woman. But being grown is my problem: this incident is further proof that I've stopped growing and have started my decline.

After a long period of reflection, I shake myself like an awakened hound. I circle the area in which I think I parked, my finger punching the button on the car remote that opens the trunk. Eventually the trunk of a Buick with Tennessee plates pops open. I still can't remember what color it is.

When I arrive at my parents' house, I don't tell them about losing and rediscovering their new car. I do tell them about Pocahontas, however, and I hand my father a piece of paper on which I've written out the generations leading back to her. As he studies it, my mother suggests that I might want to lay a bouquet on my grandmother's grave in apology. I nod contritely.

Back at the cabin, I sit on the porch in the twilight and listen to the frogs down at the pond. My neocortex is reeling with absurd scenarios as it diligently attempts to make sense of the aimless ramblings of my faceless forebears. Shipwrecked Portuguese and marooned Turks, Pocahontas and Spicie Dewdrop Vanover, escaped Africans and fleeing conversos — the whole thing is at least as far-fetched as ancestral land grants from King James I. I realize that I, too, am prey to the family affliction of mythomania.

Despondent at having wasted so much time on such utter nonsense, I watch the night erase the narrow valley while fireflies flash Morse code messages back and forth. The pulsing of the frogs gradually cheers me up, and the steady beat of their moist oratorio sets me to composing some mocking limericks about my hopeless quest. I get out my banjo and pick out a tune to accompany them. By bedtime I've finished a song I christen "The Red, White, and Black Blues." The chorus goes:

*I don't know where I've come from, and I don't know who I am.*
*My granny says Virginia, but she's just into glam.*
*They say I can't be everything, they say I gotta choose.*
*And that's why I got those red, white, and black blues.*

## Teletubbies for Christ

THE GRASS IN THE FRONT YARD of the cabin is still damp with dew. Zachary and I are toddling through it, examining clover blossoms. I'm trying to keep him quiet so his parents and cousins can stay asleep inside. A gang of calves is darting around the neighboring pasture like a shoal of hyperactive minnows.

I start pulling some weeds in the rock garden. When I look up, Zachary is squatting by the electric fence in his blue shorts and sandals. On the other side stands a small black calf. He and Zachary are staring at one another, both thunderstruck.

Suddenly the pack of roving calves sweeps past like the hoodlums in *West Side Story*. The black one pirouettes and dashes after them. Zachary stands up to watch him go, a tragic expression on his face. Then he stretches out a hand and folds and unfolds it in farewell.

I contemplate what's in store for him — a lifetime of other creatures departing before he's ready and vice versa — and there's nothing I can do to make it any easier for him. Or for myself.

Zachary's four young cousins burst from the cabin in their bathing suits. They race to the pond and clamber into my grandfather's old rowboat. Zachary and I trot into the cabin and don our suits.

By the time we reach the beach, his cousins are swarming the floating dock, cannonballing and then scrambling back up the ladder. Standing in water to his knees, Zachary watches his glamorous older cousins wistfully. I strap a life jacket on him, and he and I float slowly toward the dock. My assignment as he flails his arms and legs is to support him and propel him forward so unobtrusively that he thinks he's doing it himself, thereby gaining the confidence that will one day allow this to happen.

A flash of triple déjà vu. I swam in this pond as a child. I taught my sister Jane, the mother of two of those cousins, to swim here. I also taught Zachary's mother to swim here. Now I'm teaching Zachary. The pond remains while the children who swim in it grow up, grow old, and one day die. Yet the pond will endure, as new crops of children arrive to churn these placid waters.

A church sign pops into my head:

**BABIES ARE GOD'S PROMISE THAT THIS WORLD WILL CONTINUE.**

These mini-sermons are eggs laid in my unconscious that hatch and burrow into my awareness when I least expect it, like hookworms. The evangelicals have taken over Kroger's, and they're making inroads into my psyche. What if I one day find myself falling to my knees by the roadside, like Saul en route to Damascus? I always think of the Rapture as the Raptor. I don't want to experience it. Hot flashes are bad enough.

Ina, Nellie, and I are sitting on Ina's deck, high above the lake in which the hapless fisherman hooked the human hand. This probably isn't what Jesus had in mind when He asked His disciples to become fishers of men.

Ina is playing her mandolin, and I my banjo. We're singing a campaign song about one of Nellie's relatives, a populist governor of Alabama in the 1940s named Big Jim Folsom. When his opponents taunted him on the stump about his moral failings, he'd reply, "Anytime you bait a trap with a good-looking blond, redhead, or brunette, you're going to catch old Jim every time." Folsom finally lost the governorship during a campaign in which he appeared on TV drunk. When he tried to introduce his sons, he couldn't remember their names.

Our song, which accuses Big Jim of having fathered a child with an innocent country girl, is called "She Was Poor, but She Was Honest." We reach my favorite verse:

> *Now he sits in legislature,*
> *Making laws for all mankind,*
> *While she roams the streets of Selma, Alabama,*
> *Selling grapes from her grapevine.*

We finish just as a float boat passes below. A float boat is a carpeted platform on pontoons with padded, vinyl-covered seats and a canopy overhead. Many families on this lake own one. This particular one is teeming with fun seekers swilling beer, shrieking with laughter, and singing out of tune to a portable radio blaring a Tim McGraw song about the good old days when people ate fried bologna sandwiches and didn't speak in vocabulary borrowed from drug lords. A chubby man in baggy red swim trunks, who's standing over a smoking grill, is conducting this choir by waving a hot dog clutched in tongs.

The boat rounds the bend, and the hubbub fades into silence. It's like a scene from a Fellini film. I chuckle.

"What's so funny?" asks Nellie,

I describe the view out my condo window onto Lake Champlain, where somber Vermonters swim, paddle, windsurf, and haul heavy sails to the top of tall masts. Yankees work very hard at playing.

"I've finally figured it out," I announce.

I'm constantly trying out my theories of regional distinctions on them because no two people could be more southern, though at opposite ends of the spectrum. Nellie grew up on eleven thousand acres, tended by a black mammy, whereas Ina grew up in a setting so remote that it lacked electricity and running water.

Weighing over ten pounds at birth, Ina was a Five-Chicken Baby, delivered at home by an obese country doctor who devoured roasted chickens throughout a delivery. Neighbors judged the difficulty of a birth by how many he consumed.

Ina and Nellie are waiting for my pronouncement. My most recent aphorism is that southerners like to puff people up, especially if they hate them, whereas Yankees like to put them down, especially if they like them.

"The main difference between the North and the South is that southerners enjoy being ridiculous, whereas Yankees like to feign dignity," I announce.

"It's the weather," replies Ina. "The heat addles our brains."

"And you have to keep drinking to stay hydrated," adds Nellie.

"But everybody on that boat was probably Baptist," I observe, "and Baptists aren't supposed to drink."

"Many Baptists are Baptist only on Sunday," explains Ina, herself a recovering Baptist.

I smile grimly. Golf on Sunday is just the tip of the iceberg of southern sin. My high school classmates have recently started reminiscing about alcoholism, physical abuse, and mental illness. It seems our sunny little town was actually a snake pit, and the charming snakes were adults I liked and respected.

Ina has told me about Kingsport's answer to the Bowery, the apartments across the street from the train station, entered through a battered green door, where men drank, gambled, and whored their paychecks away, while their wives or children stood in the doorways begging them for grocery money.

Recently an article in Nellie's newspaper exposed a drug and prostitution ring conducted out of a storefront on Broad Street. The kingpin had disguised it as a grocery store by placing several dozen cans of baked beans on the shelves. The police asked the businessman next door if he hadn't found it strange that a grocery store would display only a few cans of beans.

The businessman replied, "Well, hell, I thought he had him a bean store!"

That's how I feel about these revelations of private crimes that should have been obvious to us all: I thought we had us a bean store.

But this phenomenon isn't restricted to any one region or religion. If you live long enough, all your fondest illusions about humans being created in the image of God will crumble into dust.

I'm sitting in Diane's chair while she describes how a champagne-colored rinse she calls her "special" will take on my particular shade of gray. I promise to think about it. She warns me to make a double appointment so she'll have enough time to apply the dye. I worry that my resolve to remain hoar-headed is waning.

Her cell phone rings, and she puts on her headset. After listening for a while, she starts giving advice in a low voice. Since my last appointment, she's apparently started channeling Oprah. Unfortunately, I can hear only one side of the discussion.

I study her in the mirror as she snips away, talking into her mouthpiece about how to handle abusive men. She's tall and slender with a fair complexion. It's hard to know what color her hair might be without her special rinse, which has turned it the attractive pale champagne that I've begun to covet. Does she really have Indian ancestry, or is she another wannabe? Do I — or am I? Is this Pocahontas thing for real, or is there an error, deliberate or otherwise, in the research?

I force myself to face the likelihood that I'll never know. My grandparents are dead, so I can't wring confessions from them. My father is content to be either Indian or Melungeon, but he's as clueless as I am. I could spend the rest of my life in musty courthouses clawing my way through deed books and tax lists. But records don't exist for the earliest years on the frontier. And I've already discovered that some that do exist deceive. The DNA study may reveal something about Melungeons in general, but nothing specific about my family. The Melungeons are finally getting me, just as that babysitter warned. I can neither solve their mystery nor ignore it. It's like having high cholesterol.

Close to hyperventilating, I calm myself with the words of Jeanette Carter, daughter of Sarah and A. P. Carter, who recorded the first country music songs in the 1920s: "All you can do is the best you can do. You can't do no more than that."

One last circuit around the Kaaba on my Melungeon hajj, and I vow to call it quits. I drive up the Shenandoah Valley to Lynchburg, Virginia, the hometown of Jerry Falwell, founder of the Moral Majority, who blamed 9/11 on homosexuals, abortionists, feminists, pagans, and the ACLU because they offended God, who therefore allowed America's enemies "to give us probably what we deserve." Lynchburg is also the former home for the Virginia Colony for Epileptics and the Feebleminded. A coincidence, or another of God's little jokes?

During the Civil War Lynchburg's huge tobacco warehouses served as hospitals for the mutilated troops from both sides, who were transported from the Virginia battlefields in crammed boxcars. Those who arrived already dead were packed in charcoal and shipped home to their parents. If their identities or their parents couldn't be located, they were buried in Lynchburg.

I visit this sad cemetery in the heart of town, which features row after row of identical stone tablets, arranged by state, sometimes carved with only regiment numbers. All my life I've been fighting the Civil War inside my own brain. Yet this is how the Civil War — or any war — ends: barren fields of blank headstones. Will my Melungeon struggle end similarly with my anonymous ancestors still lying unclaimed in unmarked graves, despite all my efforts to find and acknowledge them?

I drive across the James River and wind up a road to the bluff on which the Virginia Colony for Epileptics and the Feebleminded sits. Now named the Central Virginia Training Center, it houses five hundred mentally handicapped patients in several handsome red-brick Colonial Revival buildings. These occupy

350 well-groomed acres that used to be a working farm run by the inmates.

I arrive at a building that was constructed in 1910 to house the first one hundred epileptics, assembled here from Virginia's mental hospitals. As I park alongside the nearby infirmary, I remember a Helen Keller quote featured on the Training Center Web site: "Keep your face to the sunshine and you cannot see the shadow." Although the sun is beating through my windshield, I can't help but see the shadow that drapes over this infirmary like a shroud.

In 1913, the Virginia Colony for Epileptics became the Virginia Colony for Epileptics and the Feebleminded. By 1926, there were 511 epileptics of both sexes and 334 "feebleminded," all women. Two were a mother and daughter, Emma and Carrie Buck.

Carrie, being illegitimate, had been taken from Emma and placed in foster care in Charlottesville. When a nephew of her foster parents raped her at age seventeen, she became pregnant. Her foster parents committed her to the Virginia Colony, where she was at last reunited with her mother. Carrie's resulting daughter, Valerie, was judged "feebleminded" at seven months and was placed with another foster family.

I try to imagine how I'd have felt if some official had taken Sara away from me and entrusted her to strangers — especially if I myself had been denied my own mother and then raped while in the care of her replacement. Or how I'd feel to have someone declare Zachary "feebleminded" and confiscate him. I might very well strangle such a person with my bare hands.

Next, the state of Virginia passed a law mandating sterilization of the "feebleminded." Carrie Buck became the test case. The U.S. Supreme Court ruled in support of Virginia's law. Justice Oliver Wendell Holmes Jr. stated in the majority opinion in 1927, "It is better for all the world, if instead of waiting to execute degenerate offspring for crime, or to let them starve for their imbecility, society can prevent those who are manifestly unfit from continuing their kind. The principle that sustains compulsory vaccination is enough to cover cutting the Fallopian tubes. Three generations of imbeciles are enough."

Carrie Buck was sterilized against her will, and without the consent of her mother, inside the building I'm looking at, a red-brick structure with white wooden two-story porches out front. Carrie's sterilization opened the floodgates. Four thousand more were performed in this building on people the superintendent of the Virginia Colony, Dr. Albert Priddy, called the "shiftless, ignorant, and worthless class of anti-social whites of the South." Many were told they were receiving appendectomies. Some didn't learn the truth until many years later, after repeated failures to conceive. The last mandatory sterilizations in Virginia were performed in 1972.

During this period, an additional 4,300 were sterilized elsewhere in Virginia. Fifty-two thousand more were sterilized in twenty-seven other states — 20,000 in California alone. At the Nuremberg trials, the chief Nazi eugenicists, who engineered the sterilization of somewhere between 360,000 and 3.5 million people, defended themselves by quoting Oliver Wendell Holmes's Supreme Court decision in the Carrie Buck case.

In 1985, Stephen Jay Gould investigated the third generation of Buck "imbeciles"— Carrie's daughter, Valerie. He found that, before dying at age eight of a childhood disease, she attended a public school, where she received superior marks for deportment and average ones for class work. Carrie herself had once made the honor roll at school.

The "feeblemindedness" of Carrie and her mother evidently consisted of their being impoverished unwed mothers, however unwillingly so on Carrie's part. But after seeing photos of the two, I've realized that there may have been an additional motive behind their incarcerations and Carrie's sterilization. Both appear partly Native American. The present-day Saponi Nation, whose original territory included what is now Lynchburg, maintains that they were descendants of a chief named John Buck.

In the early decades of the twentieth century, several

pseudo-anthropological studies of rural mixed-race communities set out to prove that the genes for degenerate and criminal behavior descend from generation to generation. The Virginia Colony in Lynchburg appears to have expanded its patient base from epileptics to the "feebleminded" so that the children of such communities could be separated from what was seen as the bad influence of their families. They were fed, clothed, educated, taught a trade — and sterilized so that in time these mixed people would die out.

One of the Virginian eugenicists behind these plans was a medical doctor named Walter Plecker. In 1912, he became the first registrar for the Virginia Bureau of Vital Statistics in Richmond, which recorded births, marriages, and deaths in the state. He, along with others, worked behind the scenes to pass the mandatory sterilization law. This law was especially important to him because he maintained that it was "feebleminded" whites who were most prone to mate with Indians and Africans. "The worst forms of undesirables born amongst us are those whose parents are of different races," he wrote.

In a tone bordering on hysteria, he continued that unless these "defective" people could be prevented from reproducing, "We have little to hope for, but may expect in the future decline or complete destruction of our civilization." He regarded the United States as "the last stronghold of the white race."

Plecker also worked for passage of the Virginia Racial Integrity Law in 1924, along with such friends as John Powell of the Anglo-Saxon Clubs of America. Until early in the twentieth century, a Virginian had been considered "colored" if he or she had one "colored" grandparent. Even the Nazis were more lenient in their definitions, designating Germans as fully Jewish only if they had at least three Jewish grandparents.

But in 1919, the Virginia code was tightened to read, "Every person having one-sixteenth or more of negro blood shall be deemed a colored person, and every person not a colored person having one-fourth or more of Indian blood shall be deemed an

Indian." How it could take only one-sixteenth of a certain heritage to make one person a Negro, whereas one-fourth of another heritage made someone else Indian, remained unclarified.

In 1924, the so-called one-drop rule, officially the Virginia Racial Integrity Law, tightened the requirements for whiteness even further: "The term 'white person' shall apply only to the person who has no trace whatsoever of any blood other than Caucasian, but persons who have one-sixteenth or less of the blood of the American Indian and have no other non-Caucasic blood shall be deemed to be white persons."

This last provision allowing those who were one-sixteenth or less Indian to be white was for the benefit of the some 20,000 descendants of Pocahontas who were scions of the First Families of Virginia — the Jeffersons, Lees, Randolphs, et al. Their proclaiming themselves Indian while the "one-drop rule" was being implemented in their home state was not unlike Marie Antoinette's donning her shepherdess costume prior to the French Revolution.

To make matters even more mind-numbing, the different southern states had different standards for determining race. In South Carolina at this same time, for example, anyone with one black ancestor five generations back was legally black, regardless of physical appearance. In Missouri, Mississippi, and Florida, a "colored" person was anyone with one-eighth or more Negro blood. Meanwhile, in South America, one drop of European blood made someone European.

But the passage of bills and their actual implementation are two different matters. In reality, many Virginians, especially those in the mountains, had no idea whether or not their ancestry included Indians and Africans. Illiteracy was rampant, and lives were short and focused on survival.

History books label the years 1880 to 1925 the Great Age of Passing. Two-thirds of the southerners listed as "mulatto" on the federal censuses lived in Virginia, North Carolina, and Tennessee. Those who looked white enough struggled to become officially white, whatever their actual ancestry, in order to side-step the Jim Crow laws passed around the turn of the century. Those remaining under the most dire threat from the new laws were those with darker skin or telltale surnames that had been listed as "mulatto" or FPC on the censuses from the mid-nineteenth century.

But Walter Plecker's efforts to stem the destruction of civilization didn't end with the passage of these restrictive bills. He began a program to remove the corpses of people he considered nonwhite from white cemeteries. In his twisted logic, he reasoned that since all the Indian tribes in Virginia had intermarried with Negroes (in his unsubstantiated opinion), and since one drop of Negro blood now made a person Negro, there were no longer any Indians left in Virginia. Therefore, anyone claiming to be Indian was, in effect, acknowledging African ancestry and then trying to hide behind Pocahontas in order to disguise it. With reasoning like this at the highest levels of government, it's a wonder the entire population of Virginia didn't become feeble-minded as they tried to make sense of it.

"Like rats when you're not watching," Plecker explained, "they have been sneaking in their birth certificates through their own midwives, giving either Indian or white as racial classification." His mission became to expose these "rats." What the Ku Klux Klan, resuscitated in 1915, was accomplishing in other southern states via lynching, Plecker was determined to accomplish in Virginia via the more genteel tools of documentary genocide and mandatory sterilization.

Like the Grinch stealing Christmas, Plecker notified a white woman in Pennsylvania that the man her daughter was about to marry had black blood. He also wrote to a new mother, "You will have to . . . see that this child is not allowed to mix with white children. It cannot go to white schools and can never marry a white person in Virginia. It is a horrible thing."

When someone finally challenged him about one such letter, he wrote to his pal John Powell, "I have been doing a good deal of bluffing, knowing all the while that it could never be legally sustained."

Not content to limit his pathology to Virginia, Plecker gave the keynote speech at the Third International Conference on Eugenics in New York in 1932, which was attended by Ernst Rudin, a German who eleven months later helped write Hitler's new eugenics law.

Dr. J. H. Bell, the new superintendent of the Virginia Colony, wrote in 1933, "The fact that a great state like the German Republic . . . has in its wisdom seen fit to enact a national eugenic legislative act providing for the sterilization of hereditarily defective persons seems to point the way for an eventual worldwide adoption of this idea."

Of the birth and marriage records Plecker assembled in Virginia, he wrote proudly in 1943, "Hitler's genealogical study of the Jews is not more complete." In that same year, Plecker sent a letter to all the health and educational professionals in Virginia warning that those he called "mongrels" were moving from county to county, trying to change their racial designation from colored to Indian or white as they went. He listed their surnames by county. All the traditional Melungeon names appear on the list, as do some Melungeon-related names, including four in my grandparents' families.

The last vestiges of the Virginia Racial Integrity Law weren't overturned until 1975. In 2002, Governor Mark Warner and the Virginia General Assembly apologized to the 8,300 victims of the eugenic sterilization policy. Some who are still living said that although the apology was very nice, it was a case of too little, too late.

My grandparents lived a hundred and fifty miles from Lynchburg when my grandfather was practicing medicine on horseback. They left Virginia for Tennessee in 1918 when my father was three years old. Were they aware of Plecker's bureaucratic noose tightening around the necks of ethnically mixed people? As a doctor and a schoolteacher, they'd have received memos from the Bureau of Vital Statistics about its activities. Did they feel personally threatened? Did they feel alarmed for their friends and neighbors, their relatives and in-laws? Could that be why my grandmother, although ostensibly proud of her Virginia heritage, rarely went back there from Tennessee? Could this be why we never met, or even saw photos of, my grandparents' relatives? Did my grandparents move to Tennessee because it was more racially relaxed, having hosted many abolitionists before the Civil War and many Unionists during it — and never succumbing to the fad of forcibly sterilizing its citizens? Or did they simply see an opportunity for advancement when J. Fred Johnson and George Eastman invited my grandfather across the border to open a hospital in Kingsport?

The latter seems more likely. But recently I found reissued copies of my grandparents' birth certificates from the Bureau of Vital Statistics. My grandfather's is signed by Walter Plecker himself. Both list my grandparents as "white." However, the Dickinson County commissioner, whose signature confirmed their whiteness, was William Vanover, my grandmother's grandfather, himself the grandson of Abby Easterd, our family Cherokee.

The early Melungeons could probably never have imagined a day when it might feel safe to acknowledge being a "mongrel." But is it really safe even now? After all, German Jews considered themselves loyal Germans for many generations prior to the Holocaust, and Muslims lived in Spain for eight centuries prior to their expulsion in 1609.

Heading back across the James River, I speculate on what would make someone behave as vilely as Walter Plecker. He was a son of the South, his father and male relatives having fought for the Confederacy. He was reared by a black slave named Delia. After emancipation, she remained with the family and was married in their parlor.

Plecker was quoted as saying, "As much as we held in esteem individual negroes, this esteem was not of a character that would tolerate marriage with them. . . . The birth of mulatto children is a standing disgrace." A fundamentalist Presbyterian, he wrote in an essay, "Let us turn a deaf ear to those who would interpret Christian brotherhood as racial equality."

His newspaper boy said of him, "I don't know anyone who ever saw him smile."

Rigid in other ways, he reportedly ate a single apple for lunch every day. And he refused to look when he crossed a street, expecting cars to stop for him. In 1947, a car — hopefully one driven by a "mongrel"— didn't stop, and he died two hours later.

Trying to figure out why Plecker found "mongrels" so threatening, I decide that he must have felt a visceral, physical affection for Delia, who'd cared for him as an infant. And this attraction may have appalled him. Just so, gay bashers are said to be unhinged by their attraction, unconscious or not, to other men. Just so did the sin-obsessed residents of Salem burn some of their fellow citizens as witches. Such people project their own tendencies onto others and then try to destroy those tendencies by destroying their designated scapegoats. As the poet Rumi puts it, "People of the world don't look at themselves, and so they blame one another."

Also, many people know who they are only by knowing who they aren't. They're not black, so they're white. They're not gay, so they're straight. Should you introduce such people to a "mongrel" or a bisexual (*quelqu'un qui va à voile ou à vapeur*, as the French put it, "someone who travels by sail or by steamboat"), they experience an identity meltdown because they're forced to realize that their ironclad categories are permeable. By designating anyone with a single drop of African blood as African, Plecker was, in effect, copying his Virginian forebears by denying that any interracial mixing had ever occurred or that any sexual taboos might have been violated.

The early Cherokee revered creatures that crossed boundaries — snakes that lived both on and beneath the ground, birds that inhabited sky as well as land, frogs and turtles that occupied land and water. Many native tribes regarded women who fought as warriors and men who dressed as women and did women's work as sacred for the same reason. Their existence confirmed, rather than undermined, the identity of the other men and women in the tribe.

I detour so as to avoid Liberty University, where Jerry Falwell is busy inoculating Southern Baptist youth with his own venom, which will confer upon them an immunity to tolerance of anyone who isn't a straight white male Jesus freak. Falwell's hatred even extends to Tinky Winky, the purple Teletubby on PBS. He's identified it as homosexual, claiming that purple is a gay color and that the triangle on the top of its head is a gay symbol. He also insists that the magic bag it carries is a purse. The next thing you know, Reverend Falwell will be sterilizing the Teletubbies.

In 2002 the *National Enquirer* (always my source of choice) reported on a circle of gay students on the Liberty campus. The girlfriend of one dragged him to the authorities after she overheard a rumor that he'd had an assignation with a male staff member. He confessed to this allegation. The administrators insisted he was lying, so he described in detail the sheets on the bed of the staff member in question. Then an assistant pastor, a bodybuilder who directed the band, resigned.

Asked to comment, Falwell said, "I was told he had problems in this area that you speak of."

The bodybuilder, however, denied being homosexual. His father, the dean of Liberty's theological seminary, said his son was leaving only because "he feels the Lord may be leading him in a new direction, a music path."

Early in the seventeenth century King James I of England said of the Anabaptists, the cousins of contemporary Baptists, that they "thinke themselves only pure, and in a manner, without sinne, the onely true church . . . and all the rest of the world to be but abominations in the sight of God."

This is the King James for whom Jamestown was named, the same James who supposedly gave land grants to the Tidewater ancestors of the Virginia Clubbers. He's also the King James who organized the English translation of the Bible that still bears his name — and the King James who had a long romance with the Duke of Buckingham.

I drive back into Kingsport, consulting the competing church marquees for some much-needed guidance after my upsetting afternoon at the Hospital from Hell.

The Presbyterians say,

**SEARCHING FOR A NEW LOOK? GET A FAITH LIFT.**

I lisp this to myself. Not helpful.

The Methodists ask,

**WHERE WILL YOU SPEND ETERNITY?**
**IN THE SMOKING OR THE NON-SMOKING SECTION?**

Also unhelpful.

The Belvue Christians say,

**HONK IF YOU LOVE PEACE AND QUIET.**

This cheers me up.

The Baptists suggest that

**FORBIDDEN FRUIT MAKES MESSY JAMS.**

I crack a smile.

But it's the Free Pentecostals who give me the lift I'm seeking:

**GOD LOVES SPIRITUAL FRUITS, NOT RELIGIOUS NUTS.**

Sitting on the porch at the cabin trying to digest my grim journey like a python swallowing a rat, I watch the steers suddenly gallop to the upper end of the valley, bellowing and rolling their eyes like stars of the silent screen. They look like they're auditioning for a John Wayne movie.

Then I spot the cause of their panic: a coyote slinks across the valley and disappears behind the dam, on his way to his den in the woods at the top of the hill. A whole mob of them arrived in our area recently, following the interstates from out west, snacking en route on roadkill, their equivalent of fast food.

Len has told me that the mother cows, placid cud-chewers of our childhood, have become black belt karate masters, lashing their hooves like cudgels at coyotes that try to dine on their calves.

I wonder if this coyote feels bad that the steers stampede whenever they see him coming. Or is he proud to have such power? Like Walter Plecker and Jerry Falwell, the coyote probably takes perverse pleasure in striking terror into the hearts of our hybrid cattle. I sometimes hear him and his slavering pack on their hillside late at night, yipping and howling at the harvest moon as though at a burning cross.

# Chief Sit 'n' Bull

SPRING SUN POURS THROUGH MY WINDOWS, and Lake Champlain is lapping at my doorstep. But I haven't gone outside in several days. I've become as addicted to my computer as a gambler at the Cherokee casino to his slot machine. I've joined an Internet discussion group that specializes in the use of DNA testing for genealogical purposes. The results from the Melungeon study will be released in a few weeks, and I intend to be ready.

Many members of my new focus group are doctors, geneticists, and professional genealogists. At first I was intimidated, so I "lurked." I read their postings, but I didn't join in. Eventually, though, I began to feel like a voyeur at a porn site, so I started posing an occasional timid question.

In time, I absorbed the fact that three types of DNA tests are available for genealogical purposes. One samples mitochondrial DNA, multiple copies of which are found in every cell, where they govern metabolism. A mother passes her mitochondrial DNA to all her children. It dead-ends in her sons, but her daughters pass it on to their children. Since it mutates very slowly, it's useful in tracing population migrations. But it gives an individual information only about his or her distaff side, all the way back to a mitochondrial Eve who lived in Africa around 150,000 years ago.

A second type of test is for males only. It uses the Y chromosome, which a man inherits from his father, who inherited it from his father, and so on, back to a Y-DNA Adam. Y-DNA mutates more quickly than mitochondrial DNA and is, therefore, useful in tracing more recent ancestry.

If you visualize someone's ancestry as a fan, mitochondrial DNA and Y-DNA provide data about only the outer stay on either side. Ten generations back, each individual's fan has 1,024 separate stays, and these tests will have sampled only two. To learn about the center of the fan, a test called the Ancestry-ByDNA has been devised, which samples non-sex-related DNA markers from the nucleus of a testee's cells.

My discussion group explains that the test is an exercise in statistics. The markers it samples are not those that determine physical characteristics but are, rather, taken from the "junk" DNA located between genes on the chromosomes. Although this type of DNA has no as yet determined function, these markers are found in varying proportions in the four major population groups — Indo-Europeans, sub-Saharan Africans, Native Americans, and East Asians. Since so much global mixing has occurred, only one marker so far discovered occurs in just a single group. The others are found in different proportions in all the groups. For example, a particular marker might appear in 15 percent of Indo-Europeans, 60 percent of Native Americans, 10 percent of East Asians, and 5 percent of sub-Saharan Africans. The averages of these readings from 176 markers are computed by a complex formula. The testee is then given the percentages of the four populations represented by his or her sample.

My group discusses the controversial nature of this test. It has difficulty distinguishing East Asian from Native American because the two populations separated so recently that not enough mutations have accumulated to make the readings for each truly distinctive. Also, because of all the panglobal mixing, the confidence contours for the reported percentages are quite wide. Single-digit readings could represent smoke from some distant ancestral campfire, or they could be just statistical "noise."

Another test called the EuroDNA uses the same technique

on 320 additional markers to break down the Indo-European component of the AncestryByDNA results into four more categories: northern European, southeastern European (Greek, Turkish, and Italian populations), South Asian (East Indian, Pakistani, and Roma populations), and Middle Eastern (including North African populations).

In answer to one of my questions, the group discusses the fact that a single Native American ancestor more than six generations back wouldn't register with this test. In other words, Pocahontas's input is no longer discernible in her descendants via the DNA tests currently available. However, the input of several Native American ancestors from that far back might be detectable.

I try to tell my father about what I'm learning, but my e-mails to him keep bouncing back. He uses an Internet provider until his free, introductory hours expire, and then he switches to a new one until their free hours expire, and so on. No one is ever able to contact him via e-mail because his address keeps changing.

Several dozen messages arrive every day from my DNA group. Many require research in the recommended textbooks I've been buying. Participation in this group starts to seem like practice for the afterlife. Everyone interacts as a disembodied essence. Yet there are still very distinctive personalities — know-it-alls, altruists, and windbags. Anyone who shows his or her fangs too insistently is cast into limbo by our moderator, who intervenes in disputes like an avenging archangel. Hell is when your computer crashes and you're cut off from your comrades altogether.

My new best friends talk a lot about the individual DNA testing that many are conducting on their families via several commercial labs. As I gain confidence, I decide to try this. I order some test kits, and soon I'm swabbing the inner cheek of every person who opens his or her mouth in my presence.

One day my group mentions Mongolian blue spots, another physical sign of non-European heritage. I leap up from my desk chair, strip off my jeans, and grab a hand mirror. Contorting myself into a position that reminds me of the days when feminists were using specula to befriend their own cervixes, I study my coccyx. I've never seen it before. I'm intrigued. I notice a blue bruise the size of a quarter. For a horrified moment, I wonder if my idiopathic thrombocytopenic purpura has returned. Then I conclude that I've merely sat down too hard.

I wait several days. Then I peek again. The bruise is still there, but it's blessedly not spreading. Day after day I study my bruise, like a Roman oracle consulting fowl innards. I try to maintain the scientific detachment forced on me by growing up in a family of physicians. Finally, I accept the fact that I have a Mongolian blue spot.

I'm enchanted, but I can't think how to share this thrill with others. Remembering the Queen Teens fashion show, I'm alarmed by the notion of what I might do at the next Melungeon conference to prove that I may be one of them.

One sunny afternoon I take time out from my cybercult to throw bread crumbs to some kamikaze seagulls along the lakeshore with an enthralled Zachary. An airplane passes overhead, flashing silver in the sun.

Zachary points at the plane and crows, "Daddy!" He once went to the airport with Sara to see Brett off on a trip, and he now thinks that all airplanes contain his father. He apparently believes that Brett spends his time, when he's not around, circling the skies like an eagle.

As we hurl crusts to the swooping gulls, I realize that tracing ancestry via DNA is based on the belief that Zachary could be descended from these screeching harpies. The wife of the Bishop of Worcester, upon learning about Darwin's theory of evolution in 1860, is reported to have said, "Let us hope it is not true, but if it is, let us pray that it will not become generally known."

I remember first being introduced to this concept in high school. Our biology teacher, Mr. Burns, took his best students aside one day and quietly asked us to spend a lunch hour with him in his classroom. Disgruntled not to be out at the drive-in restaurants with our pals, we listened glumly while he made us promise that we wouldn't tell anyone, not even our parents, about what he was going to impart to us. He warned that he could lose his job. Once we'd reassured him that our lips were sealed, he told us in a hushed voice about evolution and natural selection. We were as titillated as though he were describing oral sex.

Yet in 2001 only 53 percent of Americans agreed with the statement that "humans developed from earlier species." This is the lowest rate for this belief in the industrialized world. The figure is around 80 percent for most other Western democracies. Even thirteenth-century Turks would have agreed with that statement. Rumi himself said, "I died a mineral and became plant. I died a plant and rose an animal. I died an animal and I was man. Why should I fear? When was I less by dying?"

Creationists in this country maintain that Adam and Eve were divinely assembled about 6,000 years ago and that subsequent humans are their heirs. Geneticists support our descent from a genetic Adam and Eve whose descendants moved out of Africa to populate the globe some 60,000 to 80,000 years ago. But Adam and Eve are all that creationists and evolutionists can agree on.

Once our bread supply runs out, Zachary and I return to the parking lot of my condo. I strap him into his car seat, an exercise that confirms my superiority over seagulls, who would never in their wildest dreams be able to fasten all these interlocking belts and buckles correctly. To be fair, though, I require a refresher course from Sara each time I drive Zachary someplace.

A bumper sticker on a cranberry Altima parked next to mine reads

**SILENCE IS GOLDEN, BUT DUCT TAPE IS SILVER.**

Vermont bumpers are giving Tennessee church marquees a run for their money.

We arrive at the airport, park in the garage, and walk up to the observation deck where Brett's father works. He greets us warmly, and then Zachary and I assume our station by a window through which we can watch an endless parade of planes taxi out to runways and take off. This is Zachary's favorite pastime. I don't know if it's because he thinks his beloved father is aboard one of those planes.

A yellow dump truck comes rolling down a runway en route to a construction site on the far side of the airport. Zachary tugs at my hand, "Gram! Look!" he exclaims. "Truck take off!"

Ina picks me up at the Kingsport airport, and we head out to her house on the lake, where I'll be staying until the London geneticist announces his findings on Melungeon DNA. Ina is now almost as stressed out over her ancestors as I am over mine. I've persuaded her to order DNA tests on herself and two of her elderly uncles.

The next day, I take my mother to a luncheon to celebrate the hundredth birthday of one of her friends. When we get back, she goes upstairs to change while I sit down in my father's room. He's very pleased with himself. He says he's persuaded a Baptist prayer group in town to pray for him to win the Publishers Clearing House sweepstakes.

"I'd ask you to pray for it, too," he says. "But I get the impression you don't believe in prayer."

"I do believe in prayer," I say indignantly. "I just don't believe in prayer to win sweepstakes. I hope God is busy solving bigger problems."

"I hope God works on little problems, too, because I don't have any big ones."

He asks how the party went. I tell him it was very pleasant, that my mother spent a lot of time talking about foxhunting to the celebrant's brother, a retired surgeon from the Mayo Clinic.

"*Foxhunting?*" he snorts. "Why, your mother wouldn't know a fox from a possum!"

I study him, startled by his ferocity. "That's cute, Dad. You're jealous."

"It's just that I hate the idea of your mother as a wealthy widow, running around town in a BMW convertible," he says woefully.

Laughing, I reply, "Who says you'll go first?"

"I'd better. I'd be miserable without her."

This is the downside to a happy sixty-five-year marriage. We who spent our early years in orange crates welcome solitude — court it, even.

The red summer sun rises from behind a wooded cliff. The lake below turns the color of fresh blood. I'm standing on Ina's deck the morning of the Melungeon conference, and in a few hours the Melungeons will know who they are, after three hundred years of wondering.

My hands resting on the railing, I recall my conversation twenty-five years earlier with Buddy, the Shobes' half-Melungeon gardener, in which he said he'd been too dark for the whites and too pale for the coloreds. Nowadays, I have a better idea of what he was talking about.

In fact, I find myself close to tears as the full enormity of what the historical Melungeons experienced finally dawns on me. Regarded as wannabes by Indians, whites, and blacks alike, they were raceless in a racist society. Many spent their lives enduring ridicule and humiliation from others who were certain of their own identity (even if they were wrong).

Whether my ancestors were among them isn't really important. But I think about my grandparents anyway, whoever they were, so intent on constructing a secure and comfortable life for themselves — and for us.

The latter-day Melungeons are gathering under a tent in a park in Kingsport, determined at last to deconstruct the white identity their ancestors struggled to bequeath them. Ina, my mother, and I sit down in folding chairs facing the podium.

Wayne, the NPR executive who's president of the Melungeon Heritage Association, takes the podium and welcomes us. He reads a message of greeting and solidarity that the Turkish ambassador in Washington has sent to his Melungeon cousins.

Dr. Chris Morris, a local rheumatologist who's also a professor at the East Tennessee State University medical school, takes the podium. He discusses several patients with supposed Melungeon ancestry, including Brent Kennedy, who have now been diagnosed with familial Mediterranean fever. Most have undergone decades of ineffective treatments for Lyme disease, lupus, manic depression, chronic fatigue syndrome, PMS, etc. The National Institute of Health has identified in them a regional variant of this hereditary disease that involves recurring bouts of fever, arthritis, chest pain, leg cramps, and abdominal bloating. Normally it afflicts only Turks, Arabs, Armenians, and Sephardic Jews. Dr. Morris also mentions the discovery among purported Melungeons of several cases of Machado-Joseph disease and Behcet's syndrome, which are normally limited to those same populations.

Next, some new kids on the block present research suggesting that the original Melungeons were crypto-Jews and Moors. Beth Hirschman, a Kingsport native, is a professor at Rutgers, and Donald Panther-Yates is a professor at Georgia Southern University.

Donald describes his descent from a daughter of the Cherokee chief Black Fox, who married the first rabbi of Wheeling, West Virginia. He discusses several routes whereby Jews became incorporated into southeastern tribes, one being the Mississippi Bubble of 1718 when the poor of Paris and some Jews from Alsace-Lorraine were shipped up the Mississippi River, deposited on the shore, and never heard from again. He also presents evidence that many early Indian traders were Jews who took native wives, maintaining that their mixed children married among themselves and assumed positions of leadership in their various tribes. A trader named James Adair wrote a book in the 1760s itemizing the cultural similarities between Jews and southeastern Indians.

Beth, who reports that her nephew was born with six fingers on one hand and six toes on one foot, talks about stars of David on Appalachian headstones; menorahs used as candlesticks on Appalachian dinner tables; mountaineers bearing surnames cited in official Catholic records as belonging to Judaizers sought by the Inquisition; and her own ancestors named Israel, Palestine, Mecca, Omar, and Zion.

She compares the Melungeons to the Marranos of northern New Mexico, whose Sephardic ancestors fled the Mexican branch of the Spanish Inquisition by moving northward, where some families retained a knowledge and practice of their heritage while others went native. (Future DNA testing will show that thirty out of seventy-eight contemporary Marrano males are Cohanim, members of the priestly Jewish caste descended from Aaron, brother of Moses. The head of a leading DNA laboratory will report that between 10 and 15 percent of their clients from New Mexico, southern Texas, and northern Mexico have Y chromosomes typical of Jews from the eastern Mediterranean, as do 6 to 9 percent of people with Spanish Catholic backgrounds.)

The Melungeons' eyes glaze over. We're already suffering from Ancestral Overload. But we know we have to make room in our crowded gene pool for this new Sephardic canoe.

During the break, I spot a young man wearing a T-shirt that reads

## TRI-RACIAL ISOLATE — NEVER!

Suspecting I've found one of the racists who periodically spit venom on the Melungeon chat sites, I question him. He says he has no problem with "tri-racial." What he objects to is "isolate." He maintains that the Melungeons have cheerfully incorporated any stranger who ever turned up. And he resents those who portray them as ignorant, inbred hillbillies who've never left their own hollows.

The audience returns to their folding chairs. Tension mounts. There's none of the cheerful banter or spirited sparring of previous gatherings. We're about to learn who we are. Many of us have spent much of our lives trying to figure this out. Several look as though they're in suspended cardiac arrest. I feel a bit that way myself. What if it's all a big ruse we've perpetrated on ourselves, and we're just standard-issue northern Europeans? It will be like Dorothy awakening from her adventures in Oz to find herself back in Kansas inspecting tornado damage.

Wayne introduces Dr. Jones, but we're all well aware of who he is. He stands up from the table and moves to the microphone. A tall, handsome man with dark hair and a mustache, he's wearing a navy blue blazer and a tie.

In his clipped British accent, he launches right in: There's no one specific DNA pattern associated with the tested Melungeons (in the way that there is for, say, the Hazara of Pakistan and Afghanistan, a third of whom share the same Y chromosome as Genghis Khan, according to my DNA Internet group). But the mitochondrial DNA from one hundred Melungeons supports the concept that the name Melungeon could indeed come from the French word meaning "mixed": 5 percent of the samples are Native American, 5 percent are African, 4 percent are Siddi, and 2 percent are Turkish. (The Siddi are Ethiopians brought as slaves to northern India. Some of their free descendants were absorbed by Roma Gypsy communities.)

This doesn't mean that each individual exhibits those percentages, continues Dr. Jones, but rather that the sampled community, taken as a whole, does. Each extended family no doubt has a somewhat different mixture.

The remaining 84 percent of the mitochondrial DNA samples are generic European. Dr. Jones explains that at the moment it's impossible to separate the various flavors of European mitochondrial DNA due to tens of thousands of years of mixing there. Consequently, the question of Portuguese ancestry remains unanswered. Nothing in the study either proves or refutes it. But DNA technology is in its infancy and will conceivably be able to resolve the issue in the future.

The Y-DNA samples from Melungeon men are still being scrutinized. But the twenty that have already been analyzed support the mixed ancestry indicated by the mitochondrial DNA — Indo-European, sub-Saharan African, and Native American. In addition, two Y chromosomes are associated with Turkish populations and one with Arabs. Two are of unknown origin.

Dr. Jones adds that these twenty Y chromosomes exhibit more genetic variation than was found in a recent Y-DNA study of several hundred men from all across Ireland. The Irish study found four distinct groups, whereas the twenty Melungeon samples alone represent seven groups. It proves, he concludes, that this "tri-racial isolate" community was anything but isolated.

After a long silence and a few distracted questions, the crowd disperses. There's very little talking as everyone tries to understand and digest this.

Ina, my mother, and I drive back toward my parents' house. The sun is setting behind Bays Mountain in an orgy of flames. Dr. Jones's findings support a scenario for the Melungeons in which people with darker skin fled, or were pushed, into these mountains, where they melded with others in the same boat — and with hospitable Native Americans and paler pioneers from northern Europe. Exactly how these people first got from Africa, Turkey, Syria, and India to the Atlantic coast of North America remains unanswered. There could have been almost as many different routes as there were individuals. For one thing, England was purging itself of its undesirables, which included Gypsies, Jews, Turks, Arabs, Africans, Moors — anyone who wasn't fair-skinned enough to qualify as English.

But once in the Appalachians, those who looked African or

Native American probably drifted away to join those communities. And those who could pass for white did so, leaving behind only those of ambiguous appearance and questionable origins.

My mother breaks the silence. "So everyone's theories could be true."

"Apparently," I reply, pulling into the Dairy Queen. "Except for those who insist that Melungeons are only tri-racial."

I buy some Buster Bars at the drive-through window. They're vanilla ice cream on sticks, coated with chocolate and peanuts. It's my father's favorite food group. Back at the house we sit down in my father's room, and I pass out the Buster Bars. As we eat them, I describe the DNA results to him. Since he's a doctor, he understands the terminology.

"So what haplogroup was my Y chromosome?" he asks.

"I don't know. It was a blind study. Only the tests I've ordered on you individually will tell us that."

"When will those results come back?"

"In a few weeks, I hope."

He nods. Then he says, "I know you all often disagree with my opinions, but I think you'll have to agree that I do have some good ideas when it comes to ice cream."

We congratulate him on his discovery of the Buster Bar.

Soon the results of my private DNA testing start to roll in via the Internet. I learn that my father's Y chromosome is associated with a group who spent the last ice age in the Balkans. Afterward, some went east to Anatolia or west to Sicily, but most followed the retreating glaciers to spread out over central and northern Europe. This type of Y chromosome is thought to have been carried to Britain by Anglo-Saxon invaders around A.D. 400.

Puzzled, I gaze at my computer screen. After all this smoke — Portuguese Indians, Mongolian blue spots, Siddi, and shovel teeth — it appears that my father's flame is European.

Then I remember my fan analogy. His Y chromosome represents only one out of 1,024 ancestors ten generations back. I won't know anything about those other 1,023 until the remaining tests are completed.

To keep myself entertained while waiting, I go to the Red Cross to donate blood. I often flash back to my idiopathic thrombocytopenic purpura episode, when I lay in bed with nosebleeds that lasted for days. I wonder whether the Red Cross will even accept my blood. I'm also curious about what type it is, since no one but my grandmother and a doctor at the hospital had blood that matched mine.

The Red Cross does accept my blood, informing me that my clotting time is now faster than average. And they covet it because it's type B-positive, which is rare in the South, where the vast majority are type O or A.

Back at Ina's house I log on to the Internet and discover that type B occurs at its highest frequency in a swath across Central Asia, with hot spots among the Roma, Rajasthanis, several Turko-Mongol populations in the Altai Mountains, and some northern Siberians. Could my grandmother Reed, cofounder of the Virginia Club, have descended from Gypsies?

As I'm digesting this entertaining possibility, I come across a Web page announcing that a bloodstain on the shroud of Turin has been analyzed and that Jesus's blood type was AB, the universal recipient. This means that God's blood type is either A or B. . . .

Later that week, I go to the platelet donation center for a second opinion on my clottability. They, too, are enchanted with my swarms of platelets and my rapid clotting time. So I lie on a stretcher for a couple of hours as a needle in one arm funnels my blood through a machine that extracts the platelets and plasma, returning the depleted residue through a needle into my other arm.

Meanwhile, I watch a Harry Potter DVD in which various characters transform into rats and werewolves for reasons that entirely escape me. While disentangling me from the web of plastic tubing and binding my bruised arms with crisscrossed purple bandages, the phlebotomist coyly promises to tell me what my HLA factors are if I'll return for another donation. (HLA stands for human leukocyte antigens, which determine immunities and transplant compatibility. A prominent geneticist named Luigi Luca Cavalli-Sforza has mapped the frequencies of some of these factors in various population groups.)

As I lurch like Quasimodo from the collection center, clutching a complimentary jar of spaghetti sauce in purple-latticed arms, I wonder if I might metamorphose into a vampire that night and prowl beneath the haloed moon in search of my missing plasma. My taxi driver, eyeing my purple bandages and no doubt sensing himself in the presence of a fellow eccentric, asks me if I've ever considered the fact that, since the Bible says that love for all mankind resides in the bosom of Abraham, some- one with three nipples is a powerhouse of God's love. I confess that I haven't thought of this before. I've known people with six fingers but never anyone with three nipples.

Extending his hand for me to shake, he informs me that I now know one. He adds that his nephew is a second. I ask if he thinks this trait is genetic. He says he doesn't believe in genes, that God fashions each person specially for his or her specific function. Silently I rue my multiregional upbringing, which has bred in me an alarming unflappability that tends to attract the more colorful members of the human community.

The next day I order an analysis of my CODIS markers on the Internet. These are a set of non-sex-related DNA sites within the nucleus of the cell that the FBI uses to establish a unique genetic bar code for each convicted felon. Via Internet databases you can compare your CODIS markers to those of var- ious groups all over the globe.

Meanwhile, the results of my father's mitochondrial DNA test arrive. The DNA that he inherited from my grandmother (which my grandfather also shared) turns out to be a variety found at its highest percentage in the Altai Mountains of Central Asia, the spawning grounds of both Native Americans and Turkic no- mads, with slightly lower frequencies among Slavs, Finns, Saudis and some populations in the Caucasus. (Often — though not always — the frequency of a particular DNA marker is highest at its point of origin. Then the marker fans out geographically, like the ever fainter ripples from a pebble tossed into a pond.) Like good sausage gravy, our plot appears to be thickening.

One day I receive in the mail a CD-ROM from the lab, reporting my father's AncestryByDNA and EuroDNA results. (These are the tests that sample markers from the "junk" DNA in the cell nucleus.) I pick up my shard of quartz salvaged from the dig at Pardo's Fort San Juan, which I've been using as a paperweight, and I palm it for courage. Then I insert into my computer the disc that will at last tell me who my father is and who my elusive Reed grandparents were, genetically speaking. When I click the icon, a chart pops up. It reads:

| | |
|---|---|
| Southeastern European (Greek/Turkish/Italian) | 47% |
| Northern European | 34% |
| Native American | 15% |
| South Asian (East Indian/Pakistani/Roma) | 4% |

I sink back in my chair. Once I pull myself together again, I study the charts and graphs and read the explanatory material. I realize that these tests still don't answer the question of Portuguese input, which would be included in the Northern European percentage.

Grabbing a pad and pen, I calculate that in the mid-eighteenth century my father had sixty-four four-times-great-grandparents living along the New River in the Squabble State. Since my grandparents were cousins in two different lines, ten of those people were the same, so there were actually fifty-four of them. Eight were fully Native American, or sixteen were half-breeds, and so on. Abby Easterd, Pocahontas, Nicketti Hughes, and Betty Reeves are just the tip of the wigwam. I can hear my poor grandmother generating torque in her coffin.

In addition, two were fully East Indian and/or Roma, or several were partially so (unless their 4 percent represents just statistical "noise"). Eighteen were northern European, or more were partly so. But the real surprise is his twenty-five four-times-great-grandparents with Italian and/or eastern Mediterranean origins.

I have a vague idea who some of the Native Americans and northern Europeans were. But I have no clue about the East Indians or southeastern Europeans. None of the family data I've collected hints at such origins. Were they descended from shipwrecked Croatian sailors, or the Turkish slaves dumped on Roanoke Island? Were they the offspring of the indentured Armenian textile workers or East Indian servants brought to Jamestown? Were they prisoners from English jails deported to Virginia? Were they kidnapped urchins or paupers lured aboard ships to Virginia with promises of land? Recent scholarship unearthed by Brent Kennedy documents secret deals between Queen Elizabeth, the Ottoman sultan, and the king of Morocco to colonize the New World jointly so as to block Spanish and French efforts. Could my ancestors have been pawns in their empire-building games?

Or are these unexpected results evidence of ancient migrations from hundreds, or even thousands, of years ago? Michael Hammer, a geneticist at the University of Arizona, has recently discovered an archaic version of a genetic marker on the X chromosome in subjects from southern China that is thought to have been passed down from *Homo erectus* ancestors nearly two million years ago. Yet for all these amazing advances, DNA techniques are still in their Model T phase. They can identify only the "what"s with any certainty, and the interpretation of those "what"s is sometimes more of an art than a science. The "when"s and "where"s are still ballpark estimates that, like diet tips, are constantly shifting as new research rolls in. So all I know for sure is that Mediterraneans, and perhaps East Indians as well, appear to have left their calling cards in my father's DNA — like the imprints of prehistoric ferns that I once found in chunks of shale at the coal mine near my grandmother's birthplace in Darwin, Virginia. Or like Champ, silently snaking along beneath the speed boats on Lake Champlain.

Greek, Roma, Turkish, Italian, and East Indian were not acknowledged categories under the Virginia Racial Integrity Law. The only labels permitted were "colored" or "white." German immigrants in America weren't widely accepted as "white" until the late 1700s; the Irish, until the late 1800s; and Italians, Jews, and eastern Europeans only in the early 1900s. As recently as the early twentieth century, Arizona declared illegal any marriage between a white person and a "Negro, Mongolian, Malay, or Hindu." In practice, how someone was categorized under the Virginia law depended on his or her skin tone. If it was dark, that person was labeled "colored," and therefore African, regardless of actual origins. Even some with fair complexions were labeled "colored" if their ancestors had been designated "mulatto" in the censuses from the mid-1800s.

But certainly my father's Native American ancestry, being greater than the one-sixteenth allowed the First Families of Virginia who descended from Pocahontas, qualified him as "colored" under the one-drop rule. And in accordance with the laws of genetics, his parents, combined, would have had around twice as much Native American ancestry as he. My grandmother knew about Pocahontas, but was she aware of her more extensive Indian heritage? Is that why they left Virginia as the racial climate chilled? I'll never know, but at least I now know this much.

I walk into my father's room the next day, wearing my baseball cap that reads

**RECYCLE YOURSELF: DONATE PLATELETS.**

My parents are watching *Matlock* with my brothers Bill and Michael.

Michael has recently retired from his pathology lab in Pennsylvania and moved back home with his wife, Kathy. He's "come in from the cold," as he puts it. After an unpromising start as a blanketed bundle in a hospital window, he's turned into a strong, solid man with a wry sense of the ludicrous and the same sweet smile as when he was a boy. He's wearing a T-shirt that reads

### CLUB SANDWICHES
### NOT SEALS.

Bill has recently moved back to western North Carolina with his wife, Cici, after thirty years in California. He wants to raise their children in these mountains and valleys rather than on the beaches of La Jolla. He says there are values here he wants them to absorb.

Bill may have a point. I've succumbed to the pull of these mountains myself, for at least part of the year. I went away because I felt I didn't fit in. I discovered that I don't fit in anywhere, and neither do most people. It's called (drum roll, please) the Human Condition. The qualities I dislike in people here I found in people everywhere. But those I like, I haven't often found elsewhere.

Because money can be scarce, many people here have learned to make do with very little and not to judge others by their possessions. Because they've often been ridiculed as hillbillies, crackers, and rednecks, they've learned to laugh at themselves — and not at others. Because they've known darkness, they've learned to seek the light in most situations.

My parents can't quite believe their bad fortune. They finally get us all through school and settled into houses with mortgages we can afford, located far away. They start looking forward to some down time, alone. But here we all come back home again, determined to brighten their golden years with our presences. They smile bravely and do their best to act glad. But I'm sure they envy their friends whose children are in prison or in rehab in distant cities.

Plopping down in a chair, I report my father's DNA results.

After a moment of bewilderment over all the rogue Turks, Greeks, and Italians, my father smiles, savoring his new role as Melungeon poster boy.

My mother sighs. When she married my father in New York in 1940, she probably thought she was getting Rhett Butler, not Chief Sit 'n' Bull.

Michael starts singing "We Are the World."

"This is really annoying," mutters my father. "If only we'd known about the Native American part, Bill, Michael, and Jane could have gone to medical school for free. Do you realize how much tuition we could have saved?"

The phone rings. The Chief answers. He listens for a while, apparently to some fund-raising pitch. Finally he replies, "I'm sorry, but I can't help you. You see, I'm Cherokee, and I need to give my money to my own people."

# All-American Stir-Fry

SEVERAL QUESTIONS HAVE BEEN ANSWERED, even while new ones have arisen (which I won't have enough time to resolve in this life or the next). But the one that got me into this in the first place — Were my father's ancestors Melungeons? — hasn't been. I suppose it depends on the definitions being used. No, they weren't Melungeons, if Melungeon means those directly descended from the community on Newman's Ridge in the early nineteenth century who bore the traditional surnames.

But yes, they were Melungeons, if that means the larger population of ethnically mixed settlers in the Squabble State. Refugees from the racial and economic tyrannies of the Tidewater oligarchy, many pressed westward into the mountains of northwestern North Carolina, northeastern Tennessee, southwestern Virginia, and southeastern Kentucky, where they appear to have merged with detribalized Indians, themselves probably already quite mixed as well.

But there's also a socioeconomic element to Melungeonhood: those with enough money and social standing in their communities were allowed to be whoever they claimed to be. As one researcher puts it, "Money whitens." Whatever may have happened to them beforehand, once my ancestors were living with others like themselves, they bought and sold land, married and produced many children, died and left modest estates. Most were farmers. A couple owned a thousand acres. Cornelius Vanover VI, the half-Cherokee son of Abigail Easterd, was a miller and an herb doctor. Several were teachers or preachers. Although many signed their official documents with *X*s until the last half of the nineteenth century, Cornelius Vanover's son William was elected commissioner of revenue for his county. Within the confines of their own small world, my ancestors don't appear to have been persecuted — unless by their own fears of being unacceptable beyond their borders.

My father and we children grew up believing ourselves to be northern Europeans, and the Virginia Club agreed. This raises the question of which is more dominant — one's cultural heritage or one's genetic heritage. Some of the Cherokee membership rolls give the "blood quantum" of those on the list. Many are designated only 1/32nd or 1/64th or 1/128th Cherokee by "blood." Yet the Cherokee Nation considers their descendants, and they consider themselves, fully Cherokee. Clearly, many more factors than just genetic endowment contribute to shaping someone's sense of identity. But what happens within the psyche when one's cultural heritage and genetic heritage don't match? What happens when there are several heritages?

Luckily, my family has plenty of company in our ethnic no-man's-land. Ina's test has shown her to be:

| | |
|---|---|
| Northern European | 68% |
| Native American | 13% |
| Middle Eastern | 11% |
| South Asian | 8% |

Brent Kennedy's brother has received the following results:

| | |
|---|---|
| Northern European | 49% |
| South Asian | 24% |
| Southeastern European | 15% |
| Middle Eastern | 10% |
| Sub-Saharan African | 2% |

Others with suspected Melungeon ancestry show similar mixtures. Some even admit to having Mongolian blue spots, though I haven't checked them out in person.

So what does this hodgepodge make us, in addition to Melungeons? It makes us Americans, for one thing. Many branches of my family have been on this continent for at least twelve generations, and the Native Americans for perhaps 14,000 years. My ancestors crossed the Bering Strait from Siberia, sailed to Plymouth on the *Mayflower*, saved Jamestown from starvation, and were saved from starving at Jamestown — in addition to the thousands with unknown or less glamorous stories. I am, indeed, an Ur-American.

Yet my own DNA results show me to be:

| | |
|---|---|
| Southeastern European | |
| (Greek/Turkish/Italian) | 42% |
| Northern European | 17% |
| Native American | 13% |
| Middle Eastern | 12% |
| South Asian | |
| (East Indian/Pakistani/Roma) | 12% |
| Sub-Saharan African | 4% |

The analysis of my CODIS markers (those used by the FBI to establish genetic bar codes for felons) suggests a similar makeup, which I corroborated by scrolling through the interminable Internet databases of gene frequencies until I developed the chronic squint of a roulette croupier. The contemporary populations whose barcodes most closely approximate my own are Tuscans, southern Croatians, Moroccan Arabs, Portuguese, and Byelorussians. This doesn't mean that my ancestors necessarily belonged to these groups, since current populations sometimes don't resemble earlier ones and since gene flow has never respected geopolitical boundaries. But it can suggest generalized geographical origins.

One of my HLA factors (the human leukocyte antigens analyzed by the platelet center) reaches its highest frequency in Lapland, among the reindeer-herding Saami of northern Scandinavia and the Kola Peninsula in Northern Russia; another, in Central Asia, New Guinea, and several Amerindian populations. Despite my own moments of skepticism, I find it difficult to explain these echoes of concordance among the different types of tests, unless they happen to be pointing to some genetic truths, however ancient they may or may not be.

The famous American melting pot that historians portray as commencing with the nineteenth-century immigration from Ireland and from southern and eastern Europe actually existed here right from the start. It's a shame our founding fathers chose to portray the fledgling United States as an outpost for wayward Anglo Saxons, rather than as the panglobal mosaic it really was. Our resulting history might have been less grim.

It's particularly ironic since, as one example from many, Thomas Jefferson's Y chromosome has been classified as haplogroup K2, which is believed to have originated in the Levant. His political enemies taunted him with having a mulatto father and a half-breed mother. In fact, his mother was a Randolph, one of the families associated with descent from Pocahontas.

Several books have been written, accurate or not, tracing the genealogies of five American presidents to African and/or Native American ancestors — Jefferson, Jackson, Lincoln, Hard-ing, and Coolidge. Some researchers maintain that Lincoln was of Melungeon descent via his mother, Nancy Hanks. (To say nothing of the King himself, Elvis Presley, whose mother's ancestors came from western North Carolina and claimed Cherokee and Jewish ancestry.)

But America has never really been a melting pot, in any case. It's actually a stir-fry. Like picky children, each generation selects only the vegetables it deems palatable. My grandmother Reed speared the Tidewater ones, and my great-grandmother Pealer the *Mayflower* ones. But the other heritages were still there, however repressed or mangled, lending their scents and flavors to the entire skillet.

I ponder contacting the relatives who've helped me reach this point, to share my findings. But Hetty, Bob, Vonda, and Aunt Ura — to say nothing of my Reed grandparents — are all dead. Although this makes me sad, it's for the best. Their origin stories got them through life. To have invalidated them would have been like clipping the wings of elderly bluebirds. But history is made to be revised. I revised theirs, as I hope my descendants will revise my version when more sophisticated DNA techniques become available.

The most important lesson my exploration into the Melungeon diaspora has taught me is that it's apparently possible for congenital belligerents to live cheek by jowl in peace and love. Greeks and Turks, Irish and English, Arabs and Jews, Protestants and Catholics, Christians and Muslims, those with complexions of every hue — all can amalgamate into one people. The Melungeons have proven that the children of Cain and Abel have the capacity to become kissing cousins. All that such a transformation requires is ostracism by your neighbors and the threat of imminent extinction.

As I drive out of Kingsport, I pass a steady stream of RVs the size of small ranch houses headed into town like covered wagons converging on Dodge City during the gold rush. This is a

NASCAR weekend, and 160,000 Tomato People will soon cram the motels and campgrounds for a hundred miles in every direction. The rival churches have posted beguiling quips on their marquees in an effort to lure itinerant worshippers to their services on Sunday morning before the Food City 500 race starts. One by one, they flash past me:

**LORD, HELP ME BE THE PERSON MY DOG BELIEVES ME TO BE.**
**LIVE SO THAT YOUR PREACHER DOESN'T**
**HAVE TO LIE AT YOUR FUNERAL.**
**WHAT DID NOAH DO WITH THE WOODPECKERS?**
**BLESSED ARE THE NASCAR FANS**
**FOR THEY SHALL PAY LOCAL SALES TAX.**

It's past time for me to retreat to the shores of Lake Champlain. I've started wondering whether I could make a living down here composing slogans for church signboards. . . .

# Acknowledgements

It takes a village to write a book, and my reading list includes just a handful of the titles I consulted during my ten years of researching and writing. So I thank the ranks of anonymous explorers, historians, sociologists, archaeologists, geneticists, linguists, and genealogists whose work helped me shape and sharpen my own perceptions.

I also thank my faceless Internet colleagues at the Rootsweb Genealogy-DNA list, and especially its founder Ann Turner, who kindly fielded my many questions. Any misinterpretation of their answers is my own doing.

With their groundbreaking book *The Melungeons*, Brent Kennedy and Robyn Vaughan Kennedy blazed trails through the thickets of Melungeon myth that made my own journey easier. Many other Melungeon descendants and researchers also shared important findings with me. My family patiently put up with my shifting theories about our ancestral origins.

Robert Gottlieb gave me the idea for this memoir and generously offered useful feedback on its early drafts, as did Doris Lessing and Ramsay Wood.

The keen editorial eye of my agent, Martha Kaplan, helped me sharpen the focus of my story and eliminate digressions, and she found it a happy home at Arcade Publishing with Dick and Jeannette Seaver. My editor there, James Jayo, smoothed out the rough patches in my prose and in my logic and made the process of turning the manuscript into a finished book a real pleasure. And Casey Ebro's impressive publicity expertise has helped bring the book to the attention of interested readers.

Jan Hanford built a wonderful new stable in cyberspace for this book and my previous ones. My daughter Sara Bostwick provided my author photo and the moral support she's always given my projects. Deborah Deutschman, Nellie McNeil, Diane Patterson, Jody Crosby, Jo Carson, Steve Fischer, Merritt and Rita Shobe, and the late Idries Shah made valuable contributions to my story as it unfolded. So did my cousins Ava McCoy, Greg Vanover, Wilma Jack, the late Bob Artrip, and the late Hetty and Elihu Sutherland.

Ina Danko's colorful anecdotes about her Melungeon family have entertained and instructed me for the past decade. Knowing her has reminded me of all that I admire most about East Tennesseans.

A few names and locations have been changed to protect me from the guilty.

# Selected Reading

ON THE MELUNGEONS

Ball, Bonnie. *Melungeons: Their Origin and Kin.* Johnson City, Tenn.: Overmountain Press, 1969, rev. 1992.

Berlin, Ira. *Many Thousands Gone: The First Two Centuries of Slavery in North America.* Cambridge, Mass.: Harvard University Press, 1998.

Black, Edwin. *War Against the Weak: Eugenics and America's Campaign to Create a Master Race.* New York: Four Walls Eight Windows, 2003.

DeMarce, Virginia. "Verry Slitly Mixt: Tri-Racial Isolate Families of the Upper South — A Genealogical Study." *National Genealogical Quarterly*, March 1992.

————. "Looking at Legends — Lumbee and Melungeons: Applied Genealogy and the Origins of Tri-racial Isolate Settlements." *National Genealogical Quarterly*, March 1993, pp. 24–45.

Ehle, John. *Trail of Tears: The Rise and Fall of the Cherokee Nation.* New York: Anchor Books, 1997.

Elder, Pat. *Melungeons: Examining An Appalachian Legend.* Blountville, Tenn.: Continuity Press, 1999.

Everett, C. S. "Melungeon History and Myth." *Appalachian Journal*, Summer 1999, pp. 358–404.

Fiske, Warren. "The Black and White World of Walter Ashby Plecker." *Virginian Pilot*, Aug. 18, 2004.

Heinegg, Paul. *Free African Americans of North Carolina and Virginia.* Baltimore: Clearfield, 1997.

Hudson, Charles. *Knights of Spain, Warriors of the Sun: Hernando de Soto and the South's Ancient Chiefdoms.* Athens: University of Georgia Press, 1997.

———. *The Juan Pardo Expeditions.* Washington, D.C.: Smithsonian Institution Press, 1990.

Johnson, Mattie Ruth. *My Melungeon Heritage: A Story of Life on Newman's Ridge.* Johnson City, Tenn.: Overmountain Press, 1997.

Kennedy, Brent, with Robyn Vaughan Kennedy. *The Melungeons: The Resurrection of a Proud People.* Macon, Ga.: Mercer University Press, 1997.

———, with Joseph M. Scolnick Jr. *From Anatolia to Appalachia: A Turkish-American Dialogue.* Macon, Ga.: Mercer Press, 2003.

Reed, John Shelton, Jr. "Mixing in the Mountains." *Southern Cultures* 3/4 (Winter 1997): 25–36.

Rountree, Helen C. *Pocahontas's People: The Powhatan Indians of Virginia through Four Centuries.* Norman: University of Oklahoma Press, 1990.

Wilson, Darlene, and Patricia D. Beaver. "Transgressions in Race and Place: The Ubiquitous Native Grandmother in America's Cultural Memory." In *Neither Separate Nor Equal: Women, Race, and Class in the South,* edited by Barbara Ellen Smith, pp. 34–56. Philadelphia: Temple University Press, 1999.

Winkler, Wayne. *Walking Toward the Sunset: The Melungeons of Appalachia.* Macon, Ga.: Mercer University Press, 2004.

On DNA

Olson, Steve. *Mapping Human History: Discovering the Past through Our Genes.* Boston: Houghton Mifflin, 2002.

Oppenheimer, Stephen. *The Real Eve: Modern Man's Journey Out of Africa.* New York: Carroll and Graf, 2003.

Relethford, John H. *Reflections of Our Past: How Human History Is Revealed in Our Genes.* Boulder, Colo.: Westview Press, 2003.

Smolenyak, Megan, and Ann Turner. *Trace Your Roots with DNA: Using Genetic Tests to Explore Your Family Tree.* Emmaus, Pa.: Rodale, 2004.

Sykes, Bryan. *The Seven Daughters of Eve: The Science That Reveals Our Genetic Ancestry.* New York: W. W. Norton, 2001.

Wells, Spencer. *The Journey of Man: A Genetic Odyssey.* Princeton, N.J.: Princeton University Press, 2002.